D0219225

With Friends Like These

With Friends Like These

REAGAN, BUSH, AND SADDAM

1982–1990

■

Bruce W. Jentleson

W. W. NORTON & COMPANY

NEW YORK / LONDON

Copyright © 1994 by Bruce W. Jentleson

All rights reserved

Printed in the United States of America

The text of this book is composed in Janson
with the display set in Poster Bodoni Compressed and Bodoni Bold
Composition by Com Com
Manufacturing by Haddon Craftsmen, Inc.
Book design by Jam Design

Library of Congress Cataloging-in-Publication Data
Jentleson, Bruce W., 1951–
With friends like these : Reagan, Bush, and Saddam, 1982–1990 /
Bruce W. Jentleson.
p.   cm.
Includes index.
1. United States—Foreign relations—Iraq. 2. Iraq—Foreign
relations—United States. 3. United States—Foreign
relations—1981–1989. 4. United States—Foreign
relations—1989–1993. 5. Hussein, Saddam, 1937– . 6. Reagan,
Ronald. 7. Bush, George, 1924– . I. Title.
E183.8.I57J46   1994
327.730567—dc20   94-1610

ISBN 0-393-03665-0

W. W. Norton & Company, Inc., 500 Fifth Avenue, New York, N.Y. 10110
W. W. Norton & Company Ltd., 10 Coptic Street, London WC1A 1PU

2 3 4 5 6 7 8 9 0

To Barbara

Contents

Preface

I FIRST WROTE OF MY CONCERNS REGARDING U.S. POLICY TOWARD IRAQ in an article published in the spring of 1991. At the time, the Gulf War victory was being hailed, and deservedly so. But the success of Operations Desert Shield and Desert Storm did not negate the extent to which the very need for them was a consequence of the failure of U.S. Iraqi policy as pursued by both the Reagan and the Bush administrations over the previous decade.

The more research I did, the more convinced I became of both the validity and significance of this analysis. A number of congressional committees were holding hearings and launching investigations. Press reports were becoming more frequent and more revealing. Initial interviews I conducted were both confirming and suggestive. Indeed allegations were intensifying of wrongdoing and scandal on a scale sufficient to prompt the appellation of "Iraq-gate." While debate raged then and continues to this day over just how much of a scandal Iraqgate was, the key issue in my view is less one of political scandal than of policy blunder. Thus the focus of this book, in contrast to other books and articles on the subject, is principally on analysis of what the

Reagan-Bush policy was, how it was pursued, why it failed, and what lessons can be derived.

In April 1992 I gave a paper at the annual conference of the International Studies Association, titled "The Enemy of My Enemy . . . May Still Be My Enemy, Too," which further developed the arguments and put forward additional documentary and other empirical evidence. I presented a still more extensive paper in early September 1992 at the annual conference of the American Political Science Association.

By then, there had been significant intersecting developments in the political world. Senator Al Gore, for whom I had worked in 1987–88 as a foreign policy aide and advisor on his Senate and presidential campaign staffs, had been named to the Democratic ticket as the vice-presidential candidate. I was asked to serve as an informal foreign policy advisor and, as things turned out, to work with Senator Gore and his staff on a major speech singularly focusing on the Bush-Reagan Iraq policy. I had become increasingly convinced of the potential political potency of the prewar Iraq policy issue. Vice-presidential candidate Gore gave his speech on September 29, and it received front-page coverage in major newspapers as well as substantial attention on the evening news. The Bush prewar Iraqi policy also was a lively topic in the third debate among the three presidential candidates, the basis for tough criticisms from both Ross Perot and Bill Clinton, including Clinton's jibe that for all his reputed savvy George Bush failed to recognize that one should only assume that "the enemy of my enemy *may be* my friend," not that he automatically was. In the end, while the election was primarily about "the economy, stupid," the Iraq issue played synergistically with the Iran-contra issue to tarnish the credentials of a president who claimed mastery of foreign policy.

As I was finishing the manuscript in the spring of 1993, I knew that I would soon be joining the Clinton administration to serve in the State Department on the Policy Planning Staff.* We academics, if we are

---

*The author substantially completed the research for and writing of this manuscript, and submitted it to the publisher, before he joined the Department of State.

truthful, need to acknowledge a tendency at times to be too glib in our criticisms and questioning of policymakers. Why didn't they simply do *x*; who was the fool, or perhaps knave, who wasn't able to see *y*; what was their real agenda when they did *z*. . . . Knowing that I was about to be on the other end of things gave me an extra incentive to strive to subject the critiques and alternatives I proposed to standards of analysis, logic, and evidence comparable to those to which I was holding the Reagan and Bush policymakers. I believe the book is the better for it, both as a case history and in the broader policy lessons I draw.

No changes have been made in the manuscript as a result of his working in the Department of State. The views and opinions expressed are solely his own, and do not necessarily imply the approval of the U.S. government.

Acknowledgments

THIS BOOK COULD NOT HAVE BEEN WRITTEN WITHOUT THE SUPPORT AND assistance of some key people, organizations, and institutions. Direct financial assistance was provided by the Social Science Research Council through an Advanced Research Fellowship in Foreign Policy Studies. I also received generous research funding through University of California at Davis Faculty Research Grants, the UC Davis Institute of Governmental Affairs and its director Alan Olmstead, and the UC Davis Washington Center.

The research assistance of three individuals was absolutely indispensable: Rebecca Britton, who was as creative as she was conscientious in pursuing leads, conducting analysis, and tying up loose ends, down to the very last incomplete footnote; Jean Stratford, a research librarian extraordinaire, who kept Shields Library at my disposal despite a separation of 3000 miles; and Dr. Elvia Morales Cooney, who provided me with the same high-quality "clipping service" she helps provide for the Carter Center, not exactly the typical thing one asks from a mother-in-law.

A number of people who were involved with and/or knowledgeable of U.S. Iraqi policy generously granted me interviews and made available declassified yet difficult-to-come-by documents. To preserve the anonymity requested by many, my thanks to all. I also am very grateful to the National Security Archive for allowing me access to their extensive document collection.

Thanks to Larry Berman, Rick Herrmann, Bill Keller, Joe Nye, and Janice Gross Stein, each of whom read parts of the study; and particular thanks to Alexander George, Ariel Levite, and Louis Ortmayer for reading the full manuscript and providing ideas and insights which I hope they'll find well reflected in the book. Special thanks go to Melody Johnson, who persisted through more drafts and re-drafts than I hope she'll ever let on, with the same hard work and dedication which characterize everything she does for the UC Davis Washington Center; and to Fatima Mohamud, who has helped me run the UC Davis Washington Center from day one and particularly helped free me up during those last hectic months.

Working with Roby Harrington, my editor at W. W. Norton, has been both valuable and enjoyable. Roby is a superb editor, someone who neither loses faith easily nor takes things simply on faith. I appreciate his willingness to stick with this project, even as it changed shape along the way. Sandra Smith, his assistant, was especially helpful in the last stages. Thanks also to Debra Makay for scrubbing my language and copy editing the book into shape, and to the production staff for its fine work.

Every time I finish a major undertaking such as this, I am re-reminded why it is my family to whom I owe the greatest thanks. To my father, Ted, who throughout his life always believed in me and my work, and who would have loved to have had this one too on his coffee table; to my mother, Elaine, who has always been there for me, and who surely will have it on her coffee table; to my children, Adam and Katie, who are the very special ones in my life; and to my wife, Barbara, to whom this book is dedicated, for being so supportive of my work on the book, for never wavering (even when I might have) on the importance of finishing it and finishing it well, and for having faith.

Introduction:
"The Enemy of My Enemy . . ."

"THE ENEMY OF MY ENEMY," THE AGE-OLD AXIOM GOES, "IS MY FRIEND." Such was the idea when, in early 1982, the Reagan administration initiated an opening to Iraq, a staunch adversary for the previous quarter century. The strategy was to tilt the balance of power against the United States' two even stauncher adversaries of the day: against Iran, with which Iraq was at war, and against the Soviet Union, Iraq's principal patron but with which relations had grown strained.

Even after the Iran-Iraq war ended in 1988—indeed, right up to the very eve of the Iraqi invasion of Kuwait on August 2, 1990—the Reagan and then the Bush administrations continued to provide economic, political, and even military assistance to Iraq. U.S. policy, as stated in National Security Directive 26 (NSD-26) signed by President Bush in October 1989, was to "propose economic and political incentives for Iraq to moderate its behavior and to increase our influence with Iraq." Such a policy was said to "serve our longer-term interests and promote stability in both the [Persian] Gulf and the Middle East."[1] Iraq may have been one of the world's leading rogue states in the recent past, but the goal, George Bush declared, was to bring Saddam and his country into "the family of nations."

Vintage realpolitik it was supposed to be. Yet well before Saddam's invasion of Kuwait, there was plenty of reason to question whether this enemy of my enemy had become much of a friend:

- The Reagan administration took Iraq off the state terrorist list, and the Bush administration kept it off—but Saddam kept supporting terrorism.
- Saddam brazenly and repeatedly violated the 1925 Geneva Protocol banning chemical warfare, to which Iraq was a signatory, first against Iranian troops and then against his own people, the Iraqi Kurds—and denied doing so despite the overwhelming and horrifying evidence.
- There were numerous intelligence and other warnings about the global front company network Saddam constructed to acquire high technology and equipment for the development of nuclear, chemical, and biological weapons and ballistic missiles—but the Reagan and Bush administrations continued to accept Iraqi assurances on dual-use exports as being for civilian-commercial purposes only.
- Saddam pledged to work with the United States toward an Arab-Israeli peace—and then threatened "to make the fire eat half of Israel."
- Saddam accused the United States of seeking to "govern" the Persian Gulf, called on all "good" Arabs to oppose U.S. influence in the region, and demanded withdrawal by the U.S. "occupying naval forces"—the same naval forces that had aided his war against Iran less than two years earlier.[2]

And then he invaded Kuwait, threatening not only this small emirate but the entire Persian Gulf region, including the very oil lifeline on which the global economy depended. The threat to vital American interests was deemed so serious that it was met by the most rapid buildup of U.S. military forces since World War II, first as a "desert shield" to protect our ally Saudi Arabia and then as a "desert storm" to drive Saddam back out of Kuwait.

Thus, one of the most crucial questions left in the wake of the 1990–91 war with Iraq, irrespective of the success of the military campaign itself, was why the prewar strategy failed. Why didn't Iraq, as predicted in NSD-26, "moderate its behavior"? Why didn't the United States "increase its influence"? Why, in short, did this enemy of my enemy, far from becoming a friend, prove still to be my enemy, too?[3]

Four questions about these questions must be addressed from the outset.

First, does it matter? We, after all, won the Gulf War. "When he crossed the line," George Bush defended himself during one of the 1992 presidential campaign debates, "I stood up and looked into the camera and said: This aggression will not stand . . . What you're seeing on all this 'Iraq-gate' is a bunch of people who were wrong on the war trying to cover their necks and do a little revisionism."[4]

It did matter. It takes nothing away from the formidable military victory and diplomatic achievement of Operations Desert Shield and Desert Storm to question why we ended up in this crisis. The notion that this was a war which should not have been avoided, that American and world interests were better served than if Saddam had not invaded Kuwait, is at its best a coldly realpolitik calculus which too readily dismisses the death toll, other human suffering, economic costs, environmental destruction, and further consequences of the war.[5] Moreover, over time, as the conflicts with Iraq persisted and the heralded "new world order" did not spring forth, even the realpolitik logic came into question. Thus, along with the military lessons to be learned from how the war was fought, there *are* important lessons to be learned about why the war occurred.

Second, even if it does matter, is such questioning of the 1982–90 policy just playing hindsight? This was the claim made by Secretary of State James A. Baker III early in Desert Shield, when the outcome still was in doubt, that only "with the benefit of 20/20 hindsight are there some things that we did that we might have done differently if we had known that this was going to happen." President Bush later ratcheted up the requirement to "90/90 hindsight."[6]

The documentary record, however, as will be traced throughout this book, shows otherwise. Intelligence warnings, dissenting analyses, and alternative policy options were presented early and often. For example, as early as 1985 key Pentagon officials warned that Saddam "continues to actively pursue an interest in nuclear weapons."[7] In late 1988, during the Reagan to Bush transition, the U.S. Customs Service reported stepped-up Iraqi efforts to obtain nuclear weapons. In February 1989 the head of Naval Intelligence testified to Congress regarding his concern over Saddam's full range of nonconventional weapons and ballistic missile programs. The next month one of Secretary Baker's own very first briefing memos acknowledged that Iraq was still "working hard at chemical and biological weapons," that it continued to support terrorism, and that it "retains its heavy-handed approach to foreign affairs."[8] And in ensuing months came more warnings about what Saddam was up to from the Central Intelligence Agency (CIA), the Defense Intelligence Agency (DIA), the Commerce Department, the State Department, the Federal Reserve Board, the Export-Import Bank, the Agriculture Department, federal prosecutors of a major bank fraud in Atlanta, members of Congress, and even Israeli intelligence. In sum, far from hindsight, there were *many* things which *could* have been done differently based on information that *was* available at the time.

Third, even if there were missed warnings and the critique isn't just hindsight, was there really anything the United States could have done to prevent Saddam from invading Kuwait? Again, Secretary Baker was firm in his denial, asserting that it was "ludicrous" even to suggest "that somehow the United States was responsible for or contributed to Saddam Hussein's invasion of Kuwait."[9] Was deterrence, as some analysts and scholars have argued, "an impossible task"?[10]

To be sure, U.S. policy was not the only factor that went into Saddam's calculation to invade Kuwait. Middle East politics, we well know, have their own intense and complex regional dynamics (inter-Arab, inter-Gulf, Arab-Israeli). So, too, with Iraqi internal politics, and with Saddam's own mix of Machiavellianism and paranoia. And

France, Germany, and the Soviet Union were all much larger suppliers of arms and dual-use technologies to Saddam than was the United States. But to acknowledge that American policy was not the only factor must not be to deny that it was a key factor. "It is unlikely that Saddam Hussein would have invaded Kuwait," as a distinguished bipartisan group of experts concluded, "had he not calculated both that the regional balance of power stood in his favor and that local *and outside powers* would not react vigorously."[11] Moreover, as delineated in a Rand Corporation study conducted less than three months before the invasion, the historical pattern for Iraq generally and for Saddam in particular was of frequently "throwing its weight around," but also rather consistently being "deterred when faced with superior countervailing regional or international military power."[12] This was a country and a leader which needed to be deterred, but which were deterrable.

Finally, if U.S. policy was a factor, wasn't it all the fault of U.S. Ambassador April Glaspie and her ill-fated meeting with Saddam Hussein?

While who-lost-country-X scapegoating long has been a popular Washington parlor game, the reasons for the failure of U.S. policy toward Iraq run much deeper than a single botched ambassadorial meeting. The Glaspie-Saddam meeting was not an isolated incident. It was an affirmation of, not an aberration from, existing U.S. policy. When Ambassador Glaspie told Saddam of her "direct instructions from the President to seek better relations with Iraq," she was acting entirely consistently with existing U.S. policy. The day before the Glaspie-Saddam meeting, Margaret Tutwiler, one of Secretary of State Baker's closest aides, told the press that "we do not have any defense treaties with Kuwait, and there are no special defense or security commitments to Kuwait." Later in the week, in fact just the day before Saddam actually invaded, Assistant Secretary of State John Kelly appeared to reduce the amassed Iraqi troops and tanks poised against Kuwait to a "border dispute" and an "internal OPEC deliberation," the types of matters on which "historically, the United States has taken no position." And President Bush had just sent his own personal, less than firm cable to Saddam, reassuring him "that my administration continues to desire better relations with Iraq."[13] Saddam was free to draw his own implications.

"We committed a boner in our close relations with Iraq" was the way Ronald Reagan put it retrospectively in March 1991. This, however, was more description than explanation. The basic "why" questions remained, and with quite important lessons for U.S. foreign policy.

In his classic work *American Diplomacy,* George Kennan offers a useful way of thinking about the reasons for foreign policy failure. One possibility is that it was a failure but not a failing, that the situation was "outside the range of our influence" and that nothing we could have done could have altered the outcome.[14] This is quite a useful perspective (for scholars and policymakers alike), as a recognition that even great powers are not omnipotent—that is, as long as delimitation does not become a cover for denial, as some sought to make it in the U.S.-Iraqi case.

"To the extent that it [a foreign policy failure] was the fault of American diplomacy," Kennan goes on to ask, "what went wrong—the concepts or the execution?" Kennan meant these as analytically distinct but not mutually exclusive categories. The "concepts" dimension gets at flaws in the substance of policy and strategy, the "execution" at mistakes in the decision-making processes, policy formulation and policy implementation. In the U.S.-Iraqi case, as this book will show, there were plenty of mistakes in both.

The core concept driving U.S. policy toward Iraq in the 1980s, as noted at the outset, was "the enemy of my enemy is my friend." Initially, during the Iran-Iraq war, the strategy was to strike an *alliance of convenience* with Iraq against both Iran and the Soviet Union. This was classical "balancing" strategy, forming alliances (formal or informal) against states whose power is feared and with states which face similar threats, even in an instance such as this when that state itself had more than earned its own rogue-state reputation and had been an enemy in its own right.[15] The same thinking persisted after the Iran-Iraq war was over as the basis for a "phase two" strategy of seeking a more enduring *accommodation* between the United States and Iraq. The Iranian threat was diminished but not eliminated, and even Gorbachev's "glasnost" and "perestroika" were not yet considered sufficient to dismiss Soviet designs on an area as strategic as the Persian Gulf. Moreover, the dominant analysis, as one internal study put it, was that Iraq was moving "deeper into the mainstream," no longer the rogue state that it had been.[16] Strategy thus was based on a belief in both the value and the viability of a more enduring U.S.-Iraqi accommodation, in effect a "resocializing" of this rogue state into the "family of nations." This remained the core concept, the Bush administration's driving strategic logic, until the very moment Saddam invaded Kuwait.

Perhaps the most famous case in the history of American foreign policy of enemy-enemy-friend strategy was the World War II alliance with Stalin's Soviet Union against Hitler's Germany. "I can't take communism," President Franklin D. Roosevelt explained to the American people, "but to cross this bridge I would hold hands with the Devil."[17] This alliance of convenience was overwhelmingly successful, at least for the immediate objective of winning the war. However, there need be two caveats in generalizing from it. First, the circumstances of the time were more exceptional than typical. We were at war—"hot" war, total war. We were confronted by the formidable power and two-front challenge of the Axis alliance of our enemies, and thus in need of any and all friends we could get. And the evil of the enemies, as evident from the Holocaust and the "day of infamy," was hard to dispute. In the U.S.-Iraqi case, in comparison, as important as the security, economic, and political interests at stake were, the fact remains that we ourselves were not at war.

Second, even in the U.S.-Soviet World War II case, the argument has been made that we held Stalin's hand too long, that is, that the viability of an accommodation should not have been so automatically assumed from the alliance of convenience. "I think it can be well argued," Kennan himself wrote about the period from mid-1944 on,

that there was no adequate justification for refusing to give any attention to these developing political problems . . . at a time when there was increasing reason to doubt whether her [the Soviet

Union's] purposes in eastern Europe, aside from the defeat of Germany, would be ones which we Americans could approve and sponsor.[18]

Indeed, the central purpose of Kennan's "long telegram" and "Mr. X" article was to stress the ways in which our former adversary but recent friend was once again becoming an adversary. Resocializing this rogue state required that it be contained, not just accommodated.

One does not have to revert to a purist pursuit of absolute identity of interests to recognize that shared enemies may not always be a sufficient basis for anything more than a temporary and limited relationship between states which, like the United States and the Soviet Union in 1944–45 and like the United States and Iraq in the 1980s, themselves have been adversaries in the past and still have issues of conflict and tension between them. It cannot be assumed that the enemy of my enemy *is* my friend, only that he *may be* my friend. There is nothing automatic about the possibility of such a relationship becoming an actuality. An effective strategy is needed, one which strikes a balance between attempting to entice the other state into improved relations and guarding against the risk of being exploited by it. It is not so much a choice between accommodation and containment as it is a "mixed strategy," blending elements of both.

The fundamental flaw in the Reagan and Bush strategies was the failure to grasp this basic distinction between the "is" and the "may be" of the enemy-enemy-friend relationship, and the consequent failure of their policies to meet three crucial requisites.

First, they failed to establish effective standards of *reciprocity* in the U.S.-Iraqi relationship. The threat of the mutual enemy can take priority, but except under the most extreme circumstances must not be given exclusivity over all other issues of conflict and tension in the relationship. Perfect behavior and self-effacing concessions need not be required. But there must be a standard, there must be some conditions, there must be certain parameters for expected reciprocity.

Second, it is essential that a degree of *proportionality* be maintained between the support provided and the threat faced. Support should be sufficient to tilt the balance against the mutual enemy, but not of a type or magnitude to give the enemy-enemy-"friend" the military capabilities to pose its own threat to you. So long as other significant conflicts and tensions remain, the relationship must be viewed as a tactical maneuver and modulated as such.

Third, *deterrent credibility* must be maintained all the while accommodation is being pursued. The prospective friend must know both that cooperation has its rewards and that noncooperation has its consequences. Maintenance of a credible deterrence posture is complementary, not contradictory, to the achievement of a balanced and enduring accommodation.

I lay these out as a conceptual framework to emphasize the broader lessons for foreign policy strategy that can be drawn from the 1980s Iraqi case for post–cold war U.S. foreign policy, and particularly for the rogue-state problem. To be sure, it is easier to lay out requisites for a strategy in the abstract than to apply them to a particular policy situation. But as Alexander George stresses in an important recent book, one of the key contributions scholars can make to "bridging the gap" between the academic and policy worlds is through the "conceptualization of strategies." Such analysis, while not in itself in operational form, "identifies the critical variables of [a] strategy and the general logic associated with [its] successful use." It "is not in itself a strategy," but it is "the starting point for constructing a strategy."[19]

Given the already evident instabilities of the post–cold war world, it is especially crucial to do this. Far from a "new world order," this is a world in which alliances are more shifting than fixed, in which regional and domestic instability may be even more pervasive and violent than in the past, and in which the roster of rogue states grows longer while these states become better armed. The need for the United States to choose friends carefully and strike alliances strategically could not be greater. We need to bear in mind that the enemy of my enemy may be my friend—but he also may still be my enemy, too. Without effective statecraft, the latter is more likely to be the result.

Another set of lessons to be drawn from the Iraqi case concerns the foreign policy making process, or, to again come back to Kennan's framework, "flaws in the execution"—flaws in the formulation and implementation of policy that both help explain why the United States pursued the policies it did in this particular case and have more general implications for our understanding of the foreign policy process.

This domestic-level analysis proceeds along three key dimensions: *premises*, as held by key decision-makers; *processes*, within the executive branch; and *politics*, particularly involving relations with Congress and pressures from interest groups.

In trying to understand how they could have been so wrong about Saddam, one administration official acknowledged the prevalence of a "mind-set" which was more the manifestation of a set of premises than the product of analytic assessments.[20] While no decision-maker is (or should be expected to be) free of beliefs or other perceptual lenses, the problem arises when such beliefs are taken too strictly as premises to be accepted rather than hypotheses to be tested. The Iraq policy case is particularly telling in that alternative views of Saddam and corresponding alternative policy options were raised both from outside and from within the Reagan and Bush administrations on a number of occasions, but were consistently rejected. Nor was it that these alternative views were necessarily refuted on their merits so much as that they were dismissed out of hand. Evidence of the effectiveness of accommodation was more and more scant. Yet, despite Saddam's efforts to acquire nuclear weapons and other weapons of mass destruction, despite his intensified repression of the Kurds, despite displays of his megalomania, despite his challenges to U.S. interests in the region—that is, despite substantial and available evidence to the contrary—his willingness to play by the rules of accommodation continued to be treated more as premise than postulate.

A second dimension involves the bureaucratic politics and intra-executive branch processes by which policy was formulated and implemented. It is not just what premises and perceptions decision-makers hold in their heads, but also the processes by which they make decisions and carry out policies. In this case, these were flawed in three key aspects: in President Bush's foreign policy making style, which for all its credits in other policy areas had serious and costly failings in this case; in the roles of Secretary of State Baker and other top Bush foreign policy officials, who were instrumental at critical moments in resisting policy shifts; and in bureaucratic malfunctions, particularly in the export control system and in terms of interagency coordination.

Finally, there was the politics of the issue. Neither the Reagan nor the Bush administration was known for taking a particularly positive view of Congress's role in foreign affairs, and this issue was no different. There were numerous instances in which congressional policy initiatives were rejected at least in part because of battles over institutional discretion—yet had they been accepted they would have substantially strengthened U.S. policy. There also were damaging episodes of breaches of interbranch trust, not the least of which was the Iran-Contra episode. The challenge of making the institutional power sharing inherent in presidential-congressional relations on foreign policy a constructive relationship was not met, with consequent results. And while the level of interest group activity was less than on many foreign policy issues, agricultural and manufacturing groups with trade interests in Iraq were quite active when the various sanctions bills were proposed, notably in the "reverse leverage" they imposed during the 1988 chemical weapons sanctions debate.

In sum, the overall sense one gets in this case is similar to that of other notable cases in which foreign policy failures have been attributed at least as much to flaws in the making/execution of policy as to its strategy/concepts. The Bay of Pigs, 1961; Vietnam, 1965; Nicaragua, 1977–79; Iran, 1978–79; Lebanon, 1982–84; Iraq, 1982–90: Clearly there is much to be learned about how we can better make our foreign policy.

Plan of the Book

The book is structured into two parts: Part I (Chapters 1–4) presents the case study; Part II (Chapters 5 and 6) develops the analysis and draws the implications for both theory and policy. This ordering is, quite intentionally, the reverse of many books. The basic analytic framework and the theory and policy arguments have been sketched in this introduction as a "lens" for viewing the case, but are kept suggestive and not determinative while the case unfolds.

The story is told in its rich detail. Such a complicated and controversial case needs to be dealt with comprehensively; no other book, to my knowledge, provides such a thorough, well-documented, and analytic history of this important case. Hundreds of declassified documents, numerous interviews, and extensive public sources all have been drawn upon.

Chapter 1 reviews Reagan administration policy during the Iran-Iraq war, tracing the origins of the alliance-of-convenience strategy and its development and early controversies. Chapter 2 focuses on Saddam's August 1988 chemical weapons attacks on the Kurds and the Reagan administration's resistance to imposing economic sanctions both as an important issue in itself and as a key transitional stage in U.S.-Iraqi relations. Chapter 3 examines the development of the Bush administration's policy, starting with the underlying conceptual bases for its "logic of accommodation," going through the intelligence and other warnings sounded during the policy review as well as the major controversy over the $4 billion in illegal loans provided Iraq by the Atlanta branch of Banca Nazionale del Lavoro (BNL), and culminating in the key October–November 1989 decisions on the promulgation of NSD-26 and the $1 billion fiscal year 1990 agricultural credits for Iraq. Chapter 4 takes the Bush policy through to the invasion of Kuwait, covering numerous key incidents and developments over those months, and looking closely at decision-making during the July–August 1990 pre-invasion crisis period.

Part II follows Kennan's analytic framework of concepts/strategy (Chapter 5) and execution/process (Chapter 6) in developing the analysis of why U.S. policy failed and drawing lessons from the Iraqi case for post–cold war U.S. foreign policy more generally. Chapter 5 develops the theoretical and analytic bases for the mixed-strategy formulation of reciprocity, proportionality, and deterrent credibility, applies the framework to the Iraqi case, and establishes more general policy implications and applications. Chapter 6 draws its lessons for U.S. foreign policy making, examining the decision-making and bureaucratic processes within the executive branch as well as the politics of executive-legislative relations and interest group pressures, and shows how and why diplomacy needs to begin at home.

Part I

REAGAN, BUSH, AND SADDAM,

1982–90

■

Reagan, Saddam, and the Iran-Iraq War, 1982–88

BACK IN THE 1950S IRAQ WAS ONE OF THE CLOSEST ALLIES THE UNITED States had in the Arab world. It was a charter member (in fact, the only Arab member) of the Baghdad Pact, godfathered by Secretary of State John Foster Dulles in 1955 as the Middle Eastern component in Dulles's global system of anti-Communist regional alliances.[1] But when the old Iraqi monarchy was overthrown by a leftist military coup in 1958, the new regime of General Abdul Karim Qassim withdrew from the alliance—leaving the Baghdad Pact without Baghdad and precipitating a name change and restructuring to the Central Treaty Organization (CENTO)—and opened diplomatic relations with the Soviet Union.

Iraq threatened a total break in diplomatic relations with the United States when in 1961 the Kennedy administration joined Britain in recognizing Kuwait as an independent state. Prime Minister Qassim claimed Kuwait to be an "integral part of Iraq" based on their common Ottoman Empire provincial boundaries.[2] What Iraq especially wanted was Kuwait's near-shore islands of Warbah and Bubiyan and their coveted coastal port access to the Persian Gulf. Qassim amassed his troops along the Kuwaiti border, but backed down when Britain deployed ground troops and naval units. The Arab League also responded, although more slowly, with a multinational force composed of Saudi, Jordanian, Egyptian, and Sudanese soldiers.[3]

The United States (more specifically, the CIA) reportedly was involved in numerous attempts to overthrow Qassim, including an assassination plot using a poisoned handkerchief, which failed, and then a more successful coup which brought the Arab Socialist Renaissance, or Ba'ath, party to power in 1963.[4] Nevertheless, under the Ba'athists, U.S.-Iraqi relations were further strained. Following the 1967 Arab-Israeli war, Iraq severed diplomatic ties with the United States. And like their predecessors, the Ba'athists also proved to be pro-Soviet. They signed numerous trade and military agreements with Moscow, culminating in the April 1972 Treaty of Friendship and Cooperation. Among the treaty's provisions were Soviet access to Iraqi air and naval bases and a pledge for "comprehensive cooperation" in political, economic, cultural, and "other fields." Soviet arms supplies, which already constituted 95 percent of the Iraqi arsenal, increased in both quantity and sophistication, including TU-22 medium-range bombers (their first deployment anywhere outside the Warsaw Pact) and SCUD missiles.[5]

This also was when relations between the United States and Iran were becoming closer and closer. The Shah of Iran was cast by President Richard Nixon and his national security advisor, Henry Kissinger, as the key "regional pillar" upholding U.S. interests in the Persian Gulf. In a seminal meeting in May 1972, held as Nixon and Kissinger were on the way home from Moscow and their first summit with Soviet leader Leonid Brezhnev, the Shah was promised a virtual blank check to purchase any conventional weapons from the U.S. inventory.[6] In addition, as will be discussed in Chapter 2, the United States pledged covert support to the Shah's efforts to foment an insurgency by the Iraqi Kurds against Baghdad.

Thus, the U.S.-Soviet superpower rivalry and the Iran-Iraq regional one fed into each other. So, too, did the Arab-Israeli conflict. Iraq again fought on the side of the Arabs in the 1973 war (as it had in

1948 and 1967). When the pathbreaking Camp David Accords were brokered by the Carter administration and signed by Egypt and Israel in 1978, it was Iraq that led the "Rejectionist Front." Iraq also was one of the major sponsors of terrorism, providing funding, training, safe haven, and other assistance to the Palestine Liberation Organization (PLO) and other terrorist groups. The Carter administration made Iraq one of the first countries on its newly established list of state sponsors of terrorism, against which tough economic sanctions were imposed.

In the late 1970s, though, the strategic scenario was rocked by a series of shocks. In January 1979 the Shah of Iran, that pillar of U.S. policy, was brought down by the Islamic fundamentalist revolution led by the Ayatollah Khomeini. In November, seventy-six Americans were taken hostage at the U.S. embassy in Teheran. In December the Soviet Union invaded Afghanistan. And in September 1980 Iraq launched a war against Iran. Throughout this period there also were signs of strains in Iraqi-Soviet relations.

It was beginning to appear that perhaps there might be a basis for a U.S.-Iraqi relationship.

The Enemy-Enemy-Friend Calculus and the Alliance-of-Convenience Strategy

The opening to Iraq can be dated to February 26, 1982, when the Reagan administration took Iraq off the list of state sponsors of terrorism. The statement for the record was that this policy shift was "intended both to recognize Iraq's improved record [on terrorism] and to offer an incentive to continue this positive trend."[7] Privately, though, as the leading Defense Department counterterrorism official later conceded, "no one had any doubts about his [Saddam's] continued involvement with terrorism. . . . The real reason [for taking Iraq off the terrorism list] was to help them succeed in the war against Iran."[8]

This was to be an alliance of convenience based on the enemy of my enemy as my friend.

Iran

While officially the United States professed neutrality in the Iran-Iraq war, there was little disputing that Iran had become a significant enemy of the United States. Not only had the fall of the Shah cost the United States one of its key allies, but the Ayatollah Khomeini had cast the United States as "the Great Satan," to be despised and defied by Iranians and by devout Shi'ite Muslims throughout the region. The 444 days of captivity for the American hostages in Teheran left a host of conflicts between the United States and Iran. It also was, even more enduringly, a collective trauma of enormous magnitude for the American polity. One U.S. public opinion survey, rating world leaders on a thermometer scale, on which even Soviet president Leonid Brezhnev got an only slightly freezing 31 degrees, gave the Ayatollah a frigid 11 degrees, the lowest of any world leader.[9]

The rise of the Ayatollah also caused concern in Baghdad. Saddam and the Shah had managed to work out a *modus vivendi* in the 1975 Algiers agreement, in which Iraq agreed to divided sovereignty over the Shatt al-Arab waterway and to cease its support for anti-Shah dissidents in the western Iranian province of Khuzestan in exchange for Iran cutting off its military support for the Iraqi Kurds. In late 1978 Saddam also had tried to help the embattled Shah by expelling the Ayatollah Khomeini from his fifteen-year exile in Iraq—a move which seriously backfired as the Ayatollah relocated to Paris where he had much greater access to communications and dissident networks, allowing him to spread his message more easily into Iran.

Before the Iran-Iraq war started, the Carter administration had made some very preliminary overtures to Saddam. "We see no fundamental incompatibility of interests between the United States and Iraq," National Security Advisor Zbigniew Brzezinski stated in a television interview. "We do not feel that American-Iraqi relations need to be frozen in antagonism."[10] There are varying accounts of a possible U.S. role in or knowledge of Saddam's attack of September 22, 1980, launching the Iran-Iraq war. President Jimmy Carter states in his memoirs that "we had no previous knowledge of nor influence over this move."[11] On the other hand, former National Security Council (NSC) aide Gary Sick claims that there was a tacit strategy of "letting Saddam assume there was a U.S. green light because there was no explicit red light."[12] There even were some reports of U.S. involvement in a covert plan for a "blitzkrieg" to be launched from Iraqi territory led by some of the Shah's ex-generals "to form a provisional government under Iraqi tutelage."[13]

President Carter's denial, however, does seem credible. In fact, the timing of Saddam's initiation of the war put a possible breakthrough in the U.S.-Iranian hostage negotiations off track. A meeting in Bonn, Germany, between Deputy Secretary of State Warren Christopher and Iranian negotiator Sadegh Tabatabai the day before the war started had gone well. But the onset of the war delayed Tabatabai's return to Teheran by over a week. By the time he finally got back, his government "had shifted their attention from releasing the hostages to defending their own country against the invaders."[14]

Carter also states that his desired outcome was a quick cease-fire between Iran and Iraq. On the one hand, he wanted to avoid a beleaguered Iran doing something rash to the hostages. On the other hand, if Iran still felt sufficiently threatened by Iraq, it might release the hostages in order to enhance its international support.[15] Another tack which both Gary Sick and Zbigniew Brzezinski attest to was a proposal approved by President Carter for lifting the embargo on $150 million worth of arms, spare parts, and other military goods purchased by the Shah, yet still sitting in American warehouses, in exchange for release of all the hostages.[16] This, it should be noted, was quite different from the arms-for-hostages deals the Reagan administration sought in 1985–86. For one thing, these were all arms already purchased by Iran. For another, it was all above board. Carter even made reference to it in the October 28, 1980, presidential debate with candidate Reagan: "If the hostages are released safely . . . we would make delivery on those items which Iran owns." Once again, though, timing was off, only this time it was that Iraq's initial advances had been slowed and even reversed, so the need for the U.S. arms had lessened.[17]

Carter administration concern grew that Iran might seek to widen the war, most worrisomely to Saudi Arabia.[18] To deter such a threat, and defend if necessary against it, AWACS planes were loaned to the Saudis. Interestingly, messages also were sent to the Saudis, the Kuwaitis, and others to "discourage these nations from permitting the Iraqis to launch attacks from their lands, hoping to keep the battle area from spreading."[19]

At the beginning of the war, with the United States not yet tilted toward Iraq, a shipment of U.S.-made engines which were to be used in frigates being built in Italy for the Iraqi navy was embargoed. Iraq also was kept on the state terrorist list. However, Brzezinski does say that as the Carter administration grew increasingly frustrated with the Iranians over the hostages, he did propose "that we send signals that we might be inclined to provide some military aid to the Iraqis if the Iranians were not more forthcoming."[20] By then, though, it was December 1980. Jimmy Carter had already lost his reelection bid. And the next month Ronald Reagan would be president, and the hostages were released.

Initially the Reagan administration maintained neutrality, but by early 1982 the Iranian threat had taken on greater urgency. The war appeared to be turning in Iran's favor as its troops pushed Iraqi forces back some thirty miles, captured fifteen thousand prisoners, and reportedly came close to capturing Saddam. Iran also was becoming more and more aggressive in attempts to export its Islamic fundamentalist revolution. The message emanated from Ayatollah Khomeini's sermons:

> The Iranian Revolution is not exclusively that of Iran because Islam does not belong to any particular people. We will export our revolution throughout the world because it is an Islamic revolution. The struggle will continue until the call "there is no god but God and Muhammad is the messenger of God" is echoed all over the world.[21]

And it wasn't just preaching. There were the "deliberatively disruptive delegation" sent to Saudi Arabia in September 1981 for the traditional Mecca pilgrimage; attacks on Kuwait in October 1981; an Iranian-sponsored coup attempt in Bahrain in December 1981; and Iranian "diplomats" expelled from North Yemen in February 1982 for promoting subversion.[22]

Most especially, the Iranian Revolutionary Guards aided and fomented the radical Shi'ite forces in Lebanon. It was these forces that were responsible, on October 17, 1983, for the terrorist bombing of the U.S. Marine barracks in Beirut, killing 241 sleeping soldiers and other personnel. Six weeks later the first American hostage was seized in Lebanon, again by radical Shi'ite groups with Iranian complicity.

The Soviet Union

The enemy-enemy-friend calculus had a second component, the possibility of the United States taking advantage of strained relations between Iraq and the Soviet Union to recoup the loss of Iraq to the Soviet orbit a quarter century earlier. Despite the 1972 Friendship and Cooperation treaty, the Soviets had initially refused to increase arms supplies to Iraq during the 1974 Kurdish rebellion. For its part, Iraq provided some arms to the Eritreans fighting the Soviet-supported Ethiopian government, and denounced the Soviet invasion of Afghanistan. Even within the Middle East, while the Soviets benefited from Saddam's opposition to the 1978 Camp David Accords and sponsorship of the Rejectionist Front, Saddam's agenda was less that of a loyal Soviet surrogate than of an Arab leader aspiring to the pan-Arab mantle of being the next Nasser (see below). "We never succeeded in penetrating the Iraqi high command," lamented one Soviet diplomat.[23]

Another major issue of contention was the fate of the Iraqi Communist party (ICP). The Ba'athists had conducted major purges in 1963 and 1968, and then again in 1978, including the execution of a number of ICP leaders. Communism, Saddam said, was "a rotten atheistic yellow storm which has plagued Iraq."[24] The Soviets retaliated by withholding military aid. All told, as one analyst observed, at the time the Iran-Iraq war started, "Iraqi-Soviet relations were at their lowest ebb since 1968."[25]

The Carter administration's immediate concern was that the war not become an opportunity for the Soviets to increase their influence with *either* party. The day after the war started, Carter issued a statement calling on "all other countries, including the Soviet Union, not to interfere in the conflict."[26] This was a reaffirmation of his Carter Doctrine pronounced earlier that year following the Soviet invasion of Afghanistan and the concerns then raised about Soviet designs on the Persian Gulf.[27] Carter reinforced his words by showing the flag, expanding the U.S. Middle East Naval Force by two ships.

The Soviets countered by accusing the United States of imperialist interventionist intentions. "Keep your hands off unfolding events" was Brezhnev's retort. At the same time, Moscow tried playing its own version of enemy-enemy-friend with Iran. The war was really the work, Brezhnev said, of those "who dream about transforming Iran once again into a military base and into a *gendarme* outpost of imperialism."[28] Arms reportedly were offered to Iran. The Soviets also distanced themselves from Iraq, pledging neutrality and refusing Iraqi arms requests, even turning back two ships fully laden with arms in the first month of the war. They also signed a Treaty of Cooperation and Friendship with Syria, another of Saddam's arch rivals, in October 1980. The joint communiqué issued by Brezhnev and Syrian president Hafez al-Assad rather provocatively stated that both countries "support Iran's inalienable right to determine its destiny independently and without any foreign interference."[29]

The Iranians, however, were largely unreceptive to Moscow's overtures. The Islamic revolution was deeply anti-Communist (a "Great Satan" second only to Western imperialism). There also was the issue of Afghanistan. The Soviet invasion of their fellow Islamic nation was intolerable; in fact, when a group of Afghan *mujaheddin* stormed the Soviet embassy in Teheran in December 1980, Iranian authorities did little to stop them. Thus, by mid-1981 the Soviets were again seeking to improve relations with Iraq.[30] While not abandoning their official position of neutrality, they did once again turn on the arms spigot for Iraq. They also signed a new long-term economic agreement.

One author calls this but an "outward normalization" and stresses the extent to which Iraq remained dissatisfied with and suspicious of Moscow. "The Soviets are straddling the fence, and it's unpardonable," one Iraqi official stated.[31] The Iraqi-Soviet Treaty of Cooperation and Friendship, Saddam declared, "has not worked."[32] With such sentiments abounding, the Reagan administration saw an opening for an Iraqi re-realignment, away from the Soviets and back toward the United States.

Saddam, the "Friend"

Who was this Saddam Hussein who was to become a new friend? Even asking this question from an early 1980s perspective, leaving aside for the moment what we learned from his later actions, the profile was not a particularly pleasant one.

While perhaps not the most murderous leader ever in the Middle East, Saddam was right up there. He rose to power through a mix of guile and brutality, a "savage and able player," in the view of two biographers, in the cruel system that was Iraqi politics.[33] In 1959, at the age of twenty-two, he was the hit man in the Ba'athist assassination attempt on General Qassim. He fled to exile first in Syria and then Egypt, returning to Iraq in 1963 when the next Ba'athist coup succeeded. In 1968 he became deputy chairman of the Revolutionary Command Council and head of internal security, in effect the power behind President Ahmed Hassan al-Bakr. On July 16, 1979, Saddam became president of Iraq, chairman of the Revolutionary Command Council, and commander-in-chief of the armed forces.

Right from the start, Saddam ruled ruthlessly. He wanted nothing less than "absolute power and unconditional subservience," and unleashed "the bloodiest purge yet, executing hundreds of Party officials and military officers, some of whom were close friends and associates."[34] The British authors John Bulloch and Harvey Morris recount a telling incident from Saddam's "trail of blood":

One of his first official functions was to host a dinner for senior officials of the ruling Arab Ba'ath Socialist Party. The meal at the presidential palace in Baghdad was followed by a meeting of the party leaders at which members were invited to write down details of any meetings they had held in the previous year with two of their colleagues Muhie Abdel-Hussein and Mohamed Ayesh. The following day Saddam chaired a meeting of the Revolutionary Command Council at which it was alleged that these two men were the ringleaders of a Syrian-financed plot to overthrow the regime. . . . With tears in his voice, Saddam read out the names of the plotters and asked them to leave the hall.

Some days later, Saddam invited the Ba'ath leadership to accompany him to where their erstwhile comrades were held. And there they were handed guns, and with Saddam at the centre, formed the firing squad which shot them.

According to some accounts, gunmen of the Mukhabarat secret police stood behind the ranks of the executioners lest any should prove recalcitrant.[35]

Beyond his own borders, Saddam aspired to be the next great leader of the Arab world, the next Nasser. This in part could be traced back to Ba'athist ideology and its pan-Arabism. Ironically, though, the Ba'ath party was actually a minority even within Iraq. The Sunni Muslims, from whom the Ba'athists were drawn, constituted only about 20 percent of the Iraqi population, little more than the Kurds and much less than the 55–60 percent for the Shi'ites. Moreover, Saddam's ruling clique was drawn almost exclusively from the Tikriti sect. And while the Ba'ath party ruled in both Iraq and Syria, Saddam and Syrian dictator Hafez al-Assad were bitter rivals for pan-Arabist leadership. Plans that had been under way before Saddam became president for a Syrian-Iraqi confederation were scuttled. For Saddam, Arab unity was less a goal in itself than a means to his own personal aggrandizement and acquisition of power.

Saddam did retain that part of Ba'athist ideology that held that "the primary method of achieving this goal [Arab unity] is through armed struggle."[36] He vehemently opposed the Egyptian-Israeli peace of the Camp David Accords. The Arab League summit which excommunicated Egyptian president Anwar Sadat was held in Baghdad. Saddam also was quite strident in his attacks on the United States as "the enemy of the Arab people" because "Israel occupies Palestine through the power of the United States."[37] In February 1980 he proclaimed a "National Charter for the Arab States," intended to "convey a message to the Arab masses that Saddam Hussein was emerging as the champion of Arab unity, a new Nasser who was willing to address the grievances of the underprivileged and the disenchanted."[38] Saddam spoke sweepingly in ensuing months of Iraq's "destiny in the Arab world" and the duty of the Iraqi army to "remain strong to defend the honor of all Arabs."[39]

Saddam's decision to go to war against Iran was partly a matter of being provoked, but mostly his own opportunism. The Ayatollah was doing his best to stir up Iraqi Shi'ites with attacks on Saddam as an "infidel" and calls for a "jihad" to take back this "land of Satan."[40] This is not, however, to go as far as those who argue that the war was primarily defensive.[41] Many moderate and secular Iraqi Shi'ite leaders in fact were quite put off and were themselves threatened by the Ayatollah's fundamentalism. Moreover, the opportunist in Saddam saw a chance both to further consolidate his domestic rule and to gain that Nasser-like prestige and power in the Arab world. He calculated that the conservative regimes of Kuwait, the other small Gulf states, and Saudi Arabia all would be grateful for his taking care of the fundamentalist menace in their midst. And with Iran seemingly tied up in internal chaos, he envisioned a quick victory, his own version of Israel's 1967 six-day war triumph.[42]

Oil also was no small part of the calculus. At the beginning of the war, Iraq was producing 6 million barrels per day, second only to Saudi Arabia. Had Saddam succeeded in seizing Khuzestan Province in western Iran and the Kharg Island oil terminal, he would have almost doubled the oil production under his control to 11 million barrels per day—nearly 20 percent of world oil consumption.[43]

The point I want to stress is that Saddam Hussein had his own reasons for going to war with Iran, his own interests to be served. He was doing his own bidding, which also happened at the moment and on this issue to serve American interests. It did not, however, mean either that Saddam had changed in any fundamental way or that American and Iraqi interests more generally had converged. He was the enemy of my enemy, but with whom the resulting friendship needed to be regarded from its inception as potentially a tactical ploy.

The Opening to Iraq,
1982–86

The practical significance of Iraq being taken off the state terrorism list was that countries on the list were prohibited from receiving U.S. government-financed export credits and were subject to highly restrictive controls on arms sales and technology exports. Once off the list, export credits could be offered and export controls loosened. They were.

Trade Credits

In fiscal year 1983 Iraq was granted over $400 million in U.S. Agriculture Department Commodity Credit Corporation (CCC) guarantees with which to purchase U.S. agricultural exports. Iraq then was dependent on imports for about 75 percent of all its food supply. Yet the disruption of its oil production now two years into the war was leaving it strapped for cash. Oil revenues had plummeted from $22 billion in 1980 to $9 billion to $10 billion. The CCC financing thus provided much-needed purchasing power for food for the war-torn Iraqi people.

The newfound Iraqi market in turn was a boon to American farmers (especially those producing wheat, rice, and corn). Agricultural exports were slumping, and the Iraqi market appeared to have great potential for growth. In fiscal year 1984 CCC guarantees for Iraq increased to $513 million, amounting to 15 percent of the overall CCC program.

The Export-Import Bank, which finances manufactured and technology exports, was also being encouraged to get involved in Iraq. Under Secretary of State Lawrence Eagleburger wrote Eximbank chairman William Draper "to bring to your attention the important role EXIM can play in furthering long range political and economic interests of the United States" by financing trade with Iraq.[44] Eximbank economists, however, were concerned about the riskiness of such lending. A February 21, 1984, country risk report on Iraq stated that "due to both unsatisfactory country economic conditions and the possibility of physical damage to new projects due to the ongoing war, there would not be reasonable reassurance of repayment."[45] U.S. diplomats in Baghdad reacted with concern, even alarm, warning that an Eximbank denial "has the potential to critically affect vital United States interests."[46] But "reasonable reassurance of repayment" is an explicit requirement for lending mandated by the Eximbank charter. Accordingly, on April 15, a request for $159 million in export financing for Iraq was denied.

Of particular concern to the Reagan administration was an upcoming request for construction of a $1.1 billion Iraqi oil pipeline to the Jordanian port of Aqaba. Iraq's falling oil revenues problem was not only a matter of declining production but also of the need for a secure outlet. Its limited coastline always had meant that it relied principally on overland oil pipelines. But two of its three major pipelines ran through Syria, its rival and Iran's ally. Syrian president Assad shut these down in April 1982. The other major pipeline through Turkey was still open, but its maximum carrying capacity was only 1 million barrels per day. Saddam was forced to resort to such limited and uneconomical means as tanker trucks overland through Jordan.

The Aqaba pipeline was slated to have a capacity for another 1 million barrels per day. The key problem, though, was not just financing but that it would run very close to the Israeli border. What better insurance against an Israeli attack, Saddam calculated, than a U.S. government financial interest in the pipeline? And as with the CCC credits, American exporters also would have rather substantial stakes.

Vice-President George Bush personally intervened to lobby his Yale classmate, Eximbank chairman Draper. "Eximbank could play a crucial role in our efforts in the region," Bush's talking points memorandum read. "Early and favorable action on applications for Exim financing for these pipeline projects would be clear and very welcome evidence of U.S. commitment."[47] A week later, concerns about reasonable reassurance of repayment and bank charter criteria notwithstanding, Chairman Draper overruled his staff's recommendations and approved $484 million in credits for Iraq—one of the largest single commitments ever made by the Export-Import Bank.[48] The next month Eximbank also opened a $200 million line of short-term credits for Iraq.

Military Assistance

While neutrality still was the official policy line, in reality the Reagan administration had begun providing military assistance to Iraq. It did not directly sell Iraq weapons, but it did a number of other militarily useful things.

Once Iraq was off the state terrorist list, export controls on dual-use technologies (that is, those with both civilian and military uses) were less restrictive. As an example, the Iraqis were sold sixty Hughes MD-500 "Defender" helicopters, and then ten Bell Helicopters UH-1s, models which had been used extensively in Vietnam. And while Saddam's government promised these helicopters would be used for civilian purposes only, an eyewitness spotted at least thirty of them being used to train military pilots. Other helicopter sales followed, including forty-eight said to be for "recreation" purposes such as transporting VIPs, but which also were diverted to military uses.[49]

Another deal involved a major shipment of commercial trucks. Some concerns were raised as to whether these trucks would be diverted to military uses. One of the arguments that helped get the sale approved was its domestic job creation effect. If the export was denied, one internal memo stated, it would "sacrifice U.S. employment opportunities and foreign earnings amounting to several hundred million dollars a year. . . . [The trucks] represent the products of workers in 7 states."[50]

The Reagan administration also engaged in a policy which an NSC aide later conceded was one of "nods and winks" toward third-country arms sales to Iraq.[51] Officially, of course, at the time no such policy was acknowledged. Any semblance of neutrality would have been exceedingly difficult to maintain, especially since at the same time a U.S.-led multilateral campaign, "Operation Staunch," had been launched to tighten the arms embargo against Iran. But in October 1983 an NSC study determined that the United States should not just tolerate but, according to Elaine Sciolino of the *New York Times*, "encourage other countries to arm and finance Iraq's war effort."[52]

In fact, Washington had been nodding and winking for quite a while at French arms sales to Iraq. Saddam had first turned to France in 1974 as an alternative arms supplier to lessen his dependence on Moscow. French arms sales to Iraq over the next eight years exceeded $4.2 billion; they would grow over the course of the Iran-Iraq war to over $7.3 billion. The benefits were mutual: By 1982 Iraq accounted for 40 percent of French arms exports. The Iraqi purchase of 130 Mirage fighters was said to have saved the French manufacturer Dassault from bankruptcy.[53]

It later would be revealed that Italy got not just a wink, but a "request" to supply arms to Iraq. Then-Prime Minister Giulio Andreotti claimed that the request was personally made by President Reagan in an Oval Office meeting.[54]

In late 1983 the senior U.S. diplomat in Baghdad proposed that there be a covert selective lifting of "restrictions on third-party transfers of U.S.-licensed military equipment to Iraq."[55] Such a policy change would have been inconsistent with a position of neutrality and illegal under the Arms Export Control Act without notification of Congress.[56] While no change in official policy was made, later revelations traced U.S. arms having gone to Iraq from Egypt, Jordan, Kuwait, and Saudi Arabia. Among the weapons so supplied were TOW anti-tank missiles, Huey helicopters, small arms, mortars, and one-ton MK-84 bombs.[57] The Reagan administration also reportedly gave its tacit consent to a deal in 1983 by a notorious Miami-based black market arms broker (rumored in numerous other instances to be linked to the CIA) to hire air force reservists to train Iraqi pilots to fly an American-made Phantom F-4 fighter-bomber captured from Iran.[58]

Perhaps even more militarily valuable to the Iraqis were the intelligence data which the United States was supplying directly. In June 1982 Iraq was provided with U.S. intelligence satellite photography and other mapping of vulnerabilities in their own defensive lines. When the Iranians attacked a few weeks later, "Iraqi defenses had been significantly fortified and the Iranians were repulsed with heavy casualties."[59] Then in 1984 Reagan signed a National Security Decision Directive (NSDD) formally authorizing a "limited intelligence-sharing program with Iraq." According to some reports, CIA director William Casey was personally involved in passing some of the highly classified intelligence to the Iraqis. Robert Gates, who then was CIA deputy director and would become CIA director in the Bush administration, had "direct responsibility" for the program.[60] The U.S.-supplied data included satellite reconnaissance photos of strategic Iranian sites for targeting bombing raids, data on Iranian air force and troop positions gathered from U.S.-manned AWACS based in Saudi Arabia, communications intercepts, and other vital military information. "My sense," recalled another Reagan official, "was that such U.S.-provided intelligence saved the Iraqis from being overrun in several key battles."[61] It was supposed to be "the bait on the hook," as a Reagan official later phrased it, showing Iraq how valuable an ally the United States could be.

There also was supposed to have been some exchange on the part of the Iraqis, providing the United States with some of their intelligence on Soviet weaponry and on Palestinian terrorist groups. One such proposed deal involved four American-made howitzers to be exchanged for a Soviet T-72 tank protected by an advanced armor potentially invulnerable to American firepower. Another involved the sale of $45 million worth of 175-millimeter long-range guns and ammunition in exchange for another Soviet tank. Yet another was the sale of one hundred Hughes helicopters equipped with TOW missiles in exchange for a Soviet Hind helicopter. All, however, fell through.[62] Indeed, most of what the Iraqis gave the United States "proved virtually worthless." It's difficult to believe that the Iraqis simply didn't have any intelligence that could have been valuable to the United

States. Instead, as one observer put it, "the United States did the sharing and the Iraqis set the limits."[63]

Restoration of Full Diplomatic Relations, November 1984

Despite these and other measures, Iraq's position in the war continued to deteriorate. In February 1984 Iranian troops seized the key Iraqi oil port city of Fao. This not only extended Iranian control within Iraq but moved them closer to Kuwait and Saudi Arabia. This also was when the "tanker war" on Persian Gulf oil traffic first heated up.[64] It was a vicious cycle of Iraqi attacks on shipping to and from Iranian ports, for which Iran retaliated with attacks on shipping to and from Kuwait and Saudi Arabia which they contended were directly and indirectly supplying Iraq.[65] The Arab League, meeting in emergency session on March 14, denounced Iran and called for a ban on all military sales to it. The Reagan administration responded in April 1984 with a secret directive authorizing additional measures intended to prevent an Iraqi "collapse" and to contain the Iranian threat against Saudi Arabia and the Gulf states.[66] Part of the Reagan motivation, in the wake of the U.S. withdrawal from Lebanon just a few months earlier, was to buttress American credibility in the region. The United States also supported a June 1 U.N. Security Council Resolution (552) which condemned the Iranian attacks on neutral shipping but made no mention of the Iraqi precipitating attacks.

Concern also was growing that Soviet-Iraqi relations were improving. The Kremlin's own enemy-enemy-friend gambit with Iran had turned sour, most dramatically with the 1983 crackdown on the Tudeh (Iranian Communist) party and the expulsion of Soviet diplomats on charges of subversion. The Soviets granted Iraq a new $2 billion long-term loan, and some $4.5 billion in new weapons were bartered for Iraqi oil and otherwise sold on favorable terms.[67] NSDD-99, another key document, specifically cited the need "to counter Soviet influence" as the reason for "expansion of U.S.-Iraqi relations."[68]

Starting in late 1983, feelers about restoring U.S.-Iraqi diplomatic relations went back and forth between Washington and Baghdad.[69] The restoration came in November 1984, just weeks after Ronald Reagan's reelection. There were, of course, the for-the-record assertions that this did not mean any change in the official policy of neutrality. The tilt to Iraq, though, could hardly be denied any longer. In fact, Reagan administration officials went so far as to wax on about how "Iraq no longer regarded itself as a 'front-line Arab state,' " and that Saddam now believed that a Middle East peace "should include security for Israel." They cited Iraq's support for the relatively moderate 1982 Arab League Fez peace plan and its at least tacit acceptance of the 1983 U.S.-brokered Israel-Lebanon peace treaty. Cables came back from the region approvingly quoting Saddam as now speaking of "the beautiful atmosphere between us." "We were convinced," a key Reagan Middle East expert said, "that Iraq was changing."[70]

Nor was this just a Reagan administration view. One Washington think tank specialist on Iraq, for example, went so far as to dismiss Saddam's "butcher of Baghdad" image as a "stereotype." Signs of his moderation were enumerated, and he was billed as "a popular leader perceived by many Iraqis to be young, energetic, alert to the needs of his people and a major driving force behind Iraq's economic prosperity."[71] The new Iraqi ambassador, Nizar Hamdoon, quickly established himself as a popular figure in Washington, working the party circuit and writing op-ed articles in the *Washington Post* on "How to Survive in Washington." "Everything and everyone is workable," Ambassador Hamdoon wrote, "depending on how you approach them and how much time you spend."[72]

Early Warnings

There were, however, causes for concern, for those who were prepared to see them.

The first reports of Iraqi use of chemical weapons against Iranian military forces, according to Secretary of State George Shultz, "drifted in" in late 1983.[73] A March 1984 report issued by the United Nations provided documentation.[74] Saddam was blatantly violating the 1925 Geneva Protocol Banning the Use of Chemical Weapons in War. He unleashed mustard gas and nerve agents against Iranian troops. "Carpets of bodies" and "hell on earth" were how Western journalists described what they saw.[75] Despite all the evidence, Saddam tried to dismiss the documented U.N. report as "wild talk." Even in private meetings with U.S. officials, and even when pressing for increased U.S. financial assistance, Foreign Minister Tariq Aziz continued the Iraqi denials. At least one of Saddam's generals was a little more forthright when he told a *Newsweek* reporter, "If you gave me a pesticide to throw at these swarms of insects to make them breathe and become exterminated, I'd use it."[76] The Reagan administration confronted Iraq with its own formal protest, led the U.N. condemnation, tightened controls on chemical exports which could be used as chemical weapons ingredients, and pressured NATO allies to join the sanctions, especially West Germany, which was Iraq's principal foreign supplier of chemical weapons–related equipment and technology. Yet there were those within the administration who wanted to look the other way for fear that the "budding relationship" with Iraq could be "demolished . . . by taking a tough position in opposition to chemical weapons."[77] On most other tracks the alliance of convenience kept proceeding ahead.

His "beautiful atmosphere between us" statement notwithstanding, Saddam also kept up his virulently anti-American rhetoric. For all the U.S. economic and military assistance, Saddam kept pointing to "negative changes" in and "Zionist influence" over U.S. policy.[78] Saddam may well have had an agenda with such statements, perhaps trying to induce Washington to offer even more to convince him of its bona fides. Or he may have genuinely believed it. Either way, the contrast was striking between what he was saying and the talk in Washington about a changed Saddam.

Nor was Saddam particularly changed in how he treated his own people. The Reagan administration's own human rights report acknowledged that execution remained "an established method for dealing with perceived political and military opponents of the Government."[79] The Saddam personality cult also continued to be propagated. Parades of young children chanting poetry in his honor were shown on television. His birthday was proclaimed a national holiday. He even had "the members of the National Assembly sign . . . a compact of loyalty in their own blood."[80] He cracked down especially hard on the Kurds in the north, including, according to Amnesty International, the abduction and torture of some three hundred children from Kurdish families.[81]

Another concern involved initial indications that Iraq was diverting American dual-use technologies to military uses, apparently including the development of nuclear weapons. Even though Iraq had signed the Nuclear Non-Proliferation Treaty in 1976, this had not stopped efforts to build what Saddam envisioned as "the Arab bomb." U.S. intelligence knew of Iraqi efforts in the 1970s to recruit scientists, esepcially Arabs trained in the West, for its nuclear weapons program. What stopped these efforts, or at least slowed them, was the June 1981 Israeli attack on the Osirak reactor, which was the main Iraqi nuclear weapons site. Even then Saddam was defiant, warning that "no power can stop Iraq from acquiring technological and scientific know-how to serve its national objectives." "All peace-loving nations," was the way he put it, should assist the Arab world "in one way or another to obtain the nuclear bomb in order to confront Israel's existing bombs."[82]

Yet with the restoration of full U.S.-Iraqi diplomatic relations had come further loosening of American export controls. Kenneth Timmerman, author of *The Death Lobby: How the West Armed Iraq,* dates the policy switch to March 1985, when high-technology export licenses which previously had not been approved "started to go through as if someone had suddenly turned a switch."[83] Key Reagan State Department officials were pushing for looser export controls, including one proposal "to permit virtually all sales of non-munitions list dual use equipment to Iraq."[84] However, key Defense Department officials, notably Assistant Secretary of Defense Richard Perle, were much less sanguine, partly because of the Iraqi-Soviet relationship, and especially because of proliferation concerns regarding Iraqi nuclear weapons, chemical weapons, and ballistic missile development. In March 1985 Perle sought to require a "non-nuclear-use assurance" from the

Iraqi government as a condition for exporting two advanced computers. "Iraq is a problem country," Perle wrote. Moreover, he pointed out, Israel, our ally, already was required to make non-nuclear assurances for similar computers.[85] But Perle lost this intra-administration battle, and the computers were exported with the Iraqi government's verbal assurances only.

A few months later, Perle urged Defense Secretary Caspar Weinberger that "to protect our national security interests," an overall tightening of export controls on Iraq was necessary. Secretary of State Shultz had written Weinberger complaining about the "imposition of impractical conditions," a thinly veiled reference to Perle and his deputy Stephen Bryen. Shultz even used the argument of weaning Iraq away from the Soviets. But while Richard Perle was perhaps second only to Ronald Reagan in subscribing to the "evil empire" world view, he did not buy its application in this case. "There is a body of evidence," Perle warned,

> indicating that Iraq continues to actively pursue an interest in nuclear weapons, that the large number of Warsaw Pact nationals in Iraq makes diversion in place a real possibility and that in the past, Iraq has been somewhat less than honest in regard to the intended end-use of high technology equipment.[86]

But Perle lost this bureaucratic battle as well. His opponents derided the "dubious merits of DOD's case," and accused Perle et al. of finding the proliferation argument "quite convenient" and really wanting "to block any high-tech sales to Iraq." The prevailing view within the Reagan administration was that there would be no Iraqi nuclear weapons development program "in the foreseeable future."[87] At a July 1986 NSC meeting, the Defense Department was given "a severe dressing-down for its 'obstruction' of Iraqi high technology applications." A new National Security Directive was issued "enjoining all government agencies 'to be more forthcoming' on Iraqi license requests."[88]

Yet another warning sign was terrorism. The whole notion that Iraq no longer deserved to be on the state terrorist list, as already noted, was somewhat disingenuous from the outset. Under the immediate circumstances of early 1982, with Iraq genuinely near defeat by Iran, there was at least some legitimate enemy-enemy-friend logic to the move. But one also needs to recall the extreme severity of the terrorist threat in its own right in the early to mid-1980s. Terrorism had become "a growth industry," concluded the always sober International Institute for Strategic Studies.[89] Saddam Hussein was part of that growth industry, and the Reagan administration knew it. "Despite U.S. pressure," a July 1986 memo to Secretary Shultz from the State Department Bureau of Intelligence and Research conceded, "Baghdad's retreat from terrorism was painfully slow."[90]

Indeed, it was not much of a retreat at all. For example, on June 5, 1982, just a few months after Iraq was taken off the state terrorist list, Saddam had a hand in the attempted assassination in London of Israeli ambassador Shlomo Argov, the event which precipitated the Israeli-Palestinian-Syrian war in Lebanon. The hit man was both deputy commander of the special operations section of the radical Palestinian terrorist Abu Nidal group and a colonel in the Iraqi intelligence service. His weapon was traced by British police to the Iraqi embassy in London.[91] Scott MacLeod, a journalist with exceptional sources in the Middle East on Palestinian terrorism, claims that with his own war against Iran going so badly, Saddam was seeking to reignite the Arab-Israeli fuse.[92] This is precisely what occurred—which, however it may have served Iraq's interests, did not serve American interests, and ultimately cost the lives of 241 American marines who had been sent to Lebanon to try to stabilize the situation.

The State Department's own report the following year acknowledged continued Iraqi support for Abu Nidal and other terrorist groups. During that time Abu Nidal conducted numerous other terrorist attacks, including the bombing of Joe Goldenberg's, a popular Jewish restaurant in Paris (killing six people, wounding twenty-two), and the assassination of moderate PLO leader Dr. Issan Hartawi, who had supported a dialogue with Israel. It was only when Congress threatened to reimpose economic sanctions that Saddam forced Abu

Nidal out (even then, a year after he had promised to do so). Nor was this indicative of a more general shift away from support for terrorism. Saddam had his own animosities toward Abu Nidal and thus could make him a useful sacrificial lamb to appease the Americans. As Patrick Seale recounts,

> Abu Nidal's support derived mainly from President Bakr [Saddam's predecessor] rather than from Saddam Hussein . . . Saddam, however, tended to make light of Abu Nidal, perhaps recognizing in him a smooth operator like himself. Abu Nidal was extremely touchy and Saddam's slights were not forgotten, and the two men were not on easy terms.[93]

Once Saddam made his rapprochement with Arafat (which itself was motivated by the Arafat-Assad split and how that played into the Saddam-Assad rivalry), he could break with Abu Nidal without appearing to act against the Palestinian cause. Yet, accordingly, he kept supporting other radical Palestinian terrorist groups, such as the May 15 Organization. He also "donated" (the word was Yasir Arafat's) howitzers, anti-aircraft guns, and armored combat vehicles to reequip the PLO army.[94]

Then came the October 1985 hijacking of the cruise ship *Achille Lauro* and the murder of an American citizen, the elderly wheelchair-bound Leon Klinghoffer. The main perpetrator, Abu Abbas, escaped capture with Iraqi assistance.[95] The American ambassador in Baghdad formally requested Abbas's arrest and extradition, but was told "Iraq would not withdraw Abbas' diplomatic passport or accept any request for his extradition." On the top of this came the attempted terrorist attack at the Rome airport. Again, the report came back:

> The two terrorists arrived in Rome on an Iraqi Air Flight from Baghdad. One told Italian police that they had come to Rome to attack an American target, "any one". . . . He had bought his Baghdad-Rome-Baghdad ticket (return open) from a travel agent in Baghdad![96]

These events came just after the Reagan administration had pressured Congress to drop a bill to put Iraq back on the state terrorist list. The bill was passed by the House, led by Congressman Howard Berman (D-California). Secretary Shultz wrote to Berman contending that "Iraq has effectively disassociated itself from international terrorism," and that his bill "would be seen and resented in Baghdad as a foreign attempt to dictate Iraqi policy, severely disrupting our diplomatic dialogue on this and other sensitive issues." Shultz went on, "I assure you, should we conclude that any group based in or supported by Iraq is engaged in terrorist acts, we would promptly return Iraq to the list."[97] In agreeing to drop his bill, Berman explicitly cited Shultz's letter and its reassurances of a firm commitment.

In fact, though, while the Reagan administration protested the *Achille Lauro* hijacking and Leon Klinghoffer murder, it did not "promptly return"—or return at all—Iraq to the terrorism list. "We take reports of terrorist activities very seriously," one of Shultz's assistant secretaries wrote to Berman. They are "of deep concern to us." We will keep "conveying to the government of Iraq the depth and breadth of our concerns."[98] Concerns, yes, but actions, no.

Yet Iraqi support for terrorism continued. A State Department study dated July 1, 1986, even noted that, to the extent that there had been some decrease in Iraqi support for terrorism, it was less a concession to the United States than a tactical move based on shifts in its own self-interests within Arab regional politics:

> Terrorism, which had been used by the more radical Iraq of the 1970's largely to intimidate Arab moderate governments and moderate elements within the PLO, had become less useful as an instrument of Iraqi policy by the early 1980's. Widespread use of terrorism against Arab targets was largely inconsistent with Iraq's pan-Arab leadership aspirations in the pre-war period. Later, the war and Iraq's accelerated drift toward the moderate Arab camp made terrorism an even less useful—indeed, counterproductive—weapon.[99]

This was the same secret memo that made the "painfully slow" acknowledgment. It went on: "Even very recently, however, there have been developments that suggest that Iraq remains reluctant to cut completely its links to terrorist groups."

Saddam was going on with terrorism, but the Reagan administration still kept him off the terrorist list. Whatever utility this had against one security threat (Iran) the United States faced, it wasn't very helpful against another (terrorism). It also may have been interpreted by Saddam as indicating what he could get away with under the umbrella of a mutual enemy.

All the while, CCC agricultural credit guarantees continued to grow. By fiscal year 1987, the annual levels reached $652.5 million. This amounted to almost one-fourth (23 percent) of the total CCC credit guarantee program. All told, CCC credit guarantees to Iraq exceeded $2 billion. A large chunk of the guarantees were going to a little known bank in Atlanta, a branch of the Italian Banca Nazionale del Lavoro, or BNL.

With such large and growing markets at stake, agricultural interest groups flexed their lobbying muscle when a sanctions bill sponsored by Congressman Berman was being considered by Congress. "We want you to be aware of our serious concerns," the National Association of Wheat Growers wrote to Berman. "Iraq has been a very good customer for U.S. [W]heat and other agricultural commodities in recent years. . . . We would be strongly opposed to any steps that needlessly jeopardized that relationship."[100]

The Export-Import Bank, in contrast to the CCC, was still less than enthusiastic about its government financing for trade with Iraq.[101] In 1985 it did offer $50 million in medium-term guarantees, only to have Iraq reject them as insultingly small. But in March 1986 when Iraq fell $3.5 million behind in payments on its short-term credits, this line was suspended. Two months later U.S. Ambassador to Iraq David Newton met with John A. Bohn, Jr., the new Eximbank chairman. Ambassador Newton pressed for reopening the short-term credit line and for making a more substantial offer of medium-term guarantees. Chairman

Bohn's response was that his interest in "doing any new business in Iraq varies from zero to not much."[102] Indeed, commercial banks considered Iraq such a risk that they were quoting interest rates of 15–25 percent.

Not only was the alliance-of-convenience strategy running into such complications, but the war itself still was not going very well for Iraq. In July 1986, Assistant Secretary of State Richard Murphy alerted Under Secretary Michael Armacost that concern

> over Iraq's ability to sustain its defenses has substantially risen over the past three weeks. . . . The trends in the war, developing at an ever faster pace since the Iranian success at Faw in February, underscore our long-held view that the longer the war continues, the greater the risk of an Iraqi defeat.[103]

But what Assistant Secretary Murphy didn't appear to know was that the latest Iranian military advances had been made possible in part by *U.S. arms sales!* Enemy-enemy-friend, meet arms for hostages.

The Arms-for-Hostages Gambit with Iran

The first arms-for-hostages proposal actually was made during the Carter administration. In early 1980 Israeli Defense Minister Ariel Sharon proposed that Israel secretly sell arms to Iran, including U.S.-made arms from its own stockpile, as a double gambit to help gain the release of the American embassy hostages being held in Iran and as part of Israel's own regional balance-of-power strategy of forging alliances with the non-Arab but Moslem periphery (for example, Iran, Turkey, the Kurds). Carter, however, "angrily said no."[104]

The American hostages were released on the very day of Ronald Reagan's inauguration. The terms negotiated included the unfreezing of Iranian financial assets in the United States. At the time, Secretary of State Alexander Haig "categorically" stated that "there will be no military equipment provided to the government of Iran." However, a well-placed State Department official (the Israel desk officer) later testified during the Iran-Contra investigations that Secretary Haig by then had secretly given Israel permission to sell Iran arms, including such U.S.-made ones as spare parts for F-4 fighter planes.[105] The exact levels of these sales remain murky, but investigative reporter Seymour Hersh cites both Israeli and American intelligence sources for an estimate of several billion dollars.[106] These weapons were a key reason why the Iraqi blitzkrieg strategy failed to bring quick victory.

In late 1983, with Iran threatening to turn the tide against Iraq, and in the wake of the Iranian role in the terrorist bombing of the U.S. Marines barracks in Beirut, the Reagan administration initiated "Operation Staunch," a high-priority effort to gain multilateral support for an arms embargo against Iran. As an indication of the priority given to this effort, over four hundred cables were sent by the State Department between January 1984 and January 1987 to U.S. overseas missions with instructions and guidance for enforcement of Operation Staunch.[107] And while far from perfect, in the view of Secretary of Defense Weinberger, Operation Staunch did prove to be "an excellent means for slowing the flood of weapons to Iran to a more tolerable level." Weinberger credits Operation Staunch for hurting "Iran's ability to acquire sophisticated weapons and ammunition for the continued prosecution of its war with Iraq," and thus ultimately helping force Iran to accept the United Nations cease-fire.[108]

The very effectiveness of Operation Staunch was one of the key reasons Weinberger opposed the 1985–86 arms-for-hostages deals with Iran. The first American hostage in Lebanon (Frank Regier, a professor at the American University in Beirut) had been taken on February 10, 1984. A second American hostage (Jeremy Levin, Beirut bureau chief for CNN) was seized on March 7, 1984. A week later it was the Beirut station chief of the CIA (William Buckley). Over the ensuing six months another six Americans were seized (Reverend Benjamin Weir, a Presbyterian minister who had lived in Beirut for thirty years; Peter Kilburn, a University librarian; Father Lawrence Jenco, director of Catholic Relief Services; Terry Anderson, an Associated Press correspondent; David Jacobsen, director of the American University Hospital; and Thomas P. Sutherland, dean of the American University's School of Agriculture).

Official U.S. policy voiced a tough line. "It is my purpose to remind terrorists and to keep them on notice that no act of violence against Americans will go without a response," National Security Advisor Robert McFarlane stated. "The United States," President Reagan declared, "gives terrorists no rewards and no guarantees. We make no concessions. We make no deals."[109] In fact, though, shortly thereafter the arms-for-hostages deals with Iran began.

In August 1985, President Reagan authorized a first shipment of American-made TOW anti-tank missiles to Iran via Israel in what was supposed to be an exchange for the release of most if not all of the American hostages in Lebanon. But not a single hostage was released. Nevertheless, another arms shipment was made the next month—one hostage, Reverend Weir, then was released, but no more. Vice-President Bush met Reverend Weir at a U.S. Army hospital in Frankfurt, Germany, and, according to Weir, "told me that I had been released through the efforts of the American government but that he could not explain what [those efforts] were."[110]

In November the ante was upped, the next arms shipment including HAWK anti-aircraft missiles. Again, no hostages were released—although in an entrepreneurial twist introduced by NSC aide Colonel Oliver North, an $800,000 overcharge for the missiles was used to fund the Nicaraguan *contras*. In January 1986, despite the continued strong dissent of Secretaries Weinberger and Shultz, President Reagan now authorized direct U.S. sales to Iran without even the Israelis as middlemen. Another thousand TOWs were sent—no hostages released. In May more arms were sent including HAWK spare parts, and this time they were delivered personally by McFarlane, North, and Company (along with the famous Bible and chocolate cake!). Two months later Father Jenco was released.

Maybe, CIA director Casey calculated, the Iranians needed to need the American arms a little more. In a stratagem that would have made Machiavelli himself proud, Casey sent a message to Saddam Hussein via Vice-President Bush and through King Hussein of Jordan and Egyptian President Hosni Mubarak that Saddam should step up his bombing attacks on Iran. To help the effort, Casey provided Saddam with additional military intelligence including satellite photographs of bombing sites. Sure enough, in just the two days following Bush's meeting with Mubarak, the Iraqi air force flew 359 missions, many of which struck more deeply into Iranian territory than ever before.[111] Now, maybe, Iran would want U.S. arms enough to release all the hostages.

On yet another track, though, Oliver North was not just carrying cakes and Bibles to the Iranians. In a secret meeting on October 29 in Mainz, West Germany, with the Iranian intermediaries, North went so far as to promise to help Iran get rid of Saddam.

> We also recognize that Saddam Hussein must go . . . I cannot tell you exactly day by day or step by step. . . . Yet the general outline follows those steps that I gave you last night.[112]

But none of this worked—and soon the whole operation unraveled. On October 5 a transport plane laden with arms for the *contras* was shot down over Nicaragua. On November 2 one more hostage was released. But the next day a Lebanese newspaper broke the arms-for-hostages story. American newspapers picked it up. The Iran-Contra scandal had begun. And, among other things, the Reagan administration found itself exposed as having worked with the country against which it supposedly had been working with the country with which it was at war. Convoluted, indeed.

Kuwaiti Reflagging, 1987–88:
De Facto Military Alliance with Iraq

One of the effects of the revelations of the arms-for-hostages deal was to make the Reagan administration move even closer to Iraq. This was in part to relieve the political fallout at home, in part to regain credibility with Saudi Arabia and other Arab allies, and in part to assuage "the sense of betrayal felt by the Iraqis." "It is difficult to refute the Iraqis' underlying accusation," Assistant Secretary Murphy wrote Secretary Shultz, "that the U.S. has armed Iran to kill Iraqis."[113]

As both gesture and substantive measure, another push was made to further loosen export controls on dual-use equipment and technology. A letter from Under Secretary of State Armacost to Acting National Security Advisor Alton Keel (John Poindexter, the previous national security advisor, had been forced to resign by the arms-for-hostages scandal, along with Oliver North) states the case:

> In light of recent events, Iraq and the other Gulf Arabs are looking for signs of American seriousness about their region. Tangible steps, such as breaking the logjam on licensing for Iraq, would give us something to point to as we attempt to reassure the Gulf states about U.S. policy in that region.[114]

As to the concerns about proliferation still held by some within the Defense Department, Armacost dismissed these as "exaggerated."

A similar view appears to have been held by Vice-President Bush. The talking-points memorandum prepared for a March 2, 1987, meeting between Bush and Iraqi ambassador Hamdoon states that the Iraqis viewed DOD delays in many of the dual-use export licensing cases as "capricious," and that "we agree with that assessment." Bush was to assure Ambassador Hamdoon that "a special look" was being taken at the Iraqi export cases.[115]

Bush also was enlisted to lobby a reluctant Export-Import Bank. Even though Iraq had made up its arrears, the bank's vice-president for country risk analysis still recommended that Iraq be kept "off cover." It was noted that eight other major Western countries also were refusing to lend to Iraq.[116] Nevertheless, Vice-President Bush telephoned Eximbank chairman Bohn. Again, from the talking-points memorandum:

> Iraqi Ambassador Hamdoon is calling on me soon, and I expect him to raise the issue of short-term Exim credit insurance for Iraq. I

would like to be as responsive as possible . . . I urge you and your colleagues on the Board to give that favorable consideration. As you know there are major U.S. policy considerations at work on this issue.

Shortly thereafter, the Eximbank board approved a new $200 million short-term credit program for Iraq.

It also was in the spring of 1987 that the Kuwaiti reflagging operation was launched. According to Defense Secretary Caspar Weinberger, American intelligence knew by September 1986 "that Iran had singled out Kuwait as the focal point of the pressure it elected to use against the Gulf Arab States."[117] Its attacks on Kuwaiti-bound shipping had escalated.[118] It also had increased covert efforts to foment unrest among Kuwait's Shia minority. In February 1987 U.S. intelligence picked up evidence of sites being constructed along the Iranian coast near the Strait of Hormuz for new Silkworm anti-ship missiles obtained from China.[119]

Protecting Kuwaiti oil tankers under the American flag and with U.S. Navy escorts thus was consistent with the long-standing U.S. commitments both to contain Iranian aggression against moderate Arab states and to defend the principle of freedom of the seas and the vital economic interests at risk from another major disruption of world oil supplies. Yet it also must be acknowledged that the reflagging of Kuwaiti oil tankers amounted to a de facto military alliance between the United States and Iraq. While Kuwait was not a declared party to the war, it also was not an innocent bystander. It was, after all, providing billions of dollars in financing to Iraq. This is not to justify Iranian aggression against Kuwait, but it is to acknowledge that coming to Kuwait's defense was not simply standing up for a neutral.

Moreover, the threat to Persian Gulf oil shipping was coming not only from Iran but also from Iraq. Iraq had launched more attacks than Iran in the "tanker war" in the period immediately leading up to reflagging. It then used the American naval presence as a protective shield behind which it increased its attacks on shipping almost three-fold. Even Saddam's "friendly fire," sorry-it-was-an-accident claim for the May 1987 attack on the U.S.S. *Stark*, killing thirty-seven American sailors, was readily accepted by the Reagan administration.[120] There was, of course, no official talk of military alliance. All of this was, however, much more than a "tilt."

Another contributing consideration was the fear of "losing the Gulf" to the Soviet Union. Initially Kuwait had approached both the United States and the Soviet Union simultaneously about reflagging their oil tankers. The initial U.S. response "was characterized as matter-of-fact: positive in principle but only if Kuwait would qualify under stringent U.S. codes and regulations for such a procedure." The Soviets, in contrast, offered "full cooperation."[121] A high-level Kuwaiti delegation went to Moscow in January 1987 to negotiate the terms. Kuwait had closer relations with the Soviets than most traditional Arab monarchies, relations which included a $327 million arms deal signed in 1984. It was only when the Reagan administration learned of the Soviet offer to reflag Kuwait's tankers that it had a change of heart. It tried to condition its offer on Kuwait denying the Soviet navy access to its port facilities. When Kuwait rejected the condition, the Reagan administration dropped it. "If we don't do the job," President Reagan warned, "the Soviets will."[122] When the United States did begin the reflagging operation, the Soviets denounced it as "sinister" and "impermissible."[123]

What may have been even more significant in the long run was that "special look" at dual-use technology export controls that Vice-President Bush had promised Ambassador Hamdoon. "The instruction was issued," according to an internal Commerce Department memo, "to treat Iraqi applications favorably."[124] Stephen Bryen claimed that the Defense Department objected to about 40 percent of the license applications for dual-use exports to Iraq sent to it for review. By way of comparison, the DOD objection rate at that time for dual-use export license applications to the Soviet Union was about 5 percent.[125] According to Commerce Department record, submitted to Congress and obtained by me, 241 licenses were approved for dual-use exports to Iraq and only 6 were denied during the last two years of the Reagan administration. Among the exports approved were:

- precision machine tools for "general military repair," which ended up being used to upgrade SCUD missiles for longer-range firing;
- a hybrid digital-analog computer ostensibly for materials research, yet which was comparable to those used at the White Sands, New Mexico, missile test range and despite DOD's recommendation for denial because of "high likelihood of military use";
- computers and other equipment to the "Arab Company for Detergent Chemicals," which turned out to be a chemical weapons producer;
- numerous exports to the Iraqi Atomic Energy Commission;
- bacterial and fungus culture exports, ostensibly for research purposes;
- quartz crystals and frequency synthesizers as "components in a ground radar system," instead used for missile guidance systems;
- high-speed oscilloscopes, essential for maintaining radar systems but also crucial for missile guidance systems as well as for capturing the brief signals from a nuclear weapon test;
- fuel air explosive technology, capable of producing bombs ten times more lethal than conventional bombs and especially useful in large open areas such as deserts (although very little of the fighting in the war with Iran was in deserts).[126]

It wasn't only the nature of the exports involved. It also was the identity of the Iraqi customers. Exports "were knowingly sent," according to a former White House official, "to Iraqi nuclear installations." Take Sa'ad 16, the military-industrial complex which proved to be Iraq's largest and most important site for missile and nonconventional weapons development. Sa'ad 16 was said by Saddam's government simply to be a university research unit and industrial facility. Lots of labs, but as an analysis by the Defense Department's Office for Non-Proliferation concluded, "almost all of the labs named deal with areas applicable to missile research and production. . . . A lab for 'seismographic soil test' is also listed, possibly indicating nuclear research." Of course, these labs were guarded by anti-aircraft batteries, patrolled by Iraqi intelligence agents in armored cars, and fully equipped with video cameras, electronic sensors, and guards posted on watchtowers. At least by November 1986 (possibly earlier), the Defense Department had tagged Sa'ad 16 as the main site for the Condor II and other missile development programs.[127]

Then there was the Ministry of Industry and Military Industrialization (MIMI). Saddam created MIMI in April 1988 to bring together numerous civilian and military projects. One of the objectives was to enhance his control. To that end, he put his son-in-law, Hussein Kamil, in charge. Kamil also was the head of the Special Security Organization (SSO), in charge of Saddam's personal security and also of overseeing the other intelligence organizations. The other objective was to provide more of a cover through the civilian projects for the military ones. Thus, MIMI used a major dam project (Badush Dam) as a front for purchasing equipment for the Condor II missile being developed nearby. The Reagan administration knew much of this; it also had information linking MIMI to nuclear, chemical, and biological weapons programs. Yet dozens of dual-use technologies were licensed for export to MIMI.[128]

Another major Iraqi customer was the Nassr State Establishment for Mechanical Industries (NASSR). NASSR was known since the 1970s to be a key military installation. Its role in Iraqi ballistic missile programs was known since 1987. When Commerce was considering a dual-use export application in July 1988, DOD stated in no uncertain terms that this was a "bad end-user." This export application and numerous others were licensed anyway.[129]

When they couldn't stop the exports, DOD opponents tried at least to require verification of nonmilitary end-uses. They proposed an agreement with the Iraqi government allowing on-site inspections for a four-year period. But this proposal, too, was turned down. "The issue of military use of this equipment within Iraq," a State Department memorandum stated with reference to a particular application being considered in September 1987, "pertains to foreign policy and not national security. . . . Foreign policy controls do not apply to exports to Iraq, even when destined to military end-users or military end-uses, unless the export pertains to crime control and detection equipment, regional stability commodities or chemicals that can be used in the manufacture of chemical weapons."[130] While these were circumscribed categories, the "regional stability commodities" item had enough ambiguity to have been interpreted as broadly covering many of the dual-use technologies listed above. It wasn't.

The United States was not alone in selling dual-use technologies to Iraq. Germany was far and away the biggest supplier. Britain also was a major supplier. In fact, it later would be revealed that the British government allowed machines for manufacturing arms and for nuclear weapons development to be exported to Iraq. Iraqi government officials had bought a leading machine-tool company in Coventry, called Matrix-Churchill, which they were using as a front company in their global procurement network. Matrix-Churchill also had a subsidiary outside Cleveland, Ohio, a company which the commissioner of the U.S. Customs Service later stated was purchased "for the specific purpose of illegally acquiring critical weapons technology."

The "war of the cities," another escalation of the Iran-Iraq conflict, which broke out in February 1988, provided tangible evidence of the advances in missile technology Saddam had been making at Sa'ad 16 and his other military-industrial complexes. Up until then, at 550 kilometers from the Iraqi border, Teheran had been vulnerable to bombers but out of the reach of Iraqi missiles. Now, though, Iraq rained a new missile, dubbed the Al-Husayn, with a range of 650 kilometers, down on Teheran. What they had done was modify the Soviet-supplied SCUD-B to more than double its range. The Al-Husayn had first been successfully tested in August 1987. From February to April 1988, 190 of these were fired at Teheran.

In April Iraq also test-fired another new missile, the Al-Abbas. This one had an even greater range, 900 kilometers, and could carry a larger warhead. It was becoming increasingly clear that, as a Congressional Research Service team concluded, Iraq possessed "one of the largest arsenals of ballistic missiles in the Middle East," as well as "a growing research and development program."[131]

Even more explicit evidence came from "Operation Ali Baba," a Customs Service sting which on June 25, 1988, intercepted Condor II missile technology and related illegal exports. This actually was a joint Iraqi-Egyptian scheme reaching all the way to the Egyptian defense minister (who was fired as a result). The key operative was Dr. Abdelkader Helmy, an Egyptian-born American citizen who was a scientist employed at the Jet Propulsion Laboratory in California and possessor of a top-secret security clearance.[132] The list of items and materials which Helmy was supposed to obtain was, according to the analysis by the U.S. Defense Intelligence Agency (DIA), "entirely consistent with items necessary to support the manufacture of a ballistic missile." More specifically, "DIA believes Dr. Helmy was procuring these materials for the Condor missile." The Condor missile was a violation of the specifications mandated by the recently established Missile Technology Control Regime. The development of such a missile "capable of carrying conventional chemical or nuclear warheads into either Egypt or Iraq," in the DIA view,

> would increase regional tensions and add further fuel to the regional arms race. . . . The potential regional destabilization which might have been caused by Dr. Helmy's activities would be damaging to U.S. interests and peace efforts in the region.[133]

Concern also was raised around this time, as it had been three years earlier by Richard Perle, about Iraqi efforts to acquire nuclear weapons. The U.S. Department of Energy issued a report documenting Iraqi efforts to gain access to "export controlled information critical to nuclear weapons technology" from the U.S. national weapons laboratories. Through clever use of "Dear Colleague" letters, they had obtained from the U.S. National Technical Information Service reports on such subjects as precision detonators, neutron generators, and flash X-ray systems.[134]

Yet all this received very limited attention. The Reagan administration stayed fixated on Iran and the Soviet Union. With respect to these mutual enemies, the reflagging operation could be deemed a success.[135] Kuwait was protected, the sea lanes were kept open, the Soviet Union was kept out, and Iran was contained. In July 1988 Iran agreed to a United Nations–monitored cease-fire, ending the eight-year-long war on virtually the same terms it had previously rejected. There were costs, such as an estimated $250 million to run the naval operations. There were casualties, including the 290 passengers on a commercial Iran Air flight mistakenly shot down by the U.S.S. *Vincennes*. And there were risks at a number of junctures, as Professor Janice Gross Stein put it, "of becoming trapped in a process of escalation it [the Reagan administration] could not control."[136]

Summary

The basis for the alliance of convenience the Reagan administration struck with Iraq was the shared, or at least coinciding, interests made for by mutual enemies. Given the severity of the Iranian threat and continuing U.S.-Soviet global competition, the basis unquestionably was a strong one.

But even then it was not a complete one. Issues such as terrorism still were points of tension. There were signs of Iraqi military ambitions exceeding just survival of the war with Iran. And Saddam Hussein had some praise but still mostly virulent rhetoric for the United States, and some reform but still mostly repression for his own people.

Nevertheless, these early warnings for the most part were dismissed or discounted. Making the enemy of my enemy my friend appeared to have worked. And so it continued.

Saddam Gasses the Kurds:
Why No U.S. Sanctions?

THE CHEMICAL BOMBS BEGAN TO FALL ON THE IRAQI KURDS ON THE morning of August 25, 1988. Villagers later would tell investigators flown in by the U.S. Congress of "yellowish clouds," of gruesome human deaths, of dead livestock, even of birds which had "fallen out of the sky."[1]

With the Iran-Iraq war over—indeed, it had ended only five days earlier—Saddam Hussein was wasting little time in mounting his "final offensive" against the Iraqi Kurds. His planes and helicopters rained chemical warfare on more than thirty Kurdish villages, while his troops blocked all escape routes except those leading up into the rugged Taurus Mountains along the Turkish border. A few days later other troops were sent in (with gas masks, of course) to raze the villages and finish off any stragglers. In one small village named Baze, "Iraqi forces opened fire with machine-guns on everyone in the village and then used bulldozers to push the bodies into mass graves."[2]

The United States Senate swiftly and unanimously passed the Prevention of Genocide Act of 1988 calling for tough economic sanctions against Iraq. "Iraq's campaign against the Kurdish people," the Senate bill stated, "appears to constitute an act of genocide, a crime abhorred by civilized people everywhere and banned under international law."[3] The Reagan administration, however, strongly opposed the Senate bill. The attacks on the Kurds were "abhorrent and unjustifiable," Secretary of State Shultz declared. But to impose sanctions was "premature," one of Shultz's deputies argued. We need "solid, businesslike relations" with Iraq, said another. The bottom line, as laid out in an administration memorandum, was that "there should be no radical policy change now regarding Iraq."[4]

This position was curious in a number of respects. First, with the Iran-Iraq war over, the enemy-enemy-friend rationale for looking the other way in the name of the alliance of convenience was now less pressing. Second, amidst the debt and devastation wreaked by eight years of war, the Iraqi economy was potentially quite vulnerable to economic sanctions. Third, this disinclination to use economic sanctions for foreign policy purposes was out of character for an administration which had so vehemently opposed those who advocated sticking to "solid, businesslike relations" as a strategy of influence when it came to sanctions against the Soviet Union, or against Nicaragua, or against Libya.

Finally, not only was chemical warfare morally reprehensible, it was a clear and blatant violation of the 1925 Geneva Protocol Banning the Use of Chemical Weapons in War, to which Iraq was a party. And not the first such Iraqi violation, as noted in Chapter 1. Moreover, according to U.S. intelligence sources, several American-made helicopters, supposedly imported for crop dusting, were used in the chemical attacks on the Kurds. They sprayed mustard gas, not pesticides, and at people, not on plants.[5]

Why, then, no U.S. sanctions? This question is key because, even beyond the intrinsic importance of the immediate issue raised, the sanctions issue marked a critical test of the underlying logic of the Reagan policy and the sanctions debate was a key transitional stage in U.S.-Iraqi relations. The reasons that sanctions were not imposed in late 1988 help us to understand both the strategy and the politics of the policy course on which the Bush administration would set out in 1989.

Historical Context: Saddam, the Kurds, Chemical Weapons, and U.S. Policy

This was not the first time—nor would it be the last—that the Kurdish issue would pose a major policy dilemma for the United States. Or, for that matter, for the international community generally. A bit of historical background puts the issue in context.

Historically the Kurds have been a people without a state. The region known as "Kurdistan" spreads not only through northern Iraq but also across parts of Turkey, Iran, and Syria. The Kurds are Muslim (predominantly Sunni), but they have their own language, culture, and ethnic identity, separate from Arabs, Turks, and Persians (Iranians). They are the fourth largest ethnic group in the Middle East, numbering 20 million, with about 10 million in Turkey, 6 million in Iran, 4 million in Iraq, and smaller numbers in Syria and in Armenia.

The Treaty of Sevres, signed in August 1920 as part of the post–World War I deconstruction of the Ottoman Empire, called for the creation of an independent Kurdistan. This was the same treaty that defined the states of Syria and Iraq. But while both these states eventually were created (Iraq in 1932 after a period of British mandate, Syria in 1946 after a period of French mandate), Kurdistan never was. The Turkish nationalist leader Ataturk (Mustafa Kemal) reasserted claim to Turkish Kurdistan, and the British insisted on keeping the oil-rich province of Mosul as part of their mandate-controlled Iraq. The League of Nations, however, did require that the Kurds in Iraq be given a degree of autonomy. This was significant because it gave the Iraqi Kurds a standing in international law that other Kurdish populations have never had.[6]

However, the central authorities, first British and then Iraqi, never lived up to these guarantees. Insurrections and guerrilla warfare by the Kurdish *pesh mergas* ("those who face death") can be traced all the way back to the 1920s. The British, the Iraqi monarchs (Kings Faisal I and II) who ruled from 1930 to 1958, the military government of General Qassim, and the Ba'ath regimes since 1968—all made promises of autonomy to the Kurds; all broke them; all resorted to military force to suppress Kurdish rebellions; none ever totally succeeded.

Kissinger, the Shah, and the Kurds, 1972–75: A "Cynical Enterprise"

In 1972 the Kurds found a friend—or at least they thought they did—in the Shah of Iran. If the Kurdish insurgency could be strengthened enough to tie up and weaken the Iraqi regime, the Shah calculated, his pursuit of regional preeminence would be well served. He thus began providing military and financial aid to the Iraqi Kurdish insurgency.

Even more important, he drew the United States in. This was the height of the American courting of the Shah. At the same seminal May 1972 meeting in Teheran at which they granted the Shah a virtual blank check on U.S. non-nuclear arms, President Richard Nixon and National Security Advisor Henry Kissinger also agreed to the Shah's request for covert U.S. aid to the Kurds.[7] Iraq had just signed its Treaty of Friendship and Cooperation with the Soviet Union, and while Nixon and Kissinger were in the midst of their pursuit of détente (indeed, their stop in Teheran was on the way home from a Moscow summit), their definition of "détente" encompassed continued competition through regional surrogates.[8]

Between 1972 and 1975 the CIA provided $16 million in aid to the Kurds. But as investigations by conservative columnist William Safire and the House Select Committee on Intelligence (the Pike Committee) made abundantly clear, the strategy never really was to help the Kurds win.[9] The Shah, who long had had his own restive Kurdish minority, was not interested in setting a precedent of genuine Kurdish autonomy. He simply wanted to tie the Iraqis up, drain their resources, sap their will to contest the broader Persian Gulf rivalry for influence. The same held for Nixon and Kissinger. A CIA memo dated March 23, 1974, stressed the benefit to both the United States and Iran "in a stalemate situation . . . in which Iraq is intrinsically weakened by the Kurds' refusal to relinquish their semi-autonomy. Neither Iran nor ourselves wish to see the matter resolved." As cold-hearted as such a statement was, it hardly compared to the axiom offered by Kissinger himself: "Covert action," Kissinger remarked, "should not be confused with missionary work."[10] The Pike Committee offered its assessment:

> The President, Dr. Kissinger and foreign head of state [the Shah] hoped our clients [the Kurds] would not prevail. They preferred instead that the insurgents simply continue a level of hostilities sufficient to sap the resources of our ally's neighboring country [Iraq]. This policy was not imparted to our clients who were encouraged to continue fighting.[11]

Sure enough, in March 1975, the Shah negotiated his own separate peace with Saddam Hussein. In return for Saddam's concessions on the disputed Shatt al-Arab waterway and his agreement to end his support for anti-Shah movements in Iran, the Shah agreed to end his support for the Kurds. He even went so far as to agree to forcibly repatriate forty thousand refugees who had fled to Iran, and then to close his border to any further Kurdish flight. These promises he kept, even when Saddam violated the cease-fire, shooting down "in cold blood" some one thousand *pesh merga* fighters who had surrendered and killing another five thousand Kurdish women, children, and elderly men as they scrambled to flee the country.[12]

Mullah Mustafa Barzani, leader of the Kurdish Democratic party (KDP), pleaded for assistance from the United States. "Our people's fate in unprecedented danger," read the message he sent to his CIA contact. "Complete destruction hanging over our head. No explanation for all this. We appeal to you and the U.S. Government intervene according to your promises." Barzani also wrote Kissinger directly:

> Our hearts bleed to see that an immediate byproduct of this agreement [between Iran and Iraq] is the destruction of our defenseless people. . . . We feel, Your Excellency, that the United States has a

moral and political responsibility towards our people who have committed themselves to your country's policy. . . . Mr. Secretary, we are anxiously awaiting your quick response.[13]

A cable also came back to Washington from the CIA station chief on both the political stakes and the humanitarian exigencies:

> Is headquarters in touch with Kissinger's office on this; if USG [U.S. government] does not handle the situation deftly in a way which will avoid giving the Kurds the impression that we are abandoning them they are likely to go public. Iran's action has not only shattered their political hopes; it endangers lives of thousands.

But still there was no response from Kissinger. Twelve days later the CIA station chief again cabled: "If the USG intends to take steps to avert a massacre it must intercede with Iran promptly."[14]

Barzani would later lament that all along he had been counting on the United States. "We never trusted the Shah. Without American promises we wouldn't have acted the way we did." Shortly before he died in March 1979, stricken with cancer and in exile in a suburb of Washington, D.C., when asked what was the worst mistake of his life, he responded, "my judgment about the American government that betrayed us."[15] U.S. policy toward the Kurds truly was, as characterized by the House Select Committee on Intelligence, "a cynical enterprise."[16]

Saddam vs. the Kurds

In the early years of the Iran-Iraq war, the Kurds were unable to take advantage of Saddam's attention (and troops) being diverted, primarily because of their own factional fighting between the KDP, now led by Mullah Mustafa's son Massoud Barzani, and the Patriotic Union of Kurdistan (PUK) led by Jalal Talabani. In July and October 1983 the KDP and Iran joined forces in a major offensive. The PUK, however, struck a deal with Saddam. Saddam reportedly agreed to greater autonomy and increased budget resources for a PUK-run Kurdistan region. The PUK, in return, was to establish an army of forty thousand soldiers to defend Kurdistan against "foreign enemies."[17] With the other hand Saddam cracked down on the KDP, imprisoning an estimated eight thousand members of the Barzani clan alone.

The PUK soon would discover what the KDP had already learned, that deals with Saddam Hussein were not to be counted on. Saddam didn't grant autonomy, and he didn't deliver the promised budget resources. By 1985–86 the PUK and KDP had agreed to set aside their differences and join forces with each other, and with Iran, against Saddam. The enemy of my enemy is my friend.

Saddam now felt he had his justification to unleash even more brutal repression against the "traitorous" Kurds. A U.S. Senate staff delegation which visited Kurdistan in the fall of 1987 reported "hundreds of villages leveled" across a countryside which "has an eery, deserted quality to it. Fruit trees, graveyards and cemeteries stand as reminders of the absent people and livestock."[18]

This report stirred debate on the Senate floor, but had little impact on the Reagan policy. This was the period, as discussed in Chapter 1, in which U.S. policy was tilting further and further to Iraq. The U.S. Navy was in the Persian Gulf in harm's way carrying out the reflagging mission. Export controls were being made looser, CCC credit guarantees larger. Kurdish human rights once again were relegated to peripheral status, overridden by geopolitical calculations.

It thus seems hardly coincidental timing that in February 1988 Saddam launched his even more massive "al-Anfal" campaign against the Kurds.[19] The goal was to break the Kurdish-Iranian alliance by effectively depopulating large areas of Iraqi Kurdistan. The method was wanton destruction and massive killing. Secret police records, replete with ledger books with "a cheerful flowered-pattern cover," revealed cold-blooded entries such as one which chillingly read simply, "four days ago, 24 men, 32 women and 54 children gave themselves up to a military unit.' "[20] Another file was on a sixteen-year-old shepherd who was seized while grazing his sheep, and then killed. There were photographs, such as one of "three Iraqi soldiers as they hold up the head of a man they have just executed. Sporting their rifles and flash-ing victory signs, they resemble hunters with their trophy." There also were videotapes of executions. The purpose of the videotapes? "To terrorize local populations and to show superiors in Baghdad the fine work being done in the field." The man in charge in Baghdad was Ali Hasan Majid, a cousin of Saddam and the same man who two and a half years later would be given the task of administering occupied Kuwait.

As part of the al-Anfal campaign, on March 16, 1988, the Iraqi air force strafed Halabja, a major Kurdish agricultural city and trading center about 150 miles northeast of Baghdad, with mustard gas and nerve toxins. Four days earlier Iraqi forces had lost a battle for the city to the Kurdish-Iranian forces. As weapons of mass destruction are wont to be, civilians bore the brunt.

> Entire families were wiped out and the streets were littered with the corpses of men, women and children. Other forms of life in and around the city—horses, house cats, cattle—perished as well.[21]

According to some sources, as many as five thousand people were killed: a death toll proportionate to over a half million deaths in a city the size of New York.

What Saddam was displaying was the largest arsenal of chemical weapons in the Third World. For all the fixation at the time on Libya and its Rabta plant, Iraq had greater chemical weapons production capacity and was producing more sophisticated (that is, more deadly) chemical weapons—and, unlike Libya, had made repeated use of them.[22] Iraqi efforts to build indigenous chemical weapons production capacity had begun in earnest in the mid-1970s, drawing mainly on dual-use equipment and technology imported from West Germany.[23] The 1976–80 Five Year Plan included a major "pesticides plant" to be built at Samarra, about forty-five miles northwest of Baghdad. The Samarra plant was to produce a thousand tons a year of organic phosphorous compounds. These chemicals were of such high toxicity that most Western nations had banned them years earlier as pesticides.

They also, though, had use as precursor chemicals for Sarin and Tabun, two deadly nerve gases.[24]

Nor was this the first time that Saddam had used chemical weapons. Four times during the Iran-Iraq war, the United Nations found evidence that Saddam used chemical weapons against Iranian troops. The first time was in March 1984, when doctors in Belgium, Sweden, and West Germany confirmed that the Iranian soldiers sent to them for treatment were victims of mustard gas. In April 1985, February–March 1986, and April–May 1987, U.N. missions sent to the region found further evidence of Iraqi use of chemical weapons.[25] This time the horrors not only were seen by a U.N. commission, but were reported in the Western media.

The Reagan administration did respond to the Halabja attacks by sponsoring a condemnatory resolution in the U.N. Security Council (as it had done three times previously) and tightening export controls on some items specifically related to chemical weapons manufacture.[26] But these were issue-specific retaliations rather than a more general policy reassessment—and not nearly the level of response against Libya. Moreover, as detailed in Chapter 1, a number of controversial dual-use exports were allowed to go through. At the same time, on the diplomatic front, a "no-contacts" policy toward the Kurds was adopted. Shortly after the Halabja attacks, two mid-level State Department officials had met in Washington with Kurdish leader Jalal Talabani. This meeting elicited an "explosive reaction" from Baghdad, in response to which Secretary of State Shultz—who had not authorized the meeting—issued an edict "mandating no contact with the Iraqi opposition." When Talabani came back to Washington in August, he was "cold-shouldered" by the State Department.[27]

The Iran-Iraq cease-fire took hold on August 20. Just three days earlier, Amnesty International had issued a human rights appeal to the United Nations (its Subcommission on Prevention of Discrimination and Protection of Minorities). The appeal stressed "grave fears that in the aftermath of the war a further significant deterioration in human rights could occur in Iraq." And it raised special concerns about "a systematic and deliberate policy . . . to eliminate large numbers of Kurdish civilians."[28] Within days the chemical attacks began, and this time on an even more massive scale.

Here, then, was a country which was a signatory to the Geneva Protocol yet was known to be producing weapons of mass destruction on a massive scale, *and* had used them *repeatedly.*[29] Indeed, they used them quite effectively. The Ayatollah Khomeini's eventual consigning to make peace with the infidel Saddam despite his vows never to do so was in part due to the demoralizing effects of having had an estimated fifty thousand Iranians killed by Iraqi chemical weapons and the attendant fear that more would follow. Similarly, the chemical warfare against the Kurds did weaken their insurgency—at least until Desert Storm, and even then the Kurds again found themselves subject to Saddam's attacks, and as in 1974–75, with less support from the United States than they believed was promised.

Thus, one way or another, the stage was set for a precedent to be established in the fall of 1988. Firm action could have an effect on Iraq and, more broadly, send a message of U.S. commitment to global nonproliferation. Weaker action risked sending a very different message to Saddam and to others.

The Sanctions Debate

S.2763, the Prevention of Genocide Act of 1988, was quite a hard-hitting bill. It would have embargoed all dual-use technology exports, cut off CCC and Export-Import Bank credits, banned U.S. imports of Iraqi oil, and mandated U.S. opposition to any loans to Iraq by the International Monetary Fund (IMF) or other multilateral financial institutions. All this in a bill the co-sponsors of which were Senator Claiborne Pell, chairman of the Senate Foreign Relations Committee and a staunch liberal, and Senator Jesse Helms, ranking Republican on the committee and the staunchest of conservatives. "Iraq's conduct is a crime against humanity," Senator Pell declared. "It must be met with the toughest possible response." "The United States must not sit idly

by," Senator Helms affirmed. "This legislation. . . . will help demon-
strate to the Iraqi regime just how serious our country views its campaign against the Kurds. In addition, it will help assure that United
States tax dollars do not subsidize the Iraqis."[30]

The Senate voted the day after the bill was introduced. The vote
was unanimous. Indeed it was, as one seasoned journalist wrote, "a re-
markably fast and serious response to human rights violations overseas. Congress often passes resolutions condemning acts by foreign
governments but rarely takes such a strong step so quickly."[31]

From there, though, the bill slowed down, was weakened, and ultimately died. Opposition came both from the Reagan administration
and from within the House of Representatives. To summarize the legislative history: The Reagan administration immediately announced
its opposition to the Senate bill. It worked with Senate bill opponents
in the House to weaken the companion bill. When the House did approve a bill on September 27, it contained the same dual-use technology sanctions as the Senate bill, but other measures such as suspension
of CCC credits, the ban on oil imports, and the mandatory vote
against loans to Iraq by multilateral financial institutions were left to
the discretion of the president.

On September 30 the Senate passed a compromise bill weaker than
its own original measure but stronger than the House bill. It put the
anti-multilateral loans provision back in, and set a sixty-day deadline
within which the president would be required to impose the additional sanctions unless he got assurances that Iraq would no longer use
chemical weapons. The House rejected the compromise.

On October 7 another compromise was broached. The terms were
similar except that the sixty-day deadline was extended to ninety
days. Also, a specific exemption for agricultural goods was added. But
this compromise also fell apart, in part because it got caught up in
end-of-session wrangling on non-germane issues being tacked on and
in part due to pressure from the Reagan administration. The bill died
on the last day of the congressional session.

The Reagan administration did not doubt that Saddam Hussein
had used chemical weapons against the Kurds. Secretary Shultz re-

counts that "I called in the Iraqi minister of state for foreign affairs, Saadoun Hammadi, and blasted him." Authorization was given to disclose the U.S. intercepts of Iraqi military communications, which was the "incontrovertible evidence" that chemical weapons had been used.[32] Nevertheless, the administration position was to threaten to veto any bill that passed and to state only that the president would impose sanctions "on his own" if Iraq again used chemical weapons. But no sanctions now for the attacks on the Kurds. And no legislation, mandate, or requirement even on next-time terms was acceptable. The administration didn't even withdraw the American ambassador from Baghdad, something which, for example, it had done around the same time against Communist Bulgaria to protest the Bulgarian treatment of ethnic Turks, which, while repugnant, was hardly of the same magnitude as ethnic chemical warfare.

Publicly the administration made the argument about sanctions being "premature." Diplomacy, both bilateral and through the United Nations, should be tried first. Moreover, beyond just the timing, sanctions risked being "counterproductive" both to "our effort to maintain a dialogue with the government of Iraq" and more broadly "to our efforts to deal with the use of chemical weapons in the Gulf region."[33]

While these concerns did have some credence, they did not adequately explain the Reagan administration's position. Concerns about counterproductivity hadn't dissuaded the Reagan administration from imposing sanctions against the Soviet Union, or Nicaragua, or Libya. Indeed, arguments about counterproductivity made by opponents of these other sanctions were dismissed as apologias. As Senator William Proxmire (D-Wisconsin) stated, "If Nicaragua were using chemical agents against its own population or a neighboring state, the outcry by the public, politicians and our own Government would drown out all other news."[34]

It also was hard to accept the idea that taking action now against a country which had used chemical weapons so many previous times still was premature. By Secretary Shultz's own account, this was not the first time he personally had protested to Iraqi officials about the use of chemical weapons. He takes credit for the March 5, 1984, protest against Iraqi use of chemical weapons against Iranian forces; for telling Tariq Aziz on November 26, 1984, the day U.S.-Iraqi diplomatic relations were normalized, that "the United States was unalterably opposed to the use of chemical weapons and that we would be watching Iraq carefully"; and again to Tariq Aziz on March 26, 1985, following intelligence reports on Iraqi construction of a new chemical weapons plant, that "the U.S. deplores and deeply opposes the production, acquisition and use of such weapons; Iraq must understand this and act accordingly."[35]

Nor was this latest round of bilateral diplomacy yielding much. The Iraqi ambassador's response to Secretary of State Shultz's criticisms was that the charges were "baseless." While Foreign Minister Aziz did pledge that Iraq "respects and abides" by all international agreements and commitments with regard to chemical weapons, Defense Minister Adnan Khairallah acknowledged "the rule" but also stated that "each rule has an exception."[36] The official Baghdad media attributed the Senate bill to the work of "Zionists" and other "potentates of imperialism and racism."[37] In Baghdad following the Senate vote, Saddam bussed 18,000 people in 150 double-decker buses to the U.S. embassy for a three-hour protest denouncing American "interference" in Iraqi internal affairs.[38]

Two more fundamental factors were at work—one a function of domestic interest group politics, the other a matter of geopolitical strategy.

Interest Groups and the
Paradox of Reverse Leverage

One of the main arguments all along for increasing trade had been that expanded economic relations would be a source of U.S. political leverage. The more Iraq came to value and depend on trade with the United States, the greater the purported potential U.S. influence on Iraqi policies. As proponents of sanctions saw it, now was the time to tap that potential.

The Iraqi economy was in dire straits. The toll from eight years of war was an estimated $450 billion.[39] To be sure, with his police state apparatus at his disposal, Saddam did not have to worry about Iraq's consumers marching in the streets. But Ba'athist party political domination traditionally had been part of a Faustian-like bargain the Iraqi people had been willing to make in return for a much higher level of public services and standard of living than in most other Arab countries. After the deprivations and disruptions of eight years of war, there was an expectation of a "peace dividend."

Yet for a country already some $80 billion in debt, new credit was tight. Western commercial banks, if they were willing to lend at all, were asking interest rates as high as 15–20 percent. Most Western governments had put Iraq "off cover" for medium-term and even short-term financing. Iraqi arrearages were over $100 million to Italy, $90 million to France, $65 million to Britain, $36 million to West Germany, and "unreported but large" to Japan.[40]

Nor was there much relief in sight from world oil markets. The combination of declining world prices and the disruptions of the war had pushed Iraqi oil revenues down from $22 billion in 1980 to a low of $7.8 billion in 1986. In 1988 they still were only $11 billion, half of the prewar level, not even taking inflation into account.

The relative value to Iraq of its trade with the United States thus was quite significant. American CCC credits had not followed the general credit-tightening pattern; in fact, they had grown to exceed $1 billion per year. Additional food exports were provided through the USDA's Export Enhancement Program and Targeted Export Assistance and Cooperation Programs. All told, for an economy which was dependent on imports for 65–70 percent of its agricultural products, this was tremendously important trade.[41]

The United States also had become a major customer for Iraqi oil. Back in 1981, before the tilt to Iraq began, the United States did not import a single barrel of Iraqi oil. Even as late as 1987, U.S. imports of Iraqi oil were no more than 30 million barrels. But in 1988 this figure increased more than 400 percent to 126 million barrels. Part of the deal was a $1 per barrel discount off world prices for U.S. companies. Even with the discount, U.S. purchases brought in $1.6 billion. The United

States had gone from non-customer to small customer to buying one out of every four barrels of Iraqi oil exports.[42]

However, as U.S.-Iraqi trade had expanded, it wasn't just the Iraqis who derived economic benefits. There are, after all, two parties (at least) to every economic transaction. One of the parties was an American farmer, an American worker, an American corporation. Their interests were in the continuation if not the expansion of this trade— surely not in its disruption by economic sanctions.

This was especially true for American agriculture. The very mention of sanctions evoked bitter memories of the 1980 grain embargo against the Soviet Union following its invasion of Afghanistan. Ronald Reagan had made "the Carter grain embargo" a major campaign issue back in 1980. His administration had signed a new grain trade agreement with the Soviets in August 1983 which included the firm and explicit pledge never to embargo grain again.[43] August 1983, it should be recalled, was still the days of the Soviet Union as "evil empire." On virtually all other fronts the Reagan administration was vigorously prosecuting the cold war. The nuclear arms buildup was going at breakneck speed. The president had only months earlier given his "Star Wars" speech. NATO was deploying the Pershing and cruise missiles. The CIA was funneling aid and arms to anti-Communist guerrillas in Nicaragua and Afghanistan. Sanctions had been used to try to block the new Soviet natural gas pipeline, including secondary sanctions against our Western European allies who refused to go along on this issue.[44] But for grain, the one American export on which the Soviets relied heavily in trade with the United States, the interest group pressure was not to be bucked.

As with the Soviet market in the 1970s, the Iraqi market had grown rapidly in the 1980s. It was now the twelfth largest overall market for American agricultural exports. For some crops such as rice, it was the number-one export market. Iraq was second only to Mexico as a recipient of CCC export credit guarantees. Another $1.1 billion in guarantees were slated for the fiscal year about to begin, on top of the $1.1 billion the previous year and $3.4 billion cumulative since fiscal year 1983. Looking even more to the future, the Agriculture Department was convinced of "Iraq's enormous market potential for U.S. agricultural exports."[45]

Here, too, there was a minority view. The Kurdish issue aside, some Reagan administration officials were becoming increasingly wary of the economic risks. At a meeting in August of the National Advisory Council on International Monetary and Financial Policy (NAC), the key interagency group which advises on credit and other international financial programs, both the Treasury Department and Federal Reserve Board representatives had proposed a $600 million limit on fiscal year 1989 CCC credits for Iraq. They acknowledged that up to this point Iraq had maintained a good repayment record to the CCC. But they were growing increasingly concerned that Iraq had set up a "Ponzi-type scheme" in which the Iraqis repaid debts only to those who offered additional credit.[46] In its own country risk assessments even the Agriculture Department did acknowledge some concerns about repayment risks. There also had been a criminal investigation the previous June by the Agriculture Department inspector general in conjunction with the Department of Justice into irregularities and improprieties in the CCC program. Yet in late September, with fiscal year 1988 drawing to a close, and separate from the $1 billion in new credits awaiting them on October 1, the CCC reallocated another $30 million in additional loan guarantees to Iraq from other country programs.

The Iraqis were quick to recognize the potential to reverse the direction of who had leverage over whom in the U.S.-Iraq trade relationship. They threatened both to turn elsewhere for their future agricultural imports and to renege on the roughly $1.5 billion outstanding CCC debt. The Reagan administration did less countering of such threats than conveying them to Capitol Hill. The message was received. Iraq was "a large and growing market for U.S. agricultural exports," noted House Agriculture Committee Chairman E. "Kika" de la Garza (D-Texas). "In light of the difficulties our nation's farmers have faced over the past few years, I am deeply concerned over any possible loss of a major market for U.S. agricultural commodities." Of course, de la Garza added, "at the same time I in no way wish to condone the use of chemical weapons by Iraq, or any other country."[47] Agriculture Chairman de la Garza and other Democrats from agricultural districts joined with Republicans in the House to block the original Senate sanctions bill with its suspension of the CCC program. "Recognizing political reality" was how one journalist described the concession by Congressman Howard Berman, principal sponsor of the House companion to the Senate bill, to delete CCC sanctions. The closest the House bill came to agricultural sanctions was a loose requirement that the president impose "appropriate additional sanctions" if Iraq again used chemical weapons.

It also was business as usual on the manufacturing and dual-use technology export side. Actual trade levels in manufactured goods were not as high as in agriculture, but they were growing. Billions of dollars in contracts had begun to be signed in such sectors as petroleum, electricity generation, petrochemicals, steel, and transportation.[48] Not only would these be lost if sanctions were imposed, but Iraqi reconstruction from the war was just beginning and U.S. companies would be excluded from the anticipated boom. The Commerce Department estimated the potential for $3 billion of U.S. nonagricultural exports annually, for the foreseeable future.

The U.S. Chamber of Commerce urged House Foreign Affairs Committee Chairman Dante Fascell that we "set aside the emotions of the moment" and ponder the economic costs of sanctions against Iraq.[49] Particularly active in the anti-sanctions lobbying was the U.S.-Iraq Business Forum.[50] This group had been established in 1985. The president was Marshall Wiley, a lawyer and former U.S. ambassador to Oman and the ranking U.S. diplomat in Baghdad in 1975–77. A key board member was Richard Fairbanks, who had held a number of top Middle East policy positions, including the head of Operation Staunch, and who now independently was a paid and registered lobbyist for the Iraqi government. Member companies included numerous oil companies now heavily involved in importing the discounted Iraqi oil (Amoco, Mobil, Exxon, Texaco, Occidental), defense contractors (Lockheed, Bell Helicopter–Textron, United Technologies), and other Fortune 500 companies (AT&T, General Motors, Bechtel, Caterpillar).

The Forum exemplified the reverse leverage phenomenon even more graphically than the CCC credits lobby. While not formally a lobbyist for the Iraqi government, its ties to the Iraqi embassy in Washington had been quite close since its inception. Even before the Forum had its own office, Iraqi ambassador Nizar Hamdoon had written to the CEOs of several major American corporations on its behalf. "Any United States company interested in doing business with Iraq . . . would do well to join the Forum." Ambassador Hamdoon later made the link tighter, telling a group of CEOs that "our people in Baghdad give priority—when there is competition between the two companies—to the one that is a member of the Forum." The purpose of the Forum, Wiley told an interviewer, was to help American business leaders and Iraqi government officials "get to know each other better."

The Forum also had close ties to the Reagan administration. At one of its conferences earlier in 1988, one Reagan official told Forum members that the administration looked to them "to help preserve—and expand—the overall U.S.-Iraqi relationship through its commercial side." Richard Fairbanks, in addition to his other positions, also was heading up the Middle East policy task force for Vice-President George Bush's presidential campaign. "I talked to senior officials in the administration," Wiley later stated. "I asked if they had any objections to what we were doing. We were told that not only were our goals consistent with U.S. policy, but what we were endeavoring to do served to enhance their policy. The administration wanted closer diplomatic and commercial ties to Iraq, the very same things we wanted."[51]

The U.S.-Iraq Business Forum weighed in heavily on the sanctions debate. Wiley wrote a letter to President Reagan expressing opposition to any sanctions. He and other Forum board members lobbied against sanctions in the House. And Wiley responded to a pro-sanctions column by *Washington Post* foreign affairs columnist Jim Hoagland with a letter to the editor decrying "Hoagland's emotional article [which] contains more heat than light." The Forum did not, of course, support the use of chemical weapons, but "the real issue is whether imposing unilateral sanctions on Iraq will be effective. . . . Morality is an essential ingredient in foreign policy in a democratic society. But morality detached from reality is stupidity."[52]

All told, as one congressional staff aide put it, the lobbying against sanctions "was obscene." All "the special interests," Senator Pell lamented, "got into the act."[53] Whatever leverage the sanctions may have brought the United States over Iraq was being constrained by the leverage that groups with vested interests in trade with Iraq were exerting in reverse.

Saddam and Iraq:
"Into the Mainstream"?

It would be simplistic, though, to reduce the Reagan administration's opposition to sanctions against Iraq just to economic interest group politics. There also was the geopolitical calculus that, as one internal analysis put it, Iraq's foreign policy was moving "deeper into the mainstream." Numerous Iraqi actions and attitudes were cited as evidence of a "moderating policy trend":

> Iraq's shift toward moderation, cooperation with neighbors and mainline Arab positions on Palestine seems *permanent and deepening*.

> In the likely case that the Iran-Iraq war ends in an armed truce rather than a peace treaty or a decisive victory, Iraq will be vulnerable, hence *unlikely to embark on foreign adventures* in the Gulf or against Israel.

> Iraq has developed *good working relations with Kuwait and is no longer trying to encroach on Kuwaiti territory*.

> *Fears of Iraqi aggression seem exaggerated.*[54]

While this study was written before the chemical weapons attacks on the Kurds, its analysis was based on trends which it identified as dating back all the way to 1978. Moreover, other administration analyses contemporaneous with the chemical weapons attacks took the analysis even further, arguing that even Saddam himself was changing. His "world view" still was "that of a conspirator who believes that power comes from the barrel of a gun." His rhetoric at times still was "Qadhafi-like," and he still tended to be "more mistrustful of the U.S. than are most other Arab heads of state." Nevertheless, he was said to have "a streak of pragmatism" and was credited with recognizing that he "has a long-term interest in developing political and economic relations with the U.S."[55] He thus was deemed the type of leader with whom one could pursue a strategy of "persuasion," to whom one could make the case that he "has more to gain from conforming to international standards than flouting them."[56]

The Washington policy community generally shared this bullish view. We needed to overcome our "blind spot" toward Iraq, wrote one Washington think tank expert. "Iraq's former hostility to Western and U.S. interests in the Gulf and its subversive position towards the conservative Arab States of the Gulf are conditions that no longer exist."[57] The main impediment to closer and better relations, another noted expert advised, was "American reticence." We needed to recognize the new "congruence in American and Iraqi interests." Iraq had changed "in fundamental and enduring ways." Saddam and his regime had been "mellowing," there was "perestroika in Iraq"; indeed, "it is probably not just idle chatter when Iraqi officials express a hope that the end of the war will bring more democracy affirming that Saddam Hussein is 'much concerned about democracy.... He thinks that it is healthy.' "[58] After all, before the Iran-Iraq war, Saddam "was a popular leader perceived by many Iraqis to be young, energetic, alert to the needs of his people and a major driving force behind Iraq's economic prosperity."[59]

The prevailing view thus was that while the war-induced need for an alliance of convenience had subsided, new and expanded bases for a U.S.-Iraqi relationship were developing. The moment was a transitional one, and in that respect and from that viewpoint the sanctions debate could not have come at a worse time. Imposition of sanctions would "undermine relations and reduce U.S. influence on a country that has emerged from the Gulf War as one of the most powerful Arab nations." They risked being taken as an indication that U.S.-Iraqi relations were "fragile," and could in Saddam's eyes "discredit the views of the few Iraqi officials who understand our system and try to explain our actions."[60]

Thus, not only was the Reagan administration seeking to head off the sanctions legislation, which would have prohibited such exports once passed, records show that it was granting new licenses for dual-use technology exports at a rate more than 50 percent greater than *before* Saddam's gassing of the Kurds. Paul Freedenberg, who at the time was under secretary of commerce for export administration, gave sworn testimony to a congressional committee that when he proposed that sanctions be imposed, he was told that policy was to continue to be one of "normal trade":

> In the summer of 1988, a number of licenses were pending with regard to technology transfer to Iraq. I asked for official guidance with regard to what licensing policy would be to Iraq, since by that time there was credible evidence of the use of poison gas by the Iraqis against their own people and also against the Iranians in the war. I suggested that the imposition of foreign policy controls be considered as a way of justifying the denial of export licenses to Iraq. That summer, I was told by the National Security Council that the licensing policy with regard to Iraq was that of normal trade and that under normal circumstances, on an individual, case-by-case basis, should clear the licenses that were pending to Iraq. I passed that information on to the licensing officers, and the few dozen licenses that were pending at that time were approved and licenses were issued for exports to Iraq.[61]

Reagan administration records show that between September and December 1988, 65 licenses were granted for dual-use technology exports. This averages out as an annual rate of 260 licenses, more than double the rate for January through August 1988 (85 licenses, for a 128 annual rate).[62] In one case, computers "for a graphics design system used in tooling designs" were approved for export to the Nassr State Establishment for Mechanical Industries (NASSR). Even aside from the Kurdish chemical warfare issue, the Pentagon had opposed this export because of its assessment of NASSR as a "bad end-user." The importer, it pointed out in an internal memo, "is a subordinate to the Military Industry Commission and located in a military facility. . . . Also, this system could contribute directly to increasing Iraq's military force capability." Both the State and Commerce departments supported the export, and they prevailed. The fact that NASSR was "under the Military Industry Commission is not grounds for denial," the acting director of the Commerce Department Office of Export Licensing wrote in a memorandum to his DOD counterpart. "The Nassr Establishment is a multi-functional complex."[63]

The U.S. Customs Service later would testify that it already had its own investigations under way at this time. Customs inspectors had "detected a marked increase in the activity levels of Iraq's procurement networks. These increased levels of activity were particularly noticeable in the areas of missile technology, chemical-biological warfare and fuze technology."[64] One particular investigation, a joint British-American one, was of Iraqi efforts through its British front companies to acquire nuclear "triggers" (electronic detonator capacitators), which according to a later grand jury indictment dated to "on or about September 6, 1988."[65] While the sting was not sprung until March 1990 (see Chapter 4), policymakers at the time should have known at least about the preliminary evidence as Customs provides both Commerce and State with a list of open investigations on a monthly basis.[66]

Saddam also had been building up biological weapons production capability. Biological weapons (that is, germ warfare) can be even more deadly and unpredictable in their use than chemical weapons. Again, West German companies played a leading role. More so than with chemical weapons, so, too, did the United States. Between 1985 and 1989, seventeen licenses were approved for exports of bacterial and fungus cultures to Iraqi government agencies. Yet at least as early as January 1988 reports of Iraqi germ warfare capabilities were appearing in the open specialized press.[67] The claim by Baghdad that these plants were really intended to produce medical vaccines was hardly credible in light of the fact that such vaccines could be much more cheaply purchased than produced by a country like Iraq. One respected American analyst confirmed that "there were growing indications in late 1988 that Iraq was producing a botulin toxin in military quantities, or some similar agent." "Everybody knows," a U.S. government official was quoted as saying, "the Iraqis are trying to develop biological weapons."[68]

However, this knowledge of Saddam's nuclear and biological weapons programs did not bring tighter export controls. Nor did other developments have any appreciable effect in questioning the deeper-into-the-mainstream geopolitical assessment.

At least two major dissents were mounted in the Reagan State Department. One was a paper written by Zalmay Khalilzad, a member of the Policy Planning Staff, questioning how much Saddam had changed and whether he might now need to be "contained" from taking advantage of the regional power imbalance left by such a weakened Iran.[69] Khalilzad had been a strong supporter of the tilt toward Iraq during the Iran-Iraq war, for reasons of regional balance of power. By the end of the war, though, intelligence briefings revealed the collapse of Iran to have been even more extensive than anticipated. In Khalilzad's view, the strategic logic remained the same, but the power balance had changed. The regional power imbalance was such, he argued, that it was perfectly natural behavior for any state which aspired to regional hegemony, let alone Saddam's Iraq, to seek to exploit such an opportunity. Nor was it just the abstract balance of power that was raising concerns about Saddam. Almost immediately after the cease-fire with Iran was in place and his need for Kuwaiti financing was lessened, Saddam again began pressuring Kuwait for concessionary long-term leases on Bubiyan and Warbah islands. He also was quick to set out to settle scores with rival Syrian leader Hafez al-Asad by stepping up arms deliveries to the Lebanese army faction of Christian general Michel Aoun. By October this included tanks, armored personnel carriers, multiple rocket launchers, artillery batteries, and some 100,000 rounds of ammunitions.[70]

The United States therefore needed to be prepared "to punish Iraq," as Khalilzad put it in a talk delivered at a think tank conference around the same time. But he took the balance-of-power logic even further, arguing that the United States also needed to be willing to assist Iran. "U.S. interests in the Gulf have changed dramatically in the past two years. Where stability once rested on keeping Iran's relative strength in check by preventing it from defeating Iraq and exporting revolution, it is now based on bolstering an economically and militarily strained Iran from Iraqi exploitation."[71]

Clearly, given the continued intensity of anti-American sentiment and radical Islamic fundamentalism in Iran at the time, there is room to question whether any retilt toward Iran would have worked. A more nuanced policy with wariness and firmness toward both Iran and Iraq may have made more strategic sense. But what is striking is that the Khalilzad paper was dismissed less by any analytic refutation of its strategic logic than on political grounds.[72] In the wake of Iran-Contra anything which could be interpreted as "soft on Iran" was politically untenable. The paper was leaked to the press in mid-September, likely intentionally, and high administration officials rushed to disown it. George Bush, in the middle of his presidential campaign and amidst allegations of his role in Iran-Contra, sought to affirm and reaffirm his anti-Iran credentials. For Secretary Shultz it was a matter of having his reputation as an ardent opponent of Iran-Contra compromised. As soon as the story appeared in the press, Shultz called a meeting in his office, angrily demanding to know who was responsible for the paper. On the cover page, in big letters, he had written "NO."[73]

Thus, whatever strategic debate there might have been was cut short by political considerations. The "soft on Iran" brush could tar a policy proposal in the same way that the "soft on communism" one had done for so long. According to one official, the political climate made such views, irrespective of their political logic, like "pissing into the wind."[74]

A final dissent came from the State Department Human Rights Bureau and its assistant secretary, Richard Schifter.[75] At most, they argued, Iraq's promise not to use chemical weapons against the Kurds would hold "for the time being"—but only because their prior use had worked so well. The Kurds were, at least for the moment, suppressed. However, there should be no doubt that since Saddam had "gotten away" with it this time, "the Iraqis may very well use them again the next time they consider such use necessary."

Moreover, the law was the law, and Saddam's actions constituted the kind of "consistent pattern of gross violations of internationally recognized human rights" which required sanctions. Not next time, but this time, according to *"existing law"* (emphasis in original).

These Human Rights Bureau views were reported in a memo to Secretary Shultz co-signed by the heads of three other bureaus (Near East Affairs, Political-Military Affairs, Legal Affairs), all of whom nevertheless recommended a veto of the Iraq sanctions bill. Our foreign policy interests "require" it. The president should go ahead with a firm statement about next time, but they doubted we would have to worry about a next time. "Our diplomatic efforts have begun to pay off." Foreign Minister Aziz had given his word, both publicly and privately, that his country "respects and abides by all international commitments" on chemical weapons. "We take these assurances seriously, and believe they indicate a willingness by Iraq to work with us on this problem."

On the other hand, if we did impose the sanctions, "Iraq has indicated it will react sharply." Our agricultural exports, the anticipated "reconstruction boom" for manufactured exports, even the U.S.S. *Stark* claims payments would be at risk—a not-so-gentle reminder of who had the economic leverage over whom. And then there were U.S. regional foreign policy interests, and the prediction that our relations with virtually all Arab states "would suffer."

In the end, President Reagan never had to veto the sanctions bill because it got tied up in the end-of-session maneuvering and gridlock on Capitol Hill. But the pen was ready. There would be no sanctions. Nor would there be any other significant measures to toughen U.S. policy. In fact, one of the Reagan administration's last acts was to allow the export of military equipment ordered by Saddam Hussein for his personal protection.[76]

The Foot Not Put Down

Later, following the Iraqi invasion of Kuwait, one former Reagan official would lament that "it would have been much better at the time of their use of poison gas [in 1988] if we'd put our foot down."[77] We didn't.

Nor was this view simply expressed after the fact. Back in 1985, in the wake of Iraq's initial uses of chemical weapons, one State Department official had expressed concern that a dangerous precedent was being set:

> a self perpetuating one, building momentum and successively smashing the bolsters of restraint which have been built up slowly over the almost 70 years since World War I. . . . Proliferators like Iraq basically pay few penalties for their irresponsible behavior, certainly not enough to dissuade others from seeking to obtain such a capability. I think we can all agree this has got to change and quickly.[78]

It didn't.

This strategic concern went beyond the Middle East to what precedents might be set globally if other states perceived Iraq as having gotten away with chemical weapons use. "Many states noted Iraq's effective use of chemical weapons against both its own Kurdish population and Iranian forces," the director of Naval Intelligence later observed. "The tacit acceptance of this development could encourage other states to obtain or improve their chemical warfare capability."[79]

And what was a dictator like Saddam to think when even the use of chemical weapons fell within the bounds of behavior which the United States considered tolerable? If this new relationship with the United States was not conditional on an issue as salient as chemical warfare—if we would not put our foot down when masses of people were gassed—then on what would it be conditional? And how credible could future threats be if and when they needed to be made?

Bush's Strategy:
The Making of NSD-26

NATIONAL SECURITY DIRECTIVE (NSD) 26, SIGNED BY PRESIDENT George Bush on October 2, 1989, established the goal, stated the rationale, and defined the strategy. The goal: To achieve "normal relations between the United States and Iraq." The rationale: This "would serve our longer-term interests and promote stability in both the Gulf and the Middle East." The strategy: Use "economic and political incentives for Iraq to moderate its behavior and to increase our influence with Iraq."[1]

The essence of the Bush strategy as manifested in NSD-26 was a belief in both the value of and the possibilities for moving beyond the wartime alliance of convenience to a more enduring *accommodation* between the United States and Iraq. The Iran-Iraq war was over, but the bases for a U.S.-Iraqi relationship—strategic, political, and economic—were seen as more robust now after six years of nurturing and amidst the continuing changes in global and regional geopolitics than when the Reagan administration had initiated the opening to Iraq in 1982. While the strategic assessment was not without its cautions and caveats, the overall thrust was toward building a fuller, deeper, and more lasting accommodation with Iraq—at least a "limited détente," as one White House official put it, with Saddam Hussein.[2]

This was, in effect, another variation on the "twin pillars" strategy of safeguarding and advancing U.S. interests in the region by seeking close relations with two major Persian Gulf states. Iran and Saudi Arabia were the original twin pillars, until the fall of the Shah. Now the Bush administration believed it had found in Iraq the potential replacement pillar for the crumbled Iranian one. The wartime alliance of convenience had been a good start; the next step was the deeper and more enduring accommodation envisioned in NSD-26.

The first section of this chapter lays out the "logic of accommodation" which underlay and drove the NSD-26 strategy. The ensuing sections raise questions about the inherent and original soundness of that logic based on information and analysis *available at the time* NSD-26 was being formulated—not hindsight. One section documents a series of warnings prior to October 2, 1989, from both within and outside the Bush administration about Saddam's development of nuclear and other weapons of mass destruction and about his continued human rights violations—warnings which went unheeded. Another brings in the "BNL affair," the uncovering two months before NSD-26 was signed of over $4 billion in illegal loans to Iraq by the Atlanta branch of the Italian Banca Nazionale del Lavoro (BNL), money which provided vital financing for Saddam's weapons development. The chapter's last section focuses in some detail on Bush administration deliberations and decisions in the key period of October–November 1989, involving both NSD-26 and a major new $1 billion commitment of CCC credit guarantees, decisions which fixed the Bush policy to a course on which it stayed until after Iraq invaded Kuwait.

The Logic of Accommodation

The Bush administration took up where the Reagan administration left off. "The U.S. transition," a pre-inaugural task force reported to the president-elect, "comes as we must choose a new direction in our policy towards Iraq. It is up to the new administration to decide whether to treat Iraq as a distasteful dictatorship to be shunned where possible, or to recognize Iraq's present and potential power in the region and accord it relatively high priority. We strongly urge the latter view."[3]

Within a month of his inauguration, President Bush issued National Security Review (NSR) 10 establishing an interagency process for a comprehensive review of U.S. policy toward Iraq. NSD-26 was the end product of this process.

Based on interviews, declassified documents, and other sources, four core concepts emerge as key to the logic of accommodation embodied in NSD-26: (1) the persistence of the threats from Iran and the Soviet Union; (2) a view of Iraq as a force for regional stability and peace; (3) gains both political and economic to be made from increased trade with Iraq; and (4) the appropriateness, as in relations with China and others, of relegating human rights issues (including the Kurds) to "low-politics" status.

Persistent Threats

The starting point was the same as for the original alliance of convenience: Iran. The enemy of my enemy is my friend.

U.S.-Iranian relations at the end of the Iran-Iraq war were in many respects worse than when the Reagan administration first tilted toward Iraq in 1982. As bad as relations had been then, there were no direct military hostilities between American and Iranian forces until the numerous incidents of 1987–88. And then came the U.S.S. *Vincennes*–Iran Air tragedy, which, while at the moment the final demoralization convincing the Ayatollah Khomeini to agree to a cease-fire with the infidel Saddam, became the basis in ensuing months for terrorist retaliations against the United States—including a bomb found under the minivan of Mrs. Sharon Rogers of San Diego, the wife of Captain Will Rogers, skipper of the U.S.S. *Vincennes*.

Then there was the death sentence pronounced in February 1989 against British author Salman Rushdie for his "blasphemous" book,

The Satanic Verses. The Rushdie death sentence was widely seen as an attack on Western culture and values writ large. Even when the Ayatollah Khomeini died in June 1989, he left in his last will and testament a call for "fierce animosity to the West, a militant assertion of Iran's Islamic identity."[4] His successor as president, Ali Akhbar Hashemi Rafsanjani, was in some respects more moderate and pragmatic. But this didn't stop him from issuing a call to Muslim faithful everywhere that for every Palestinian "killed by Israel," five Westerners (American, British, French) should be killed.

Iran also was still heavily involved in Lebanon. Americans were still being held hostage by the Shi'ite Amal, Hizbollah, Party of God, and other groups closely tied to Iran. It also was in Teheran that these groups met later in the year to announce opposition to the Arab League–authored, U.N.-endorsed, and U.S.-supported Taif Accord for a settlement of the Lebanese civil war.

As to the Soviet Union, the other original member of the enemy-enemy-friend calculus, its threat was diminished, but still in the Bush administration's view not to be dismissed. Recall that the Bush administration's initial approach to U.S.-Soviet relations was extremely cautious, no more than "status quo plus" in its own self-described terms. The question of the day still was whether Gorbachev was "for real." Plans initially were continued for NATO to deploy a new generation of short-range Lance nuclear missiles in Europe. Bush and Gorbachev did not hold their first summit until December 1989, and even then it was scripted more as a get-to-know-you session than with a substantive policy agenda.

In the Persian Gulf and Middle East, the Soviets still were seen as very much the formidable rival they had been for decades. Their relations with Iran were in another upswing. The Soviet withdrawal from Afghanistan, the last troops leaving in February 1989, removed a major conflict from Soviet-Iranian relations. Whereas a few months earlier the Ayatollah Khomeini paired references to the "criminal" Soviet Union with the "world-devouring" United States, in February he received Soviet Foreign Minister Eduard Shevardnadze and signed on to a joint statement calling for improved relations.[5] Shortly after

Khomeini's death, Rafsanjani went to Moscow and with Gorbachev proclaimed a "new stage" in Soviet-Iranian relations. One of the agreements they signed was for renewed Soviet arms sales to Iran.

Soviet-Iraqi relations had fluctuated greatly during the Iran-Iraq war. They nevertheless came through the war with a sense that, as one analyst surmised, "although disagreeing on many tactical short-term matters, Moscow and Baghdad needed each other for the implementation and success of their respective long-range policies."[6] Saddam would never be as faithful and predictable as many other Soviet clients. But even a bumpy alliance with Iraq still served Soviet interests. The same was true for Iraq. The Bush administration thus still saw the need to "wean Iraq away" from its relationship with the Soviet Union.[7]

Gorbachev and Shevardnadze also had been practicing some deft diplomacy in improving relations with many of the traditionally pro-Western Gulf states. Kuwait was the Gulf state traditionally with the closest relations to Moscow. It had rather skillfully played one superpower off against the other in getting its tankers reflagged. With the Iran-Iraq war over, it again was pursuing relations with both Washington and Moscow. Moreover, the Soviets had managed to establish diplomatic relations for the first time with Bahrain, the United Arab Emirates, and, especially significantly, Saudi Arabia.

Iraq as a Force for Regional Peace and Stability

The Bush administration saw the "deeper-into-the-mainstream" trend pointed to by the Reagan administration in Iraqi foreign policy as continuing. Some caution was counseled "because Iraq's postwar intentions are still evolving." But the possibility was pushed that "the lessons of war may have changed Iraq from a radical state challenging the system to a more responsible, status-quo state working within the system, and promoting stability in the region."[8] The goal was to reform and "resocialize" Saddam into "the family of nations."[9]

Part of the reasoning was what some referred to as the "exhaustion" thesis; that is, after eight years of war, Saddam and his people had little endurance left for further aggression, and with their huge war debt and economic reconstruction needs, were primed to be responsive to inducements to moderation. The CIA's 1989 national intelligence estimate (NIE) provided such "a message of reassurance," according to later testimony by CIA Director Robert Gates. "That estimate essentially said that we believe for the next two or three years, having just concluded a 10-year [sic] war with Iran, we believe that Saddam will not launch an aggression against any of his neighbors, that he will focus on rebuilding internally, economically and so on."[10]

Part also was based on interpretations of signs of moderation in Saddam's recent regional policies. He increasingly was aligning with the conservative, anti-Soviet Arab regimes which were the main U.S. allies in the region. In February 1989 Iraq joined with Egypt, Jordan, and North Yemen to create the Arab Cooperation Council (ACC) as a new regional economic and non-military grouping. Even though it was Saddam who took the lead in setting the ACC up and its founding summit was held in Baghdad, the assumption was that the creation of the ACC was more a sign of Iraq moving toward the pro-Western orientation of the other members than the reverse.[11] It thus was considered by the Bush administration a complement to the six-nation, Saudi-led Gulf Cooperation Council (GCC), a further entrenchment of the strength of moderate forces in the Arab world.

Saddam also reestablished diplomatic relations with Egypt and provided key sponsorship for getting Egypt invited in May 1989 to its first Arab League summit in almost a decade. This was a watershed in finally ending the post–Camp David ostracism of Egypt in the Arab world. Saddam also signed bilateral nonaggression pacts with Saudi Arabia and Bahrain, ostensibly to allay any fears they might have of Iraq's regional ambitions now that its war with Iran was over. The accord with Saudi Arabia established the principle of "non-use of force and armies between the two states."[12]

One regional issue on which the Bush administration had more concerns was Lebanon. As noted in Chapter 2, Saddam was supplying arms and providing other support to the rebel Christian general

Michel Aoun, who was challenging Syria's continued military occupation and the Syrian-supported Lebanese government. In March 1989 the fighting escalated, the artillery shelling the heaviest in Beirut in three years, leaving some ten thousand additional refugees. When Secretary of State Baker met with Iraqi Under Secretary for Foreign Affairs (and former U.S. ambassador) Nizar Hamdoon later that month, Lebanon was one of the issues on the agenda.

Of all the regional issues, the main one on which the Bush administration wanted Iraqi cooperation was the Arab-Israeli peace process. Saddam was supporting PLO Chairman Yasir Arafat in his recognition of Israel's right to exist and opening of an official PLO–United States dialogue. The initial breakthrough had been achieved in December 1988 in the closing days of the Reagan administration. It was up to the Bush administration to sustain and develop the dialogue. Given the opposition of other longtime rejectionist forces (for example, Iran, Syria, radical PLO factions), Saddam's support was considered crucial.

The Bush administration, and Secretary of State Baker personally, invested quite heavily early on in an Arab-Israeli breakthrough. The administration made its first peace process proposal in March 1989. In April, Israeli Prime Minister Yitzhak Shamir, Egyptian President Hosni Mubarak, and King Hussein of Jordan each came to Washington (separately) to meet with Bush and Baker. But for all the activity, there was little progress. While Iraq was not expected to become a central player in the peace process, its support still could be a critical element in the overall formula. "Iraq can play a more constructive role" and "a true dialogue [with the United States] will encourage it to do so."[13] Surely its opposition would complicate, as it had done in the past, an already complicated situation.

Bush and Baker also likely were implicitly seeking through improved relations with Iraq to pressure Israel. "The depth of American irritation with Israel," as Lawrence Freedman and Efraim Karsh observe, was "striking."[14] There were times when Bush administration pressure on Israel wasn't left implicit, as with Secretary Baker's May 1989 speech to the American Israel Public Affairs Committee (AIPAC), the principal "Jewish lobby," in which Baker came out urging Israel "to renounce the unrealistic vision of a greater Israel."[15] At a personal level the Bush-Shamir relationship was notoriously poor in its chemistry. As a matter of policy, Bush heard "lo" from Shamir far more than he heard "nyet" from Gorbachev.

The point is not that the Bush administration was abandoning Israel or seeking a comparable friendship with Iraq. But it was trying to structure a broader base for U.S. relationships in the region—to rebuild those two Arab pillars. To pressure Israel in the process was hardly atypical of the Byzantine maneuvering of Middle East diplomacy.

Gains from Trade

One set of gains to be made from increased trade with Iraq was political. "Trade is the best key to political influence," the transition team report held. "Economic incentives," NSD-26 affirmed, were to be proposed "for Iraq to moderate its behavior and to increase our influence."

The 1988 chemical warfare sanctions experience was not seen as contradicting this logic. The problem was considered less one of reverse leverage than misguided leverage. In the Bush strategic view, sanctions targeted at another state's human rights or other internal policies just don't work: not for the Iraqi Kurds, not for Chinese dissidents. But expanded economic relations could contribute to improved political relations on foreign and other external policies. In the Iraqi case, they were expected to reinforce and further the trends toward moderation in regional affairs.

More CCC credit guarantees were to continue to be one of the principal economic incentives. Iraq's need for agricultural imports kept increasing, but its ability to pay for them kept decreasing. The United States was not Iraq's only agricultural trade partner, but its market share had been growing by 30–40 percent a year. In addition, U.S. credit terms were among the most favorable, especially now that some other countries had put Iraq off cover because of its mounting debt.

There also was a sense that nonagricultural trade could, and should, take off. *"To Iraq, technology is our most important asset."*[16] It came up repeatedly in both diplomatic and business meetings with Iraqi officials. Postwar reconstruction was expected to set off a boom in Iraqi demand for industrial equipment and technology, construction projects, oil equipment, and other sectors in which American companies were highly competitive.

The transition team report had raised concerns about "the potential for diversion of U.S. exports to Iraq's war machine." It did not, however, see the need for any tightening of controls on dual-use technology exports. "Current export policy," it instead recommended, "should not be changed."[17] Further encouragement was taken from Iraq's participation in January 1989 in the Paris multilateral chemical weapons conference and its reaffirmation of its pledges to abide by the 1925 Geneva Protocol. Licenses thus continued to be granted by the Bush administration for a wide range of dual-use exports. According to Commerce Department records, only nine applications were denied in the months leading up to NSD-26.

The other gains to be made from the trade were of course economic. "I'd be very wealthy," an NSC aide later remarked about interest group pressure, "if I could have a dollar for every company that called me [during the drafting of NSD-26]." She added, "the same was true for members of Congress," pushing the interests of constituents and political supporters.[18] Since 1985, U.S. agricultural exports to Iraq consistently had grown at a faster rate than for overall agricultural exports. In 1988 the increase had been a rather impressive 54 percent. For rice exporters, it was their largest market. It also was a major market for wheat, feed grain, oilseed products, cotton, sugar, dairy products, poultry, and tobacco.[19]

The stiff competition American manufacturers faced from European counterparts led them to push even harder for looser and less cumbersome export controls as well as export promotion assistance. The U.S.-Iraq Business Forum was quite active in this period, holding meetings bringing member executives together with Bush administration officials and also organizing trips to Iraq, at least one of which included a meeting with Saddam. This was said to be the first time

Saddam had ever met with a commercial delegation. The meeting was "cordial," according to the U.S.-Iraq Business Forum chairman. Saddam "expressed his interest in expanding normal commercial relations with the United States."[20]

Especially lucrative was the growing U.S.-Iraqi oil trade. Beginning in late 1988 American oil companies had been receiving from Iraq a discount of $1 per barrel below the prices being charged to European oil companies. This amounted to about $37 million in the last quarter of 1988, and another $123 million through the first three quarters of 1989. The per-barrel discount was increased to $1.24 in January 1990, for savings of another $241 million, on imports that actually continued for over a month after the Iraqi invasion of Kuwait.[21]

Here, too, there may have been an attempt to use trade to enhance political influence. By the time of the invasion of Kuwait, the United States was buying one out of every four barrels of Iraqi oil exports. Even at the discounted rates, oil sales to the United States in 1989–90 earned Iraq over $5.2 billion. It seemed to fit the logic of accommodation quite well to calculate that such mutually beneficial economic relations would reinforce and further foster the goal of *"businesslike, profitable and above all stable relations."*[22]

The Kurds and Human Rights: Low Politics

"Human rights considerations" are included in NSD-26 as something which "should continue to be an important element in our policy toward Iraq." This, however, is a statement which cannot be accepted at face value.

First, it is difficult to see from whence this continuation was to be. From the Reagan-Bush opposition to the chemical warfare sanctions? Second, other Bush administration documents indicate much less importance being given to human rights. The very language in which the policy choices were delineated in the "Guidelines for U.S.-Iraq Policy" cited earlier as either "treat Iraq as a distasteful dictatorship to be shunned where possible" or "recognize Iraq's present and potential power in the region and accord it relatively high priority" was revealing. Option A was for the unrealists, those who set foreign policy strategy on the basis of tastefulness, and who even then just would not find it always possible "in the real world" to shun the offending regime. References were made to those who supported sanctions in 1988 as having acted out of "aroused great emotions," and of those who push the human rights issue as having a hidden agenda of searching simply for "a convenient hook" to "scuttle" the whole U.S.-Iraqi relationship. Option B, on the other hand, was for realists, those who were hard-headed enough to understand the need for the "high politics" of power imperatives to take precedence over the "low politics" of human rights and other idealist concerns. And that was it, two options only, dichotomous and mutually exclusive, no room for the former if one recognized the exigencies of the latter.

On the Kurdish question, this meant opposition to the more egregious methods of suppression but also an implied acceptance of the "legitimacy" of the objective of suppression.

> We should oppose Iraqi military activities against the civilian population and the destruction of hundreds of villages in Kurdistan. But bearing in mind the historical context, *in no way should we associate ourselves with the 60 year old Kurdish rebellion in Iraq or oppose Iraq's legitimate attempts to suppress it.*[23]

The emphasis is in the original.

In other parts, the "Guidelines" paper descriptively reads like an Amnesty International report: "Saddam Hussein will continue to eliminate those he regards as a threat, torture those he believes have secrets to reveal, and rule without any real concessions to democracy." Prescriptively, though, they differed immensely. Bushian realism was not to debate whether human rights abuses existed but to limit the priority of the issue and limit the pressure for change.

> Our efforts should concentrate on slow, steady pressure and a *realistic* appraisal of our leverage . . . [F]ew expect a humane regime to

come to Iraq any time soon. We should therefore be *realistic* and demand of Iraq what we do of its neighbors—in tune with our aim to rope Iraq into a conservative and responsible alignment in foreign policy [emphasis added].

The resemblance to the Bush policy toward China following the June 1989 Tiananmen massacre is strong. Geopolitical factors take precedence. Quiet diplomacy is preferred to sanctions. Expectations are limited. The main concern is avoiding human rights becoming an obstacle to the strategic and economic bases for accommodation.

Summary

These were the core concepts on which the Bush strategy as manifested in NSD-26 rested. They constituted the strategic logic which deemed an accommodation with Iraq both possible and desirable. Yet over the course of the period leading up to the signing of NSD-26 on October 2, 1989, repeated warnings were sounded about Iraqi actions, capabilities, and intentions. These warnings were quite inconsistent with the logic of accommodation, and they went unheeded.

Warnings Unheeded

In mid-January 1989 ABC News broke a story about Iraq's development of biological weapons. Despite being a signatory to the 1972 Biological Weapons Convention, Iraq had programs under way to develop weapons capable of spreading typhoid, cholera, and anthrax massively throughout a targeted population. Iraqi Ambassador Abdul Amir Anbari of course denied all such reports, calling them "totally false and uninformed," and claiming that Salman Pak, the small village south of Baghdad identified as the main location for the biological weapons laboratories, instead was nothing more than a riverside resort town especially popular among honeymooners.[24]

In fact, though, the reports were confirmed by U.S. government and other sources. Anthony Cordesman, a noted military analyst, commented that "regardless of where you go in the Middle East or for that matter which Western intelligence agency you would talk to, they would all confirm that Iraq has biological agents in actual production and is stockpiling them for military use."[25] Iraq's biological warfare programs actually dated back to the late 1970s, but it was in the late 1980s that large-scale production had begun. One of the main biological agents being produced was botulinum toxin. Botulinum toxin had a potency about three million times greater than even the chemical nerve agent Sarin. One SCUD missile warhead loaded with botulinum toxin, according to Pentagon calculations, could contaminate a 3700-square-kilometer area.[26] This was more than enough to be of major concern to Israel. And the Bush administration knew it, as Israel reportedly asked the United States "to pass a warning on to Iraq that if it continues [its] biological weapons program, the Israelis will act to destroy it."[27]

Testimony to Congress on continuing Iraqi chemical weapons programs came from top U.S. intelligence officials as early as February and March 1989. CIA Director William H. Webster pointed to Iraq as the single largest producer of chemical weapons in the Third World. Its main facility was the one previously identified at Samarra (see Chapter 2), but there now also were "a number of other production facilities" which all told had produced "several thousand tons of chemical agents." Moreover, despite the end of its war with Iran, Iraq continued to stockpile chemical weapons, to amass a variety of delivery systems (bombs, artillery shells, artillery rockets, and battlefield missiles), and to keep acquiring dual-use technologies in an effort "to make its program entirely independent of foreign assistance."[28]

In another hearing, Rear Admiral Thomas A. Brooks, director of Naval Intelligence, testified that Iraq was among those states "actively pursuing a capability" for nuclear weapons. At a time when we were making unprecedented progress in strategic nuclear arms control with the Soviet Union, the admiral stressed, we must not allow nuclear proliferation to otherwise degrade our security. Iraq was not the only threat, but it was on Admiral Brook's list in no uncertain terms.[29]

Secretary of State Baker was duly warned. He was to meet on March 24 with Under Secretary Hamdoon. The meeting was intended, according to a briefing memorandum Baker received, "to express our interest in broadening U.S.-Iraqi ties." Baker also was cautioned, though, about some disturbing trends, including that Iraq "is working hard at chemical and biological weapons and new missiles."[30]

Over at the Department of Energy (DOE), concerns about Iraqi nuclear weapons development also were mounting.[31] Over the second half of 1988, according to William A. Emel, who headed the Proliferation Intelligence Program within DOE's Office of Foreign Intelligence, information had been accumulating "that heightened concerns about a possible Iraqi nuclear weapons program." These concerns were strongly articulated at a December 13, 1988, classified intelligence briefing conducted by the Technology Intelligence Branch of the DOE Office of Foreign Intelligence, joined by experts from Lawrence Livermore National Laboratory. Iraq (along with Iran, also a subject of the briefing) "deserve[s] special attention," the DOE nonproliferation officials were told. It both was "highly motivated to pursue nuclear weapons" and "probably can command the resources to constitute a serious effort." Sometimes a country had the intentions but not the capabilities; other times, the capabilities but not the intentions; the two together were a dangerous combination.

In February 1989, DOE proliferation expert Emel attended a special intelligence conference with counterparts from other Western governments. At this conference, he later testified, "Iraq was identified as of significant concern." Upon his return to the United States, Emel pushed for greater attention on Iraq. He found a bureaucratic ally in A. Bryan Siebert, Jr., who headed DOE's export control branch (Office of Classification and Technology Policy, Defense Programs).

Siebert had been the principal author of the March 1988 DOE report mentioned in Chapter 1 criticizing the lax system which had allowed the Iraqis to acquire "export controlled information critical to nuclear weapons technology" through open reports and even visits by

Iraqi "scientists" to Los Alamos on Reagan administration–approved visas. Siebert also had attended the December 1988 intelligence briefing, and since then, he and his deputy Roger K. Heusser were being "peppered" by calls from nuclear proliferation experts at the national labs who were alarmed by what they kept uncovering about Iraq's "shopping list." "When we put these 'pieces' of information together," Heusser stated, "it was a clear signal to me that Iraq had a major effort to develop an atomic bomb." "There was evidence," Siebert concurred, "of a broadly-based, sophisticated nuclear weapons effort underway by Iraq."

Others in DOE still believed the situation to be less urgent. Conventional wisdom held Iraq to be at least ten years away from nuclear weapons capability. Siebert and Heusser not only read the specific evidence on Iraqi activities differently; they also read recent proliferation history very differently. Hadn't India developed its nuclear weapon more quickly than predicted? And Pakistan? And, going back to the late 1940s, the Soviet Union?

Siebert and Heusser concluded that the situation was of such magnitude and urgency that it required the "immediate and personal attention" of Energy Secretary James D. Watkins. Under the provisions of the Nuclear Non-Proliferation Act, the Energy secretary has principal authority for advising the president and cabinet on nuclear proliferation. While Iraqi procurement efforts were global, the United States was being targeted for key components such as nuclear capacitators. "It is eerie," Siebert later testified, "how closely the items on the Iraqi shopping list matched up—practically one to one—with key components in U.S. nuclear weapons systems." Moreover, any prospect for getting multilateral collaboration depended on U.S. leadership, which in turn required a strong and consistent U.S. policy. Indeed, beyond just Iraq but also with respect to the rest of the nonproliferation agenda, there was concern that inaction "would injure its [the United States'] valuable nonproliferation credentials."

Thus Siebert and Heusser worked over a weekend in early April 1989 to prepare a hard-hitting memorandum for Secretary Watkins. The language was clear and the statement strong: "Recent evidence indicates that Iraq has a major effort underway to produce nuclear weapons." Their recommendation was for full-scale consideration by the National Security Council. Secretary Watkins was to contact Secretary of State Baker and National Security Advisor Brent Scowcroft to set in motion a priority interagency review and action plan.

The next step was to get their immediate superior, Deputy Assistant Secretary for Security Affairs in Defense Programs Charles M. Gilbert, to sign on. Gilbert concurred but wanted to get his counterpart, Deputy Assistant Secretary for Intelligence Programs Robert J. Walsh, on board before proceeding. Walsh, however, felt the Siebert-Heusser memo was an overreaction. Yes, Iraq was "acquiring nuclear technology and related equipment," but these "also have peaceful applications." Yes, the nuclear technology they have been acquiring was "excessive for traditional domestic application," but recent reports "overstate their capabilities." The matter was not of such urgency that it required the secretary's attention. Iraq was "10 years away" from a nuclear bomb.[32] The Siebert-Heusser memo did not go forward.

The following August (1989) the Ninth Symposium (International) on Detonation was held in Portland, Oregon, under DOE sponsorship. The general subject was explosive detonation technology, which DOE acknowledged was "a dual use technology with both commercial and military applications in the areas of conventional munitions applications as well as nuclear weapons applications." Indeed, one DOE official later acknowledged that this conference "was the place to be if you were a potential nuclear proliferant."[33] Yet among the attendees were three Iraqi scientists from the Al-Qaqaa State Establishment, a site already identified by U.S. intelligence as part of Saddam's nuclear weapons complex. Among the presentations they were able to attend were ones on HMX, "the high explosive of choice for nuclear detonation," and on flyer plates, key equipment which helps generate the precise shock waves needed to ignite atomic bombs. U.N. inspection teams later would find HMX and flyer plates at Iraq's main nuclear weapons complex.[34]

Secretary Watkins later expressed his own dissatisfaction with his own department's intelligence programs. "DOE's intelligence program was not effective, not well known or respected in the Intelligence Community, and not responsive to Departmental needs."[35]

In April 1989 the Consarc Corporation, a small but specialized New Jersey manufacturer of high-technology industrial furnaces, began filling a $10 million order placed by Iraq.[36] The furnaces were said by the Iraqis to be for manufacturing prosthetic limbs for soldiers maimed in the war with Iran. Consarc executives knew that their furnaces had potential dual uses for nuclear weapons and ballistic missiles. In a letter to the Bush Commerce Department requesting an advisory opinion, Consarc pointed out that "there is nothing to stop them from melting zirconium, the major use of which is cladding material for nuclear fuel rods." The titanium which was the stated material to be melted for the prosthetic limbs also had uses for missile nose cones. Melting plutonium and uranium for nuclear bomb cores was another possible diversionary use. Indeed, the four furnaces together which were part of the deal constituted "a 'Cadillac' production line for atomic bomb and missile parts."[37]

But the Bush Commerce Department told Consarc that they did not even need a license to export the furnaces, let alone a review of the case. All they needed was end-user certification from the Iraqi customer stating the intended civilian use. The Iraqis readily provided the piece of paper. Commerce apparently made its ruling without interagency review, or solicitation of outside expert opinion, or any significant focused investigation of its own.

Before signing the contract in April, Consarc again contacted Commerce with some "worrisome information" from its British subsidiary which had been reading in the open press about Iraq's Condor II ballistic missile program. The Bush administration gave "a reassuring response." Consarc went ahead and signed the contract with the Iraqis. "Hooray for you," read a cable from a U.S. embassy official in Baghdad who had been assisting Consarc in the negotiations.[38]

With great fanfare, elections for a new National Assembly were held by Iraq in April 1989. For once, Western journalists were eagerly received. Saddam wanted to get a message out that Iraq, too, was part of the global wave of democratization. A few months earlier in a speech to the Iraqi Bar Association he had declared a pardon for all political prisoners and pledged to establish a democratic multiparty system. Half of the representatives elected to the National Assembly were billed as "independent." He had allowed a "Freedom Wall" at the University of Baghdad. "There is no censorship in Iraq," his new minister of information and culture proudly proclaimed.[39]

One State Department official who visited Iraq around this time, and who was among those expressing concern about whether Iraq needed to be contained more than accommodated, commented on Saddam's skill at creating a "Potemkin facade" over his Stalinist core. "This made it harder to argue that underneath the facade, there lurked a monster."[40] There were signs, though.

The State Department's own recent human rights report had concluded that "Iraq's abysmal human rights record remained unacceptable." In late February 1989 Amnesty International issued a report on Iraq which should have shocked even those who might have grown inured to stories of human rights violations. The report was subtitled "Children: Innocent Victims of Political Repression." It detailed stories of schoolchildren "who had been apprehended, lined up and summarily shot in public"; of a nine-year-old Kurdish boy being imprisoned since he was six; of one political prisoner pressured to confess by witnessing the torture of twelve relatives, some between five and thirteen years old; of two others, a husband and wife, whose baby was kept in a nearby cell and "deliberately deprived of milk." Amnesty had mounted a special appeal to the U.N. Commission on Human Rights accusing Saddam's regime "of the most flagrant and massive violation of human rights." Even in the world as imperfect as Amnesty knew it to be, "we can think of none which cries out more for international attention and action."[41]

As to other components of Saddam's ostensible democratization, the independent representatives in the National Assembly were prohibited from including anyone defined as "dangerous to the state." The lifting of censorship, as the minister of information and culture went on to say, did not include "issues of national security."[42] Both, of course, can be reasonable restrictions. They also can be sinister loopholes. It all depends on who gets to define them.

Saddam also again moved against the Kurds. This time it was a massive "relocation" program, clearing out Kurdish settlements in a twenty-mile-wide zone running along almost the entire eastern border with Iran. The stated reason was to protect the Kurds "from the security threat of additional Iranian bombardments."[43] Yet there had been no such bombardments since the August 1988 cease-fire. Estimates were of as many as half a million Kurds being forcibly relocated. The Senate Foreign Relations Committee proposed economic sanctions. The Bush administration opposed them.

April also was Saddam Hussein's birthday. This year's commemoration was the First Baghdad International Exhibition for Military Production.[44] Two hundred companies from twenty-seven countries exhibited their latest arms and military technology. There was no official U.S. government exhibition, although some American companies sent private delegations. U.S. embassy staff also came.

"Defense equipment for peace and prosperity" was the official slogan. But what they saw "was a shock" even for many of the arms traders and government officials who had been dealing with (and selling to) Iraq for a long time. On exhibit not only were foreign weapons but Iraqi-made weapons of surprising sophistication and quantity. They included at least ten different Iraqi-built ballistic missiles, including the al-Husayn and al-Abbas; the al-Walid, a new transporter for mobile SCUD missile launchers which so closely resembled commercial vehicles as to make surveillance more difficult; French Mirage jets modified to carry Soviet-style laser-guided missiles; three different types of fuel-air explosives; new ground-based and airborne radar systems; and long-range artillery rockets. A French general in attendance later, after Iraq's invasion of Kuwait, would acknowledge that it was at the Baghdad arms fair that he first "began to wonder whether we hadn't gone a bit too far. I realized we had better begin paying closer attention to what the Iraqis were developing in the way of armament."[45]

Among the arms being exhibited was a prototype for the "Super Gun," a giant piece of artillery designed to be able to "shoot" 1000-pound bombs—including chemical, biological, and possibly small nuclear warheads—over distances greater than 600 miles. The Super Gun was to be, in essence, the equivalent of a ballistic missile (and, since it was reusable, at a much lower operating cost), another way of launching weapons against Israel, Iran, or other designated enemies.

The Super Gun was the brainchild of a Canadian-born weapons expert named Gerald Bull. Bull's background is worth briefly recounting as it bears upon the story.[46] In the world of arms makers and traders, he was considered a genius. A Ph.D. in aerodynamics at age twenty-two, he had spent most of his life in the design, development, and sale of advanced artillery. He once had worked on a joint U.S.-Canadian military project (the High Altitude Research Project, or HARP) to develop an artillery piece capable of firing a projectile hundreds of miles upward. Bull saw it as potentially leading to an artillery capability for launching satellites. Project funding was cut, though, and the HARP was mothballed.

Bull later became a U.S. citizen and went out on his own, setting up a company called Space Research Corporation (SRC). Among his customers was South Africa, with which he kept doing business even after the global arms embargo imposed by the United Nations in 1977. While Bull claimed that he did this at the request of the CIA, he was arrested by the Carter Justice Department, charged with arms smuggling, and sentenced to prison. This reportedly left him "just absolutely infuriated" and with much disdain for the United States. "The U.S. has obsolete conventional weapons and no morale in their armed forces," he told an interviewer in 1981. "They couldn't defeat Timbuktu in a fight."[47]

After prison he moved SRC to Brussels. He found numerous new customers, one of which was the People's Republic of China (PRC). The Chinese contracted with Bull to set up a full production line for 155-millimeter cannons. The Reagan administration directly and indirectly supported the project, which it viewed as quite consistent with its cold war triangular interest in strengthening China's military capabilities.[48] When the Bull-PRC enterprise made its first foreign sale, it was to Iraq.

Another Bull customer was Voest Alpine, the artillery division of the Austrian state-owned arms manufacturer Noricum, to which he sold some of his designs. One of Voest Alpine's main customers was Iraq, although to get around Austrian neutrality laws prohibiting weapons sales to states at war, the guns were sold through Jordan.[49] Apparently, though, the guns Voest Alpine produced proved faulty, the barrels melting under the intense use to which Iraq was putting them against Iranian forces.

The Iraqis decided to deal directly with Gerald Bull. Bull came to Baghdad in early 1988 and met with Hussein Kamil, Saddam's son-in-law and head of the Ministry of Industry and Military Industrialization (MIMI). Kenneth Timmerman describes the encounter:

> He [Bull] was like a man possessed. Bull was convinced that he could build a "super-gun" like nothing the world had ever seen, if only an enlightened leader such as Saddam Hussein would finance the project and leave him alone. . . . For just $10 million, Bull told Hussein Kamil, the gun could be built right in his own country. The idea immediately appealed to the Iraqis. Indeed, what was $10 million? It would buy scarcely a dozen Soviet tanks! And the project would give a dramatic boost to the Iraqi weapons industry. So Hussein Kamil signed a contract with Gerald Bull and his Brussels-based Space Research Corporation on the spot.[50]

In late September 1988 Saddam Hussein was quoted in the *Washington Post* as openly boasting of a new super weapon which when completed would "put Iraq among only two other countries in the world."[51] Yet despite this boasting-cum-warning (and despite the timing right in the middle of the chemical warfare sanctions debate), a number of licenses were granted for exports related to the Super Gun project in the last months of the Reagan administration and continuing in the Bush administration. For example, in the spring of 1989

SRC was granted a license to export ostensibly to its Brussels office an engineering software package (ANSYS) with both civilian and military applications. Two aspects of this case raised questions. First, the ANSYS manufacturer explicitly stated on the export license application the program's potential use for designs of "satellites and missiles." Second, it also was stated at the time of license application that the software was to be installed on a Silicon Graphics IRIS Super 380 computer. Yet a few months later in September 1989, when SRC applied for a license to re-export an IRIS Super 380 computer from Brussels to Iraq, the Bush administration granted the license. The license application designated the end-user as the Iraqi State Enterprise for Automotive Industries. The computer and software were used for vehicles all right: for the armored VSP (vehicle self-propelled) which carried the Super Gun.[52] After the Gulf War it would be at the State Enterprise for Automotive Industries that U.N. inspectors would find one of the Super Gun prototypes.

One of the other Super Gun needs was for manufacturing capacity for the huge gun barrels. Iraqi officials approached West Homestead Engineering and Machine Company (WHEMCO), a Pennsylvania company, which had retooled a 10,000-ton open die forge press acquired from a munitions factory where it had been used to manufacture 16-inch cannons for the U.S. military. The end-use, WHEMCO was told, was merely to produce barrels and other metal containers for the Iraqi petrochemical industry. DOD officials expressed concern to Commerce licensing officials: "Is there any way we could be assured that this equipment would be used solely for producing steel containers for the petrochemical industry, as stated by the applicant?" No, Commerce stated, further end-use assurance was not possible. Yet the export license still was granted.[53]

The Iraqi government kept pressuring for more Export-Import Bank financing. U.S. Ambassador April Glaspie reported back from Baghdad in May that U.S. firms had been losing contracts because of inadequate financing. Financing "continues to be a key criterion in the GOI's [government of Iraq's] consideration of bids. . . . U.S. firms will need Ex-Im project financing if they expect to win contracts."[54] Two mega-projects were highlighted, notably the $2 billion to $4 billion "PC-2" petrochemical complex in which some U.S. firms were interested.

A U.S. government interagency review of Iraq's creditworthiness was scheduled for June 13, 1989. The State Department, Commerce Department, Treasury Department, Federal Reserve, U.S. Trade Representative, Export-Import Bank, and the CIA all were involved. The Eximbank staff prepared a report for the meeting.

Its risk assessment was no more encouraging than earlier ones. Back on January 23, it had issued an "alert report": "Iraqi Payments Situation Further Deteriorates."[55] On April 24 its report had concluded that "Iraq's balance of payments picture remains bleak."[56] The best that was now said in the June report was that "if there is sustained, gradual improvement in Iraqi government policies, Iraq's arrears and rescheduling could end within ten years." However, while such policy change "cannot be ruled out, it is also not very likely. Consequently, debt arrears and rescheduling are more than likely to continue."[57]

The main policy problem being referred to was the "military absorption of Iraqi resources." The war with Iran was over, but all the major indicators showed no lessening of the priority being given to the military sector. Iraq still had one-quarter of its male labor force on active military duty. Domestic military spending constituted 39 percent of the gross domestic product and 60 percent of the government budget. Even based on official data (which excluded much of the global front company procurement network), military imports amounted to 50 percent of total imports. They ate up 42 percent of Iraq's oil revenues.[58] Indeed, the petrochemical complex PC-2 for which Eximbank credits were being pushed turned out to be one of Iraq's major nuclear weapons development sites.

Optimistic scenarios were sketched out and modeled, but more for the sake of the exercise than realistic prospects. "The Iraqi government," the report concluded, "is likely to persist in its costly military, political, economic and financial policies."[59]

In Israel, concern was intensifying over military maneuvers Saddam was making. Israeli intelligence had detected in June new fixed missile sites being constructed in western Iraq which would put Tel Aviv within Iraqi missile range. In July Iraq began aerial reconnaissance flights along the Jordanian-Israeli border. This was the latest development in increased Iraqi-Jordanian military cooperation, which also included the transfer to Jordan of captured Iranian weapons, integration of the two countries' air defense systems and the sharing of early warning data, visits by Iraqi division commanders to the Israel-Jordan border area, and plans to form a joint armored brigade.[60] A few months earlier Israel also had picked up signs that Iraq was making substantial progress in its effort to develop nuclear weapons.

Some of this intelligence was passed on to Bush administration officials. But the response was less than receptive, viewing it all largely as another Shamir government tactic to stall the peace process.

A series of top-secret high-level intelligence reports from the Defense Intelligence Agency (DIA) and the CIA in June and September 1989 showed the Iraqi military enterprise to be far greater than even the wares shown at the Baghdad arms fair or the official statistics cited in the Export-Import Bank study indicated. Saddam Hussein had developed a network of global front companies across Europe and also into the United States through which he was making key technological acquisitions for building his weapons arsenal, including nuclear, chemical, and biological weapons and ballistic missiles.[61]

The ultimate objective of the global network was openly stated by top aide Hussein Kamil as "implementing a defense industrial program to cover all its [Iraq's] armed forces needs for weapons and equipment by 1991."[62] Saddam did not want to just keep purchasing weapons, whether from the Soviet Union or France or other arms exporters. He was after the technologies themselves, to establish his own weapons production self-sufficiency. He had in mind not just conventional weapons, but the full range of nonconventional weapons of mass destruction. His source was to be Western technology, European and American. Some was being acquired illicitly on the black market. Much more was accessible through normal dual-use technology export licensing just by claiming commercial uses and then diverting to military ones.

This had been the main reason for the creation of MIMI in April 1988, merging previously separate civilian and military ministries. The "I" (Industry) was to provide better cover for the "MI" (Military Industrialization). Pesticide and petrochemical plants disguised chemical weapons ones. Pharmaceutical factories and medical laboratories fronted for research on biological weapons. A glass-fiber factory said to be for manufacturing shower stalls was in actuality a facility for producing missile casings, rocket nose cones, and parts for centrifuges to enrich uranium to nuclear weapons grade.

A great deal of intelligence on MIMI and the various military-industrial complexes it ran had been available for a number of years, as indicated in Chapters 1 and 2. More kept coming in. MIMI's version of an industrial policy, one of the September 1989 CIA reports laid out, was "to integrate proposed specialty metals, vehicle assembly and other manufacturing plants directly into missile, tank and armored personnel carrier industries." Even more telling, MIMI was said to be at the heart of "the nuclear network."[63] Similar information even was available from open sources. The German news magazine *Stern* published a detailed list of the military-related "research laboratories" at the Sa'ad 16 complex. "The best available evidence," a respected nonproliferation expert testified to Congress, "indicates that the facility (Sa'ad 16) will be used to develop a wide range of military hardware, including ballistic missiles, and chemical weapons."[64] *MidEast Markets* ran a story reporting that facilities for building the Condor II missile "are virtually complete."[65]

Yet the Bush administration had been continuing to license dual-use exports to MIMI, Sa'ad 16, and other Iraqi military-industrial complexes and directly to the Iraqi military. Some examples:

- equipment for the Arab Company for Detergent Chemicals (a front for chemical weapons production);
- bacteria samples to the Iraqi Atomic Energy Commission and University of Baghdad, both linked by the CIA to "biological warfare, support and numerous other military activities";
- nine high-power supply units, allegedly for the steel industry, but used to make weapons-grade uranium;
- vacuum pump oil, later found by international inspectors to have been used for lubricating the corrosion-preventing pumps for keeping uranium moving in the enrichment process;
- communications and tracking agreement for Sa'ad 16;
- compasses, gyroscopes, and accelerometers to the Iraqi air force, usable in missile guidance systems as well as aircraft;
- helicopter guidance and fight equipment to the Iraqi air force;
- computers to the Iraqi navy;
- command and control equipment to the Iraqi Ministry of Defense;
- manufacturing equipment to Saleh al Din, listed in the licensing records as simply "a government agency," but characterized in intelligence reports as "typical of Iraq's arms production facilities";
- helicopters and engines to the Iraqi air force for search-and-rescue helicopters, yet listed as "nonmilitary."[66]

The DIA and CIA reports also delved into the intricacies of the structure and operation of the global front company network. Another division of MIMI known as the Military Industrialization Board (MIB) put together a shopping list in consultation with the military-industrial complex. This was sent through the intelligence agent network built into Iraqi embassies and consulates and offices of Iraqi Airways. Agents worked through the front network of manufacturing and trading companies in Europe and the United States. These companies then set out to fill the orders.

Of all the front companies, the "tentacle of the octopus," as one government official called it, was Matrix-Churchill. As noted in Chapter 1, Matrix-Churchill Ltd., one of Britain's leading machine tool companies, had been clandestinely purchased by the Iraqi government in 1987. The company was described in its own literature as "a major supplier of machines for munitions production in the United Kingdom and one of the leading suppliers worldwide with some 275 munitions installations."[67] The British government knew about the Iraqi acquisition of Matrix-Churchill, but in something of a Faustian gambit allowed the deal to go through and dual-use exports to be made while planting an agent inside the company in an attempt to gain intelligence on the Iraqi network.[68] Since at least January 1988 the British knew the exports were being used for arms. By at least February 1989 they knew that some exports were going to the Iraqi ballistic missile program, and had strong suspicions that some were going to the development of nuclear weapons. When a few officials within the British Defense Ministry began pressing to end the gambit, the Trade Ministry countered that the economic benefits of the trade were too great to lose. Trade Minister Alan Clark later would testify that he even had encouraged Matrix-Churchill officials to be "economical" with the truth in their export license applications.[69] Yet the British government knew that the Matrix-Churchill machine tools had applications to nuclear weapons. "We know of course that machine tools capable of contouring in two axes, as is the case with these machines, are essential for the production of nuclear weapons," a February 1, 1989, report to the Foreign Office minister stated.[70]

Matrix-Churchill was specifically cited in the June 1989 DIA report. More than that, U.S. intelligence appears to have known about Matrix-Churchill from finished intelligence reports provided by British MI5 and MI6 as early as 1987. As of March 1989 raw intelligence drawn from interviews with the British sources inside Matrix-Churchill also reportedly was flowing. A lawyer for Paul Henderson, the main British source, claimed that his client not only had no doubt that his information was being passed on to the CIA, but also that it "was available to the White House."[71] Henderson himself testified to House Banking Committee investigators that "his handler made it clear to him that information was shared with the United States."[72] British government records show a bilateral meeting with U.S. officials in late September or early October 1989 "on machine tools and the Matrix-Churchill applications."

Nor was Matrix-Churchill just a British operation. Its American subsidiary, the Matrix-Churchill Corporation, located near Cleveland, was no less a key component of the global network. Soon after the Iraqi purchase of the parent company, one Dr. Safa al-Habobi was installed as chairman of Matrix-Churchill USA. This same "Dr. Safa" was also director-general of NASSR, the industrial complex known by the CIA since the 1970s to be a key Iraqi military installation; director of the Technical Corps for Special Projects (TECO), the division of MIMI which oversaw all public sector enterprises in defense-related industrial construction and civil engineering; on the board of the Technology Development Group (TDG), the London-based hidden owner of Matrix-Churchill Ltd.; the man in charge of the Al-Arabi Trading Company; a commander in the Iraqi military; and probably an officer of Hussein Kamil's Special Security Organization (SSO). Habobi's role was such that, according to British intelligence, he had been personally congratulated by Saddam. British sources referred to the whole Iraqi operation as "Habobi's procurement network."

The Matrix-Churchill American subsidiary had signed an agreement in May 1988 with the Al-Arabi Trading Company to act as a procurement agent and project manager.[73] It was assigned to fill orders for over two hundred projects, including many of high priority. One of these was a $14 million project for construction of a factory in Iraq to produce precision-cutting carbide-tipped machine tools. These high-precision carbide tools have commercial applications ranging from soda cans to artificial limbs. They also can make artillery shells and valves for nuclear weapons. Indeed, after the Persian Gulf War, U.N. inspectors would find (and destroy) the carbide tool factory as an integral part of a major Iraqi nuclear weapons site.[74]

Another nuclear weapons–related project brokered by Matrix-Churchill, involving glass-fiber technology, is discussed in the next chapter. Matrix-Churchill was also involved in the Super Gun, the

Condor II missile, and other high-priority Iraqi military projects. Yet despite all these activities, and despite all the intelligence community warnings about them, Matrix-Churchill would not be shut down until September 1990, a month after the Iraqi invasion of Kuwait. The commissioner of Customs then would charge that the company had been bought by Iraq "for the specific purpose of illegally acquiring critical weapons technology."[75] But this was what the DIA report was warning about over a year earlier. Yet Matrix-Churchill stayed open, and export licenses continued to be granted for its sales and projects.

Nor does it appear to have been a question of these reports not reaching top Bush administration officials. The June DIA report, according to the *Los Angeles Times,* went to "high level Administration officials." The *Los Angeles Times* reporters were even more specific with respect to the CIA report of September 3. It went "to 38 Administration officials, including seven at the National Security Council and 10 at the State Department," including Secretary of State Baker. Another CIA report the very next day (September 4) was written in "stronger and more definitive" language; apparently, there was some concern whether the previous day's listing of nuclear technologies being acquired made the point strongly enough that what all this was about was the building of nuclear weapons. This, too, went to Secretary Baker and other top officials. And while not certain whether it was this report, one of the earlier ones, or still others, two *New York Times* reporters state that evidence of the Iraqi arms buildup was presented directly to President Bush at an NSC meeting.[76]

A few weeks later Jerry Kowalsky, president of CSI Technologies, a California-based company, met in London with Iraqi officials as the next step in "Operation Quarry." This was the Customs Service sting launched the year before (see Chapter 2) when Kowalsky passed on to Customs and the CIA his concerns about Iraqi purchase offers for his firms' highly specialized electronic capacitators called krytrons, with potential dual uses as triggering devices for nuclear weapons.

Kowalsky had been asked by the Customs Service to go ahead and make the Iraqis an attractive proposal. The culmination was the London meeting. When Kowalsky asked the Iraqis about the intended end-use, he was told that they were for "computer room air conditioning units." As he later recounted in testimony to a congressional committee, "Whenever a probing question was asked regarding the application, the Iraqis would lapse into Arabic and discuss between them before they would answer any questions. A translation later had Ali Daghir [one of the Iraqi officials] saying, 'You see Americans are naive, stupid.' "[77]

Kowalsky also was told that the Iraqi customer was a research facility named Al-Qaqaa. The name "meant nothing to me" at the time. But only a few weeks earlier there had been a major explosion at this Al-Qaqaa facility which Saddam's government had tried to keep quiet but which an Iranian-born British journalist named Farzad Bazoft set out to investigate.

Kowalsky signed the contract with the Iraqis for CSI to manufacture the electronic capacitators. When delivery was made a few months later, in March 1990, U.S. and British Customs agents were there to bring Operation Quarry to fruition. But in the fall of 1989, Operation Quarry did not have any more impact than the June DIA or September CIA reports, or any of the other warning signs, in injecting greater caution and concern into the Bush administration's overall strategy toward Iraq.

BNL: Saddam's Banker

"For the attention of Mr. C. Drogoul," read the telex dated March 26, 1989:

> I would like to express my greetings and personal good wishes for you and your family and all your staff at Del Lavoro Bank–Atlanta on the occasion of the Easter festivities. Wishing you all happiness, good health and prosperity.

It was signed Hussein Kamil Hasan, MIMI director-general and son-in-law of Saddam Hussein.[78]

Mr. Christopher Drogoul, vice-president and manager of the Atlanta branch of the Italian Banca Nazionale del Lavoro (BNL), knew
very well the reasons for this hearty greeting. Others would only
begin to know a few months later when on August 4, 1989, acting on
tips from informants, the FBI raided BNL-Atlanta. What they found
was evidence of the largest bank fraud in U.S. history (a record then
broken by the Bank of Credit and Commerce International, or BCCI).
Far beyond the $720 million in CCC credits for Iraq which it had been
guaranteeing, BNL-Atlanta had made over $4 billion in unauthorized
and largely unsecured loans to Iraq. And not just for more wheat, rice,
and corn. Much of this money was used by Iraq to acquire materials,
equipment, and technology for nuclear and chemical weapons and
ballistic missile programs. BNL had been acting as the principal
banker for Saddam's global front company network.

BNL was Italy's largest bank. It had 424 branches worldwide and
was 96.5 percent government owned, its principal executives political
appointees. The Atlanta branch had been opened in 1982. It lost money
its first two years, until Drogoul, then thirty-four years old and
"known in Atlanta's international banking community for his intense
drive and ambition," took over.[79] Drogoul turned BNL-Atlanta
around in part through shrewd use of the CCC program. He would
offer extremely low interest rates, as little as ¹⁄₁₆ percent above the
LIBOR (London Inter Bank Offering Rate), while using BNL's coveted AAA bond rating (a rating only one American bank had) to bor-
row short-term at or below LIBOR. BNL-Atlanta financed CCC programs to Eastern Europe, the Far East, and the Middle East, including
(and especially) Iraq. By fiscal year 1985 BNL-Atlanta had 20 percent
of the Iraqi CCC program; by fiscal year 1987, 92 percent.

There was a problem, however, with bank headquarters in Rome.
Bank policy limited exposure for CCC lending to a single customer at
$150 million. Iraq had reached the limit. Drogoul requested an in-
crease in allowable exposure. But he was turned down in part because
of a dispute then current between the Italian and Iraqi governments
over a $2.65 billion contract for the sale of naval frigates. It was at this
point that Drogoul came up with his "gray book" scheme. He kept

making new loans to Iraq but tracked them in a separate set of books; he called these "Perugina," after a popular Italian candy.[80] And quite a lot of "candy" he had: $556 million in additional CCC credit financing in fiscal year 1986, $619 million in fiscal year 1987, and $665 million in fiscal year 1988.[81] There were the additional benefits for BNL-Atlanta of the profits on these loans being tax free, since there was no reporting to the Internal Revenue Service or the state of Georgia, and for Drogoul of bribes, kickbacks, and other side payments.

Drogoul went further. On February 22, 1988, he signed the first of four medium-term loan agreements (MTLs) with the Central Bank of Iraq. This initial agreement was for $200 million with the liberal terms of five- to seven-year maturities and two- to five-year grace periods. It supposedly was for "reconstruction projects and hydroelectric dam along the Tigris at Badush"—the oft-used cover for the Condor II missile program. The partner was MIMI. The three other MTLs were signed October 6, 1988; December 3, 1988; and April 8, 1989. The sums ranged as high as $1.15 billion. They were also with MIMI, and were also being funneled to priority weapons development projects. The cumulative value of these four MTLs was approximately $2.1 billion. About half had been disbursed prior to the August 4, 1989, FBI raid.

The timing of these loans was crucial in two respects. As already discussed, this was right when Saddam was intensifying his programs to develop his arsenal of weapons of mass destruction. Hussein Kamil's assertion that the objective was the pursuit of military technological self-sufficiency came in May 1989. It also was right when most official Western creditors were scaling back, if not turning off, their lending to Iraq. To be able to tap over $2 billion in unsecured loans with favorable terms provided by BNL-Atlanta was quite useful and timely.

The CIA estimated that at least $600 million of the BNL money was used for the acquisition and development of weapons technology. Congressman Gonzalez puts the figure even higher at $800 million.[82] The weapons-related BNL financing included such exports made by U.S. companies and licensed by the Reagan and Bush administrations as a $40 million brass-refining factory used for manufacturing artillery shells for the Super Gun; the $14 million carbide-tipped machine tool factory built at the Al-Atheer nuclear weapons complex; a $53 million petrochemical-plant-cum-weapons-factory; a $26 million ductile-pipe plant used to manufacture barrels for the Super Gun; $12 million worth of machine tools for the Hutteen munitions complex near Baghdad; and about $53 million worth of technology and machinery for the Condor II missile. BNL-Atlanta also financed numerous exports by European companies of equipment for nuclear centrifuges and other nuclear machines and materials, for the Condor II missile, for SCUD missile enhancements, for the short-range Ababel rocket, for 210- and 155-millimeter howitzers, for military night vision equipment, for the artillery fuse factory, and for numerous other weapons systems. Matrix-Churchill was involved in many of these, and BNL even made a $600,000 direct loan to Matrix-Churchill for the company's own operating expenses.[83]

The BNL case would drag out over the full four years of the Bush administration, stirring such controversy and allegations of official involvement and cover-up as to be dubbed "Iraq-gate." There is some evidence of prior knowledge of BNL activities in the intelligence agencies. The National Security Agency (NSA), which specializes in electronic surveillance, was said to have accumulated "voluminous" information on BNL through its monitoring of telex traffic and tracking of money flows. The CIA "had monitored relations between BNL and Iraq for years.... 'The CIA knew about it, and so did the Defense Intelligence Agency,' said a U.S. intelligence official."[84]

And even if Bush administration policy-makers didn't know before August 1989, they knew now. DOD officials informed the FBI of their own suspicions of BNL's role in Iraq's procurement network. The Customs Service wrote the U.S. Attorney, Northern District of Georgia, who was charged with the legal investigation, of their suspicions that BNL had "provided loans to various U.S. firms for the illegal export to Iraq of missile related technology to be used in the Condor II project." The Assistant U.S. Attorney prosecuting the case told Federal Reserve officials that "she believes that BNL-Atlanta made loans to Matrix-Churchill ... to finance the purchase by Iraq of missile casings."[85] A State Department briefing memo acknowledged that "the money does appear to have been used to finance a wide range of imports and projects, probably including the acquisition of sensitive technology."[86] The Agriculture Department's inspector-general was so concerned about the revelations of corruption in the CCC program that he advised scaling back the upcoming fiscal year 1990 CCC program at least on an interim basis. A Federal Reserve Bank aide wrote Chairman Alan Greenspan on September 28 that indictments were expected "in the next 30 days." Secretary of State Baker was "most interested" and was receiving "frequent briefings."[87]

The Iraqi government expressed "surprise" at the whole outcry. All its financing arrangements with BNL, it insisted, were "correct and legal." And the money was spent "purely for civil use."[88]

The Die Is Cast:
NSD-26 and Fiscal Year 1990 CCC Financing

The interagency review process which led to the promulgation of NSD-26 later was characterized by one Bush administration official as an effort "to go back to basics and rethink the premises on which we operate." According to other participants, though, it all was quite consensual. When NSD-26 finally was signed on October 2, it was but "a linear extension of interim policy." Basic agreement had been reached as early as April 12 at the Deputies Committee meeting chaired by the deputy national security advisor at the time, Robert Gates. An NSC review was held on June 26, also with little apparent debate. Debate, if anything, was over "whether we were being too stringent." The "message of reassurance" mentioned earlier from the CIA's fall 1989 NIE reinforced this tendency. The result, far from a return to basics or a rethinking of premises, and despite all the warnings, was "more of the same. Wean the Iraqis away from nuclear and chemical proliferation; tie them economically closer to the U.S. and the Western world; try to use carrots, rather than sticks, in moderating their behavior."[89]

The point, of course, is not just that a piece of paper was signed by the president. National Security Directives are much more than that. They are the *end products* of extensive and priority deliberative processes, and as such, while often relatively short in actual length, reflect more complex and complete strategies. Also, once promulgated, they become *instruments* to be invoked as authoritative sources of support and justification in intra-administration policy disputes. As one veteran State Department official observed, "Once it [an NSD] is signed by the President, opposing the policy is no longer a matter of bureaucratic in-fighting but willful opposition to the President."[90] The argument that a particular position is consistent with the mandate established by the president in a National Security Directive often can be the margin needed to prevail over a contending position. This is very much what NSC-26 manifested, and how it was used.

The other key decision made by the Bush administration around the same time involved the allocation of $1 billion in new CCC credit guarantees to Iraq for the new fiscal year 1990. The meetings and memos involving the issue are quite revealing and had telling implications. They thus are reviewed here in some detail.

Back at the August 10 meeting of the National Advisory Council on International Monetary and Financial Policy (NAC), the interagency group with jurisdiction over CCC and other international financial policies, the Agriculture Department had proposed the additional $1 billion for Iraq for fiscal year 1990.[91] USDA and its farm constituency had quite a lot at stake in the Iraqi market. Sales in the previous year had been $180 million in rice (the number-one market for U.S. rice exporters), $173 million for wheat and wheat flour, $94 million for feed and other grain products, $71 million for cotton, and substantial sales of other crops. But this NAC meeting was less than a week after the BNL raid. At the insistence of the representatives of the Treasury Department and the Federal Reserve Board, the NAC deferred any recommendation.

At a meeting on October 3, the day after NSD-26 had been signed, USDA came back with its $1 billion proposal. As part of its case, it raised the specter of lost export earnings, that a "lack of timely, positive action . . . would induce the Iraqis to take their agricultural purchases elsewhere." But both Treasury and the Federal Reserve remained strongly opposed. According to the minutes of the meeting:

> The Fed [representative] had reservations with regard to Iraq's overall creditworthiness. In this connection, he noted that Iraq had continued undertaking selective, unilateral rescheduling with its official creditors. Moreover, despite increases in oil revenues since the end of the Iran-Iraq war, Iraq's foreign exchange earnings were still insufficient for it to service its external debts properly and fully. . . . He contended that these questions together with the still-unfolding BNL scandal, suggested that USDA should adopt a "wait and see" attitude before going ahead with a program of the magnitude proposed.
>
> The Treasury desk officer for Iraq, noting that the CCC and the U.S. and U.K. export financing agencies were the only official credit institutions open in Iraq, said that Iraq's international creditworthiness was very low. . . . He continued by saying that it was well known in the international financial community that Iraq only paid those creditors from which it received new credits and, viewed in this manner, the CCC could be contributing to a Ponzi-type scheme.
>
> The Treasury attorney stated that she had spoken at length with the Assistant United States Attorney (AUSA) in Atlanta who is in charge of the BNL investigation. From the AUSA, the Treasury attorney understood that indictments relating to the BNL affair would definitely be sought.[92]

The State Department, however, "was particularly forceful in arguing that programming should go forward." State stressed "that Iraq had great strategic importance to the United States."[93] With USDA, it offered a compromise proposal of a first tranche of $400 million with a second tranche possible pending the results of the BNL investigation. This was approved by the NAC in a 5 to 2 vote, with Treasury and the Fed dissenting.

Two days later (on October 5), the Iraqi delegation arrived in Washington for negotiations with the USDA. They were not pleased with the reduced $400 million offer, and negotiations stalemated.

The next day Foreign Minister Aziz met with Secretary of State Baker. This was the first meeting between Baker and Aziz. It began with mutual pledges to foster good relations, including Aziz's statement that

> Iraq has said clearly that it wants to maintain the whole region intact—including the individual countries—and that it has no bad intentions against any of them. He stressed that Iraq's objective was and is good relations with them all, particularly Saudi Arabia and Kuwait.[94]

Aziz, however, qualified his remarks with the concern vis-à-vis the United States that "frankly speaking in the spirit of friendship, Iraq has not seen 'enough improvement' in the relationship since the [Iran-Iraq] ceasefire." The United States "seemed to have a negative approach to Iraqi post-war efforts to develop its industry and technological base," he stated with reference to dual-use technology export controls. Iraq's industrial and technological programs were "for our people," he assured. "No objective directed against any other country" lay behind them. Accusations and implications otherwise were part of "a propaganda campaign against Iraq in the U.S.—particularly by the Congress." Nor had Iraq done anything illegal in the BNL affair. "The Minister made it clear that this [the CCC-BNL linkage] was not a sign that the U.S. wanted improvement in relations. It is in fact a setback and GOI [government of Iraq] is very unhappy." Aziz set the new CCC financing as a test of the relationship.

Secretary Baker acknowledged that the United States did have concerns about proliferation, but despite the recent DIA and CIA reports and other warnings about Iraqi nonconventional weapons programs, Baker couched these as only general "worldwide concerns." On the BNL issue, one of his aides interjected that there was at least some evidence of wrongdoing by Iraqi government officials. Aziz denied this, but offered that "if Iraqi officials were implicated, the GOI wanted to know immediately. He stressed Iraqi pride in rooting out corruption and said GOI would surely act on any information available to it." Secretary Baker then asked if U.S. investigators could question any Iraqi government officials so implicated. Aziz "said he did not know. It would depend on the information."

Baker pressed his own main agenda, which was gaining Iraqi support for the Arab-Israeli peace process. The Bush administration was pushing the Mubarak plan, a new ten-point proposal made by the Egyptian president to bridge the gap on Palestinian autonomy issues. Iraq could help simply by its support lending legitimacy in the Arab world to the Egyptian position, if not with pressure on the PLO to support the Mubarak plan. But in the meeting with Baker, Aziz only would provide a private assurance of his support, refusing to make a public endorsement on the alleged grounds that it was Iraqi policy "to refrain from public statements on the peace process." This was curious, since Iraq had not exactly refrained from quite public and quite strident criticisms in the past, including hosting in Baghdad the first Rejectionist Front meeting following the signing of the Camp David Accords in 1978. Moreover, ten days later, after Secretary Baker had also broached his own plan, the meeting at which the PLO Central Council rejected the "Baker Plan" and instead called for an escalation of the *intifada* was held in Baghdad.

Baker nevertheless had pledged to Aziz in their meeting that he "would immediately look into what could be done" on the CCC package. Just in case Baker hadn't gotten the message from Aziz, Nizar Hamdoon reinforced it in meetings in Baghdad on October 7 and 8 with U.S. Ambassador April Glaspie and chargé Joseph Wilson IV. "With his mailed fist still in his velvet glove," as Wilson recounted the meeting, "Hamdoon then pointed out that Iraq does have alternative sources of supply to which it could turn." Wilson also picked up on the threat "implicit in Hamdoon's remarks" that Iraq might default on its already existing CCC debts (then about $1.7 billion). His message, Hamdoon stressed, came from the "highest authorities in the Iraqi government."[95]

As part of his looking into the matter, Secretary Baker received a memo from an aide on October 11. The memo recommended proceeding "with caution and prudence." Nothing had been proven yet, but Baker was apprised that the allegations were of "widespread and blatant 'irregularities' in the CCC program," as well as of diversion of CCC funds "for arms purchases." The BNL scandal "is directly involved with the Iraqi CCC program and cannot be separated from it."[96]

That same day the USDA sent two of its officials down to Atlanta to meet with the prosecutors in the U.S. Attorney's Office. According to Gale McKenzie, the key prosecutor in the case, the picture she presented to the USDA investigators was a bleak one:

> Criminal complicity of certain Iraqi government officials, BNL-Atlanta officers and employees, and Entrade [a Turkish-owned trading company in New York] in a multibillion dollar scheme to defraud BNL.
>
> Use by Iraqi government officials of non-CCC guaranteed, unsecured scheme proceeds to purchase products useful for military purposes, including machines that could, among other things, remove burrs from nose cones of missiles and compress nuclear fuel;
>
> Kickbacks. . . .
>
> Barter, transhipment or other diversion [of CCC guaranteed commodities] from consumption in Iraq;
>
> After sales services. . . .
>
> Criminal complicity of certain Iraqi government officials . . . to defraud USDA.[97]

The next day, based on this information, the USDA pulled even the $400 million CCC package off the table and suspended negotiations with the Iraqi delegation "pending further notification."[98]

The next morning (October 13) Secretary of State Baker was told of the USDA action at his regular 8:40 A.M. senior staff briefing. According to notes taken at the meeting, Baker responded that withdrawing the $400 million "is step in wrong direction." The same notes indicate Baker's order to "get it back on the table." Another State Department official told congressional investigators that he was told by Baker " 'in no uncertain terms' to 'get on with the program.' "[99]

That same day Frank Lemay, special assistant to the under secretary of state for economic affairs, was sent over to the USDA "to find out what was going on." Lemay, a career foreign service officer, was chosen because, as his boss put it, he was "number one bird-dog in the office." His memo directly quotes his USDA briefers as saying that "the investigations are at the explosion stage" and that they feared that the BNL case could "blow the roof off the CCC." He warned that "as investigators dig further into the paper morass, more and more indications of significant wrongdoing on the part of BDLA [BNL] and Iraq are surfacing." At minimum, he stated, the Iraqi government "knew of the illegal dealings of the BDLA but found it convenient to continue using its good offices." They also appeared to be doing quite a bit of their own skimming through "consulting fees" to Matrix-Churchill and "after sales services," which exporters were required to provide free of charge, and assorted kickbacks. Most significant, though,

> it appears more and more likely that CCC guaranteed funds and/or commodities may have been diverted in exchange for military hardware ... (including) nuclear related equipment.

Lemay acknowledged that all this was not yet substantiated, but he left no doubt as to how serious he considered the preliminary evidence: "If smoke indicates fire, we may be facing a four alarm blaze in the near future."[100]

Lemay's memo, according to congressional investigators, went to Baker. The secretary was not happy. In a shoot-the-messenger-type move, he took the issue away from State's Economics Affairs Bureau and put Robert Kimmitt, under secretary for political affairs and one of his most trusted aides, in charge. He also brought in legal advisor Abraham Sofaer to work with the USDA and the Justice Department on the legal aspects. All told, according to the notes of a Treasury Department official in close contact with State, Baker was "putting pressure ... *insisting* on being kept informed."[101]

Baker was after not just getting the $400 million CCC partial package back on the table, but the full $1 billion. He was assured by aides, including his legal advisor, Sofaer, that as long as he could get Iraqi Foreign Minister Aziz to affirm his promise to cooperate with investigators and to agree to monitoring and safeguards on the new CCC trade, they could "wall off" the new fiscal year 1990 $1 billion program (split in two tranches to ensure periodic review) from the BNL investigation. Moreover, there were the "foreign policy grounds" of NSD-26 and its mandate of improved economic and political relations with Iraq to be invoked. Baker's aides recommended a personal call to Agriculture Secretary Clayton Yeutter to make this case.[102]

Baker apparently was at his persuasive best. A handwritten note at the bottom of his talking-points memo reads "10/31. Done. CY [Clayton Yeutter]: 'I think we're seeing it the same way you guys are. I'll get into it.' " The note is initialed "JAB III."[103]

The White House also had gotten involved at this point. Stephen Danzansky, the director of cabinet affairs, worked closely with the USDA in late October and early November to get the $1 billion package through the NAC. On October 26 Danzansky, along with two other White House aides (Nicholas Rostow, counsel to the National Security Council, and John Schmitz, deputy to White House Counsel C. Boyden Gray), met with USDA Counsel Alan Raul "to discuss the Iraq situation and the nature of the CCC process."[104] On October 30 Raul sent Danzansky a new USDA position paper on Iraq. This paper put much less emphasis on the allegations and charges which Lemay said had been stressed to him by his USDA contacts, and which Atlanta Assistant U.S. Attorney McKenzie said she had stressed to the USDA. It acknowledged risks and uncertainties but stressed the lack of "hard evidence."[105]

The next day Raul followed up with a fax to Danzansky of what he characterized as an "Iraqi assurance." It was a press release from the Iraqi embassy which expressed "astonishment at these unfounded reports" regarding BNL and CCC, and which claimed that Iraq had used BNL funds only for agricultural and other projects of a "pure civil nature."[106] The next day the USDA requested that the NAC reconvene to consider its revised proposal for the full $1 billion in CCC credit guarantees split into two $500 million tranches. The second tranche "would be contingent on resolution of the BNL affair." But the evidence at this point was "not sufficient reason to delay a program for Iraq any longer."[107]

NAC members were sent an eleven-page USDA report which claimed that "no wrongdoing is indicated at this time." Arthur Wade, the chief USDA investigator working on the case in Atlanta, would later testify to Congress that while this report was not technically false in saying nothing had yet been proven, it was crafted "artfully" and for a "definite purpose." "I viewed what I had as evidence; we were definitely beyond the speculation point," a fellow investigator added.[108] As for Frank Lemay, who came under fire when his memo was revealed to Congress and, among other things, had his veracity questioned, he testified to having no doubt as to the accuracy of his memo. "I took careful, sometimes verbatim, notes on what was said, I asked for clarification of points that were unclear, and I drafted the memo on the day of the meeting from those notes." Richard McCormack, the under secretary for economic affairs, later confirmed that "Mr. Lemay's representations to the committee were entirely accurate."[109]

At the NAC November 3 meeting, though, Baker's representative strongly supported the USDA proposal. He "was satisfied that there was no evidence at this time that warranted disapproval of the FY 1990 program." Moreover, he stressed, "officials *at the highest level* wished to proceed with it."[110]

Nevertheless, the NAC again balked at recommending the new CCC program. Treasury and the Fed remained opposed, still for the same reasons. State and USDA decided to buck the matter up to the next level. Another NAC meeting was called, this time not at the staff level but of deputy secretaries. State turned its lobbying up a notch. Treasury was key since it chaired the NAC. Deputy Secretary of State Lawrence Eagleburger called his counterpart, Deputy Treasury Secretary John Robson, "to urge acceptance of the full program." Robson agreed but asked for a statement in writing of the rationale. "Dear John," Eagleburger wrote in a confidential letter, "Further to our discussion, *on foreign policy grounds* we support the Department of Agriculture's proposal for a full, billion-dollar program" of CCC guarantees. "The CCC program is important to our efforts to improve and expand our relationship with Iraq," which, Eagleburger reminded, had been *"ordered by the President in NSD-26."*[111]

The White House also stayed involved. Danzansky kept in touch with the USDA. He was also present at the November 8 NAC deputies meeting. This was highly unusual, according to some sources "the first time that a White House official sat in on a NAC decision to grant credits to a foreign country."[112] It was also around this time that Jay Bybee, another aide to White House Counsel C. Boyden Gray, placed a call to the Atlanta prosecutor. Both the intent and the content of this call have been disputed. Bybee claimed that the call was intended only as an inquiry about any "potential embarrassment to the White House" from the BNL investigation and not an attempt to influence the investigation. Gerrilyn Brill, the senior U.S. Attorney on the case, interpreted the message of the call as stressing the "policy implications" of the BNL case. Bybee claimed that he was told that there was no basis for holding up further the fiscal year 1990 $1 billion CCC credit guarantees. But Assistant U.S. Attorney McKenzie later complained that the information she had provided was "discounted" in the decision to go ahead with the $1 billion.[113]

On the eve of the NAC deputies meeting, another complication arose. A report from the CIA dated November 6 added further evidence that Iraq was diverting BNL funds, possibly including CCC guaranteed loans, to nuclear weapons technology and other military purchases. The CIA report stated that Iraq had used BNL credits "to buy military and dual-use technology." Indeed, BNL had been "by far Baghdad's largest source of credits" and thus key to its "complex procurement networks of holding companies in Western Europe to acquire technology for its chemical, biological, nuclear and ballistic missile development programs." The CIA report also stated that "we believe Iraqi intelligence is directly involved in the activities of many holding companies funneling technology to Iraq."[114]

The CIA report reached a sobering conclusion. Iraq should not be expected to give up its global front company network just because its financing had been disrupted:

> We believe Iraq will work hard to establish new military procurement networks to replace those disclosed by the press and by the U.S. and Italian investigations as part of the fallout from the BNL affair. Baghdad highly values these networks to obtain technology that might otherwise be denied to it if the end uses or purposes were revealed.[115]

The minutes of the November 8 NAC deputies meeting show no concern expressed about the November 6 CIA report. The USDA stuck to its own revised report and the position that the BNL investigation had yielded only "allegations of wrongdoing" and that "there was not any evidentiary basis for withholding approval of a new CCC transaction." Besides, the others were reminded, in the United States "innocence is assumed until proven otherwise and it therefore was improper to penalize the Iraqis for unproven allegations." Yes, there were some risks, but "these possibilities had to be weighed against the value of $1 billion in export sales."[116]

State was represented by Under Secretary Kimmitt. Invoking NSD-26, Kimmitt argued that to cut CCC "would clearly run counter to the President's intentions." Iraq was nothing short of "key to the achievement of our objectives in the Middle East, the Gulf and Lebanon." He also made mention that Treasury already had changed its position. He conveyed the assurances of Iraqi Foreign Minister Aziz "that Iraq would cooperate fully with the [BNL] investigation." In sum, he argued that "despite possible future revelations, overwhelming foreign policy considerations led him to urge support of the proposal."[117]

The NAC, finally, approved. Iraq was to receive $1 billion in fiscal year 1990 CCC credit guarantees split in two $500 million tranches. But the USDA was still concerned about the risks, coming around only under the pressure brought on Secretary Yeutter by Secretary Baker, as reflected in a letter from a top Yeutter aide stating that "Secretary Baker has personally informed Secretary Yeutter that significant foreign policy initiatives of the United States in Iraq and the Middle East could be jeopardized."[118]

The next day Kimmitt wrote Baker, "Your call to Yeutter and our subsequent efforts with OMB and Treasury paid off." You should also "break the good news to Foreign Minister Tariq Aziz, since he raised the issue with you, and you promised to take a personal interest in it."[119] The decision to grant the full $1 billion in new CCC credits, read Baker's telex to Aziz, "reflects the importance we attach to our relationship with Iraq."[120]

In that same cable, Secretary Baker laid out a quid pro quo. It would "be useful," he told Aziz, "if you could weigh in with [the Palestinians] and . . . urge them to give a positive response. . . . We are at a critical point in our diplomacy."[121] Even the Shamir government had now come around to endorse the Baker Plan. Finally there seemed to be a chance for progress in the Arab-Israeli peace process.

But far from providing the "weighing in" quo for the $1 billion CCC quid, shortly after the Baker cable the Iraqis announced the creation of the "Popular Arab Front" dedicated to supporting the *intifada*. On even this issue of such importance to the Bush administration, the Iraqis were not being very accommodating.

Not to mention the global front company network, or the BNL scandal, or the treatment of the Kurds. None of this squared with the "logic" of accommodation.

And all of this was quite visible *at the time* that the die was being cast.

Saddam's Strategy: Into Kuwait, Not the Family of Nations

THE WHOLE IDEA, GEORGE BUSH WOULD LATER CONTEND, WAS TO BRING Saddam Hussein "into the family of nations." That was what the Reagan administration had started trying to do. That was what NSD-26 was all about. And that was what the Bush administration kept trying to do, right up to August 2, 1990, when Saddam invaded Kuwait and showed how far outside the family of nations he was intent on remaining.

December 1989 and January 1990: More Warning Signs

In December 1989, only two months after NSD-26 was promulgated and one month after the new $1 billion CCC commitment, U.S. intelligence picked up evidence of Iraqi tests of two new ballistic missiles. One was called the Al-Abid, or Worshiper, the other Tammuz I (for the nuclear reactor at Osirak bombed by Israel in 1981). These were long-range ballistic missiles, with two to three times greater range than the intermediate-range missiles (Al-Husayn, Al-Abbas) used in the war against Iran. These new long-range missiles had the potential to attack Israel from sites deep within Iraq. Moreover, the Tammuz I also had the payload capacity to carry a large nuclear or large chemical or biological weapon.[1]

The Tammuz I test was conducted virtually at the same moment that a Missile Technology Control Regime (MTCR) meeting was taking place in London. Whether this was purely coincidental or an intentional act of defiance, the fact was that the testing of such a long-range missile was of significant international concern. *Al-Jumhuriyah*, Baghdad's official daily newspaper, deemed any such concern as "illegitimate" and something that "would not minimize the Iraqis or the Arabs joy over this great accomplishment." Part as warning and part as maxim, it also declared that "in terms of technology, the Iraqis are coming as a power that must be taken into account. No real independence can be achieved without mastering technology."[2] Saddam Hussein made the same points himself in a speech the next month to an Arab League conference in Baghdad. We need to "guarantee that our weapons are self-made," Saddam said, in order "to secure prospects for victory and maintain that our society is impregnable."[3]

There also were further reports on Saddam's nuclear weapons programs. The Joint Atomic Intelligence Committee (JAIC), the principal U.S. interagency intelligence group monitoring nuclear proliferation, had gone through a "vigorous debate" in developing its confidential analysis over how close Iraq was to building its first nuclear weapon. State and Energy analysts had prevailed with their view that it would not be for eight years at the earliest, but some in the CIA projected the Iraqis as close as two to four years away.[4] There were also reports in the open press. "Iraq is trying to build a nuclear bomb," an article in *MidEast Markets* unequivocally stated.[5] Saddam's government brushed off rather than denied such reports. "We have the right to protect our achievements because they belong not only to Iraq, but to the entire Arab nation as well," one official simply stated.

Nor were the signs from Baghdad particularly encouraging on the Arab-Israeli peace process. On December 6 Egypt formally accepted the Baker Plan as the basis for further peace talks. Israel had accepted it the previous month conditioned on a guarantee from the United States that the PLO would not have a direct role in the talks. Egypt's acceptance was taken as an indication that the PLO leadership was willing to go along with the "invisible" role Egypt was offering through its own good offices. Iraq, though, convened the Popular Arab Front's first *"intifada* support" meeting in Baghdad which issued a communiqué backing "the brave Palestinian intifadah" (as well as expressing "solidarity with the heroic people of Vietnam . . . Namibia, South Africa and Nicaragua").[6] This was followed by broadcasts from PLO central radio, transmitting from Baghdad, assailing the U.S.-led peace talks as having reached a "level of absurdity." And in his Army Day speech, Saddam hailed the "great performance of the Iraqi Army in the Arab lands and the skies of Palestine, the Golan and the Sinai"; warned against "hostile, aggressive and usurpist Zionism"; and implicated the United States directly, asserting that "if Israel carries out an act of aggression, the United States will not be able to deny the charge of encouraging Israel to carry out such an act."[7]

Yet the Bush administration continued on its NSD-26 charted course. The information on the missile tests, aides assured Secretary Baker, "is still sketchy." Nor was much stock to be put in what was characterized as "recent rehashing of allegations" regarding Iraqi nuclear weapons.[8] These, though, were curious assessments given that the interagency Subcommittee on Nuclear Export Controls (SNEC), chaired by the State Department, recently had received intelligence briefings leading it to conclude that "Iraq is acquiring nuclear related equipment and materials without regard for immediate need." A SNEC memo displays a degree of concern and even frustration over the tensions in the Bush administration policy:

> The problem is not that we lack a policy on Iraq; we have a policy. However, the policy has proven very hard to implement when considering proposed exports of dual-use commodities to ostensibly non-nuclear end users, particularly state enterprises.
>
> SNEC policy for some years has been not to approve exports for

Iraq's nuclear program. . . . However, at the same time, U.S. policy, as confirmed in NSD-26, has been to improve relations with Iraq, including trade, which means that exports of non-sensitive commodities to "clean" end users in Iraq should be encouraged.

Yet the cleanliness of most if not all Iraqi state enterprise end-users was suspect, given that most if not all were "involved in both military and civil projects."[9]

Moreover, SNEC members were informed of the intelligence community's presumption that "the Iraqi government is interested in acquiring a nuclear explosive capability." They also were shown supporting evidence that "Iraq is acquiring nuclear related equipment and materials without regard for immediate need." Yet, as Alan Friedman recounts it, such doubts were "brushed aside" by Baker's State Department, and "within twenty-four hours of the intelligence briefing, State . . . recommended seven of the nine exports for immediate approval."[10]

Over at the Department of Energy, the task force which had been set up in July to track intelligence reports on Iraqi nuclear weapons development "died of neglect." The task force was the one achievement to come out of the intra-DOE bureaucratic battle otherwise lost by those trying to sound the warning of Iraqi nuclear ambitions (Chapter 3). It was disbanded in December, though, "due to a lack of DOE interest," according to one of its key advocates.[11]

It also was right at this time that Secretary Baker sent a memo to President Bush proposing a waiver of the ban recently imposed by Congress on Export-Import Bank lending to Iraq. Congress had included Iraq with the likes of Iran, Syria, Libya, South Yemen, Cuba, Angola, Cambodia, and Vietnam as ineligible for Eximbank financing of any kind (direct loans, credits, insurance, or guarantees). The legislation did, however, allow the president to waive the prohibition if "its application is not in the national interest of the United States."

Baker's memo was dated December 8. The next day an American diplomat met in Baghdad with the Iraqi minister of trade, who cited the Eximbank ban as an example of how "mischievous persons" were seeking to ruin U.S.-Iraqi relations. Assurance was given that the Bush administration had strongly opposed the congressional action, and that "we intended to issue the required waiver."[12]

Toward that end Baker also had a "memorandum of justification" prepared for Eximbank chairman John D. Macomber. The language was right out of NSD-26:

> It is in the national interest of the United States to maintain existing economic and political incentives, such as the short-term Exim credit insurance, to encourage Iraq to moderate its behavior and increase our ability to deal effectively with Iraq on issues of importance to the United States.[13]

The memo emphasized the "opportunities for U.S. firms to participate in the post-war reconstruction of the Iraqi economy" and that Iraq was "an important supplier of petroleum for the U.S. market." It concluded that "there have been no recent events that would justify the total withdrawal of EXIM coverage at this time"—despite Iraq's long-range ballistic missile tests and the latest wrenches it threw into the Arab-Israeli peace process.

Shortly thereafter, President Bush issued the following executive order:

> I hereby determine that, with respect to Iraq, application of the prohibition contained in that section [Section 572 of the Foreign Operations, Export Financing, and Related Programs Appropriations Act of 1990] to the Export-Import Bank or its agents is not in the national interest of the United States.

The Baker State Department also was the principal source of pressure to go ahead with the second $500 million tranche of CCC credit guarantees. "We want to move ahead on the second tranche this month, as the Iraqis have requested," a January 4 memo stated.[14] Baker apparently was ready to dismiss the allegations of violations of the CCC program raised by the BNL case. "The Secretary has personally satisfied himself that no evidence has been offered imputing the Iraqi program," the Iraqi minister of trade was told. "The allegations were baseless."[15]

Others, though, were not quite so dismissive. The BNL investigations had been uncovering numerous irregularities and possible illegalities. The U.S. Attorney's Office in Atlanta indicated that it anticipated its first indictments by early February. The USDA, with the support of Treasury, was willing to continue the first tranche without suspension but was resisting the release of the second tranche. Instead the USDA general counsel prepared a memo for State and Justice proposing a demarche to the Iraqi government for assurances of cooperation with the investigations. Foreign Minister Aziz had pledged such cooperation in his October 6 meeting with Secretary of State Baker, but it apparently had been less than forthcoming. The whole BNL issue, the Iraqi minister of trade insisted, was being "manipulated by those hostile to Iraq to damage Iraq's reputation."[16]

There was also some dissent from within State. Once again, as in 1988, a paper arguing the need to "contain" Iraq was written by members (different ones than in 1988) of State's Policy Planning Staff. The paper drew an explicit albeit limited analogy to Kennan's original strategy for dealing with the Soviet Union. Saddam's regime had to be viewed as inherently and continuingly expansionist by nature, irrespective of how exhausted it might be at a particular moment. As with Stalin's Russia, if Saddam's Iraq was forced to make choices, the regime's internal contradictions would be exacerbated. The policy being proposed was for firmer, more vigilant policies: not necessarily a return to pre-1982 strict adversarial relations, but an element of containment to firm up and balance the overly accommodationist NSD-26 approach. One proposal, with its own touch of historical irony to it, was for Iraq to be put on the agenda for the upcoming Soviet-American ministerial meeting in pursuit of something of a joint containment effort.[17]

The paper went to Policy Planning Director Dennis Ross. He "found the argument persuasive but did not act on it."[18] Ross was highly respected both within the administration and among administration critics. But as Baker's key aide also on the Arab-Israeli peace talks and the Soviet Union, Ross had his plate full. It was hard to get his attention in a sufficiently concerted fashion to intercede to change the direction of a policy which still apparently had strong support with Secretary Baker personally and in the White House.

February and March:
"The Spring of Bad Behavior"

On February 15, 1990, the Voice of America (VOA) ran an editorial transmitted into a number of Arab countries, including Iraq, reflecting on the implications of the recent freedom wave that had swept away the dictators of Eastern Europe.

> A successful tyranny requires a strong, ruthless secret police. A successful democracy requires the abolition of such a force. That is a lesson the people of Eastern Europe have learned well. . . . Secret police are also entrenched in other countries, such as China, North Korea, Iran, *Iraq,* Syria, Libya, Cuba and Albania. The rulers of these countries hold power by force and fear, not by the consent of the governed. But as East Europeans demonstrated so dramatically in 1989, the tide of history is against such rulers. The 1990s should belong not to the dictators and the secret police, but to the people.[19]

The broadcast was almost routine for the times. Not, though, to the ears of Saddam Hussein. Deputy Foreign Minister Hamdoon "convoked" U.S. Ambassador April Glaspie to protest such "a flagrant interference in the internal affairs of Iraq and the direct official [that is, by the U.S. government] instigation against the legitimate authority [that is, Saddam's regime]."[20] Of course, Hamdoon didn't mention that Saddam was said to have ordered the heads of his security services to watch videotapes of the fall of Romania's Nicolae Ceausescu, to learn from his mistakes.[21]

Compared to the annual human rights report on Iraq released the same month by State's Human Rights Bureau, the VOA editorial was rather understated. "Iraq's human rights record remained abysmal in 1989," the report declared. It was not short on details:

> For years execution has been an established Iraqi method for dealing with perceived political and military opponents of the government.... In some cases, a family only learns that one of its members has been executed when the security services return the body and require the family to pay a fine....
>
> Thousands of political prisoners continued to be arbitrarily arrested and detained.... Relations, including children of suspects, are said to be held as hostages to compel confessions....
>
> The freedoms of speech and press are not respected.... All publications are subject to censorship.... Journalists and photographers visiting Iraq at the invitation of the Government are required to present film taken in Iraq for inspection by the authorities....
>
> Public meetings may only be organized under the auspices of the Government or by the Ba'ath Party. Association for nonreligious purposes and demonstrations without government approval have met with severe repression.[22]

Iraq even had brought its police state methods into the United States in a recent attempt by Iraqi agents to assassinate an Iraqi dissident living in the United States.[23]

But instead of expressing outrage at the outlandish "flagrant interference" charges, or using the incident to raise human rights and democratization issues, the Bush administration sought mostly to assuage Saddam's hurt feelings. "This editorial could easily be read as a call to Iraqis to revolt against Saddam," Ambassador Glaspie cabled back to Washington. She received instructions (dated February 27) for an apology:

> It is in no way USG [U.S. government] policy to suggest that the Government of Iraq is illegitimate or that the people of Iraq should or will revolt against the Government of Iraq.
>
> We regret that the wording of the VOA editorial left it open to that incorrect interpretation.

Secretary Baker added an "FYI":

> Department believes that failure to clear the text of the editorial represents a violation of the understanding we have with USIA [United States Information Agency], and by extension, VOA. We intend to follow up.[24]

The next day (February 28) Ambassador Glaspie wrote the letter of apology to Foreign Minister Aziz. "I conveyed your concern to my Government, and was immediately instructed to assure you that it is absolutely not United States policy to question the legitimacy of the government of Iraq nor to intervene in any way in the domestic concerns of the Iraqi people and government." Further,

> President Bush wants good relations with Iraq, relations built on confidence and trust, so that we can discuss a broad range of issues frankly and fruitfully. I am sorry that the Government of Iraq did not inform me of its concern about the editorial sooner, so that I could have provided you with the official assurance of our regret without delay.[25]

All future VOA editorials were to be cleared by the State Department, by order of Secretary Baker.

Six weeks later, a U.S. Senate delegation led by Senate Republican Leader Robert Dole told Saddam that the VOA editorialist had been fired. This proved not to be true, but it didn't take away from the empathizers' intent. Senator Alan Simpson, the second-ranking Senate Republican and also a member of the delegation, tried to put it all in a broader context. "Democracy," he told Saddam,

> is a very irksome and confusing thing. I believe your problem is with the Western media, not with the U.S. Government. . . . The press is spoiled and conceited. All the journalists consider themselves brilliant political scientists. They do not want to see anything succeeding or achieving its objectives. My advice is that you allow those bastards to come here and see things for themselves.[26]

Baker also kept the pressure on for freeing up the second CCC tranche. An NAC meeting was held on February 22. With authorization from Under Secretary Robert Kimmitt, State's representative proposed immediate release of the second tranche. Again, though, the USDA stated that it was not yet ready to make such a move. The BNL indictments still had yet to be handed down, but were said to be imminent. An internal USDA memo expressed concern that the BNL scandal had the potential to become the CCC's equivalent of the "HUD or savings-and-loan scandal." Treasury even proposed that if any further credits were extended, there be a further split into two $250 million tranches.[27]

Pressures from Congress were mixed. On the one hand, pro–second tranche letters and calls were coming to the USDA from senators and representatives tied to agricultural groups with exports at stake. But Senator Patrick Leahy (D-Vermont), chairman of the Senate Agriculture Committee, questioned Agriculture Secretary Clayton Yeutter as to whether "foreign policy pressures have encouraged the Department to give Iraq special treatment." Secretary Yeutter denied such pressures, stating that "to the contrary, the extension of CCC guarantees in connection with sales to Iraq have recently been subject to special scrutiny because of the BNL investigation."[28] Yeutter's response was somewhat misleading. Foreign policy pressures clearly were being exerted. The USDA was resisting them at this point, but it had not done so at the key November 1989 NAC meetings (Chapter 3), and later in May 1990 would again not do so.

Assistant Secretary of State for Near East and South Asian Affairs John Kelly continued to be the principal direct exerter of those pressures. He insisted that "there is no apparent justification for continued delay." He also was convinced that the failure to deliver on the second tranche, especially on top of the VOA editorial controversy, was a key factor explaining Saddam's recent spate of anti-American speeches. We were "feed[ing] Saddam's paranoia and accelerat[ing] his swing against us. We need to move quickly to repair the damage to the U.S.-Iraqi relationship by getting this critical program back on track."[29] In testimony to the House Foreign Affairs Committee following a three-hour meeting in Baghdad with Saddam, he insisted that "it is clear that Iraq seeks improved relations with the United States." Saddam's human rights record and weapons programs were "problems," and while ours was not "an easy relationship," it was one "in which we have made significant progress in recent years."[30]

Indeed, even by his own standards, Saddam had been quite strident of late. He used the occasion of the first anniversary of the Arab Cooperation Council, the founding of which the Bush administration had pointed to as an indicator of Iraqi moderation, to launch a series of attacks on the United States. One of his basic lines was that the United States was exploiting the decline of the Soviet Union to exert a new "spirit of unilateralism." He cautioned, "If the Gulf people, along with all Arabs, are not careful, the Arab Gulf region will be governed by the wishes of the United States." He warned against the United States from its new position of strength committing "follies against the interests and national security of the Arabs." The Arab nation needed to take a "realistic approach" to ensure for themselves that "America must respect the Arabs and respect their rights and should not interfere in their internal affairs under any cover." The Soviet Union had let its Arab allies down by "giving in to U.S. pressure." Now, though, freed from their own fears of communism, the Arab nations also needed American protection less and could themselves through pan-Arabism become a force balancing "the single-superpower." The ACC, far from playing a pro-U.S. coalescing role, was to be part of this counterbalancing effort. Indeed, Saddam went so far as to say that there was no room among "good" Arabs for "the faint-hearted who would argue that, as a superpower, the United States will be the decisive factor and others have no choice but to submit."[31]

Saddam didn't need to name names. Egyptian President Hosni Mubarak was so angered by Saddam's attack on the United States and the attendant implications against Egypt as a U.S. ally that he walked out of the meeting.[32] The meeting broke up a day early.

Saddam also took a line which hardly could be construed as supportive of the Arab-Israeli peace process. "Palestine will return. Light will chase out darkness and the banners of justice shall fly over holy

Jerusalem, God willing." Israel was the aggressor, but not even just for its own reasons. U.S. strategy "needs an aggressive Israel, not a peaceful one." The "Zionist lobby" in the United States was "as powerful as ever." Arabs had "reason to feel suspicious of U.S. policy and intentions." He especially hammered away at the emigration of Soviet Jews, which was but "a sinister scheme cunningly planned by Zionists," with the conspiratorial assistance of both the United States and the Soviet Union.[33] The Baker Plan still was denounced as but a scheme "to allow the Zionist entity to escape the impasse brought about by the valiant Palestinian intifadah." Like all U.S. policies in the region, this was "fully biased in favor of the Zionist party" and part of the ongoing U.S. effort to help Israel "pursue aggressive policies against the Arab nation."[34]

Saddam also used the ACC first anniversary summit to issue demands on his fellow Arab states. One was for a moratorium on the $40 billion debt Iraq owed to other Arab states (about one-half of Iraq's total debt) from the Iran-Iraq war. In ensuing months the moratorium hardened to demands for outright debt forgiveness. Iraq fought the war against the Persians, Saddam argued, for the whole Arab world. Her people paid in blood; the other Arabs should pay the bills. The message was actually less intended for fellow ACC members Egypt, Jordan, and Yemen—politically important but not big lenders—than for the rich GCC states such as Saudi Arabia and Kuwait. "Let the Gulf regimes know," he told President Mubarak and King Hussein, "that if they do not give this money to me, I will know how to get it."[35]

Saddam also proposed that the other Arab states directly and indirectly provide Iraq with $30 billion in new economic aid. Some of this was to be through direct grants. The rest was to be through reallocations of OPEC production quotas. Iraq was to get a larger quota, other OPEC members a smaller one, and there was to be stricter cartel enforcement against overproduction cheating by countries like Kuwait, which in 1989 produced 1.8 million barrels per day, more than twice its quota.[36] Iraq's 1989 quota was 2.73 million barrels per day. At an average price of $16 per barrel, this was not even enough to service its debt.[37]

The problem being manifested was the continued deterioration of the Iraqi economy. Falling oil prices were one of the causes: Every $1 per barrel drop cost Iraq $1 billion annually. But so were Saddam's own policies, like his continuing huge military expenditures—though he had no intention of changing these policies. He turned to his Arab brethren not as supplicant but asserting what he claimed was rightfully Iraq's. And by helping Iraq, the other Arab states would help themselves. Saddam's strategic analysis was crystallizing. The pan-Arabism needed to counter U.S. unipolar designs of dominance and to defeat Israel was to be served by, and then was further justification for, assistance to be provided Iraq by its fellow Arab states. All were of a piece.

According to the Pentagon, it also was in February that U.S. intelligence detected construction of five SCUD-type fixed missile launcher complexes in western Iraq.[38] This detection did spur some increased attention to the Iraqi proliferation threat. Interagency Policy Coordinating Committee (PCC) meetings were held, including another discussion of tightening export controls. MTCR partner countries were alerted to U.S. concerns about the Iraqi missile program, and Australia Group member countries about the Iraqi chemical weapons program.

In addition, a cable was sent to American embassies throughout Western Europe and in Japan identifying key dual-use technologies on Iraq's missile and nuclear "shopping list." One of these was glass-fiber technology, which in addition to commercial uses ranging from shower stalls to fiberglass fishing boats could be used for manufacturing missile nose cones and uranium enrichment centrifuges. The embassies were told that "the USG has learned that Iraq's Nassr State Enterprise has been seeking a glass fiber production plant. Nassr has procured commodities on behalf of Iraq's nuclear and missile programs in the past." Specific companies in each country which possessed glass-fiber technology were identified, and the American ambassadors were instructed to urge the governments to review pertinent export license applications "cautiously."[39]

Simultaneously, though, licenses were still being granted by the Bush administration for dual-use exports ordered by Iraqi military-industrial complex customers. For example, another shipment of electronic equipment was approved for Salah al Din, tagged in an earlier intelligence report as "typical of Iraq's arms production facilities."[40] In another case, a license was granted for computer and related equipment designed for infrared imaging enhancement, despite CIA technical evaluations of its utility for near real-time tracking of missiles.[41] As to the multilateral demarche, while numerous countries abided by it, a few months later, the Bush administration would grant licenses for precisely the glass-fiber technology singled out for the alert (see below). And yet there still were complaints from some within the Bush administration that licensing procedures were too cumbersome, "a drag on trade with Iraq."[42]

On March 28 a shipment of 95 krytrons, also known as nuclear triggers, headed for Iraq was seized in London. This was the culmination of Operation Quarry, the joint sting begun in September 1988 by British and American Customs agents (see Chapters 2 and 3). The shipment was worth only $10,500 (the financing provided by BNL),[43] but the dollar value belied the significance of these small electrical devices which functioned as detonators inside a nuclear bomb. When an Iraqi agent arrived at Heathrow to load the krytrons in a crate labeled "air conditioning parts" on a flight to Baghdad, the sting was sprung.[44]

Official denials were of course the order of the day. The Iraqi ambassador to the United States wrote a letter to Energy Secretary James Watkins blaming "misinformation and [a] falsification media campaign."[45] The devices were "merely electrical capacitators," a government statement read, "used for many industrial, scientific and technical purposes."[46] Another one of Saddam's ambassadors claimed that it was but the latest foray of an anti-Iraq campaign being run by Britain, the United States, and "the Zionist entity." "Everybody knows that the Iraqi nuclear program is for peaceful purposes," he continued. The Zionists and their allies simply were trying "to find the necessary justifications or atmosphere for a new Israeli military aggression against Iraq."[47]

Saddam further demonstrated his disregard for world opinion when on March 15 he executed a British journalist falsely accused of spying.[48] Farzad Bazoft, an Iranian-born free-lance reporter then working for the London *Observer,* had been arrested six months earlier when he was investigating a mysterious explosion that had killed an estimated seven hundred people at the Al-Qaqaa military-industrial complex. Iraqi officials had tried to suppress word of the disaster. When it leaked out, they resorted to a cover story about an ordinary industrial fire with only a few deaths, mostly firemen. Bazoft managed to gather evidence that the Al-Qaqaa explosion was caused by HMX, or high melting point explosives. HMX is what krytrons are supposed to detonate in a nuclear bomb. It also was one of the topics covered at the Department of Energy international conference, mentioned in the previous chapter, attended by three Iraqi scientists who listed their employer on the conference program as Al-Qaqaa.

Iraqi security forces found Bazoft out, charged him with espionage, and arrested him. British consular officials were refused access to the prisoner. Prime Minister Margaret Thatcher strongly protested. When government-to-government negotiations made no progress, she appealed to U.N. Secretary General Javier Perez de Cuellar to intercede. But Saddam hanged his "spy." He and his henchmen were described as "gloating" in their defiance. "Thatcher wanted him alive," said Minister of Information Latif Nussayif Jassim. "We sent him home in a box."[49]

The Bush administration protested this execution of a journalist but did little more. Consider this exchange between top Baker aide and press spokesperson Margaret Tutwiler and a reporter:

REPORTER: Margaret . . . you all found it prudent and wise not to say anything when Iraq sentenced a British-based journalist to death. Now that he's been executed, does the United States find it timely to say nothing?

TUTWILER: We deplore Iraq's decision to ignore the many international appeals for clemency and the undue haste with which the sentence was carried out. Where human life is involved, there should always be time for additional consideration of such a sentence.

REPORTER: Are you going to do anything about it?

TUTWILER: What do you mean, are we going to do something about it?

REPORTER: Well, the British have recalled their ambassador, for instance. Are you going to protest? Are you going to—

TUTWILER: I don't know. Let me check on that. I know that we have deplored this. We have made a very strong statement. I did not think to ask, are we going to protest it or withdraw our ambassador, et cetera. I'll be glad to ask.[50]

It truly was a "spring of bad behavior," as Assistant Secretary Kelly termed it.[51] The question remained what the Bush administration intended to do about it.

April to June:
Missed Decision Points

On April 2, at a ceremony honoring his armed forces and military-industrial complex, Saddam launched into a diatribe more sweeping and scathing than even his February ACC speeches. On the United States:

Present-day America is a great nation—a great nation by material standards not by moral standards. A great person is judged by his manners. The United States is a superpower in accordance with material yardsticks. It is not a superpower in accordance with moral and ethical yardsticks. The great are great in terms of ethics, and the United States will become a superpower and enter our hearts and minds when it acts in a true ethical and legal manner. A country becomes great on the basis of its ethical leverage: that is, when it sponsors the rights of people and nations, when it defends the principles of international law, and when it defends all causes, not merely certain selected ones. . . . In practice, they are hypocrites. They are using it as a slogan for neo-imperialism, for meddling in the internal affairs of others.

On the nuclear triggers and accusations that Iraq was seeking to develop nuclear weapons:

> The British, U.S. and Zionist intelligence sent them [nuclear trigger devices] so as to say: See, Iraq is producing a nuclear bomb. This is the policy of entrapment. . . . By God, spare us your evil. Pick up your goods and leave. We do not need an atomic bomb.

On the execution of Bazoft:

> They created a big uproar about Bazoft. Therefore, the new slogan of human rights that the big powers are upholding is to protect the spies. By God, we will cut the spy who comes to Iraq into four pieces. Let those who want to listen take note of this. Those who have spies here, let them remove them.

And to Israel, a boast that "we have the binary chemical" weapon, the most lethal of all chemical weapons, otherwise possessed only by the United States and the Soviet Union—and the threat that with this weapon *"we will make the fire eat up half of Israel."*[52]

The State Department immediately denounced the speech as "inflammatory, irresponsible and outrageous." A White House statement called it "particularly deplorable and irresponsible." President Bush himself stated, "This is no time to be talking about using chemical or biological weapons. This is no time to be escalating tensions in the Middle East. And I found those statements to be bad. . . . I would suggest that those statements be withdrawn."[53]

Saddam called in Prince Bandar bin Sultan, the Saudi ambassador to the United States, to deliver a message to Washington that his speech had been misinterpreted, that he only meant a threat of second-strike retaliation if Israel were to first attack Iraq. First or second strike, though, explicit threats about using binary chemical weapons were ominous, not just inconsistent with a peace process but boding to push the Middle East conflict into nonconventional warfare. And even as he tried to convince Prince Bandar that he was only talking defensively, Saddam couldn't help but also try "to justify his verbal assault on Israel." He also blamed "the imperialist-Zionist forces" for unfounded rumors that " 'I have designs over my neighbors. I don't have designs over my neighbors.' " He also mentioned his concern that the Iraqi people were becoming too "relaxed," that " 'I must whip them into a sort of frenzy or emotional mobilization so they will be ready for whatever happens.' "[54]

Saddam requested that the Saudis get an Israeli assurance through and confirmed by the United States that it would not attack Iraq. Prime Minister Shamir had warned the day after Saddam's speech that Israel had "proven in the past that it is able to defend itself and will not be blackmailed."[55] But his government did give the United States the requested assurance that it would not attack Iraq. The Bush administration passed this message directly to Saddam.[56]

It also sent a firm demarche to be delivered to Saddam by Ambassador Glaspie at a meeting which had been arranged with the Senate delegation led by Senator Robert Dole then visiting.

> Iraqi actions in recent weeks and months have caused a sharp deterioration in U.S.-Iraqi relations. Iraq will be on a collision course with the U.S. if it continues to engage in actions that threaten the stability of the region, undermine global arms control efforts and flout U.S. laws.

The list of such Iraqi activities was long and cumulative over the six months since the October Baker-Aziz meeting: the verbal attacks on the U.S. presence in the Gulf, human rights violations, the attempted assassination of the Iraqi dissident in the United States, the nuclear trigger smuggling, questions about "Iraq's willingness to live up to its NPT [Non-Proliferation Treaty] commitments," the burn-half-of-Israel threat, the deployment of new missile launchers to western Iraq.

> Iraq is now a major regional power and should act in the responsible way such a role requires. At a time when the U.S. and the Soviet Union are methodically divesting themselves of weapons of mass

destruction, Iraq's threats to use these systems have become a major impediment to the kind of relationship with the United States that Iraq says it wants.

Your government must take some concrete steps particularly in areas involving human rights and illegal procurement activities to address these concerns and act to reduce tensions. Without such measures on your part what little support that is left in the U.S. for Iraq may further erode.[57]

The Dole delegation (which included five senators, four Republicans and one Democrat) also delivered its own letter expressing "our very deep concerns about certain policies and activities of your Government, which stand as a major barrier to improved relations."[58]

On April 16 a key meeting was convened in the White House Situation Room. The group was the interagency Deputies Committee, chaired by Deputy National Security Advisor Robert Gates. This was the first meeting at such a senior level to assess relations with Iraq since the issuance of NSD-26.

Positions had started to change. Under Secretary Kimmitt, representing State, now opposed release of the second CCC tranche. Kimmitt also favored rescinding the waiver on Export-Import Bank lending issued in January. "Technically, political considerations are not supposed to influence CCC or EXIM lending decisions," he wrote in a note to Secretary Baker,

but in fact those decisions have to be made in the broader political context. If we go forward with CCC and EXIM, I think Saddam Hussein will regard that decision as a positive political signal, which will lead him to downplay other efforts we might undertake to stop his proliferation campaign.[59]

Even before this meeting the Commerce Department had imposed a new requirement for review of all license applications for export to Iraq by the assistant secretary for export administration. Under Secretary of Commerce for Export Administration Dennis Kloske, according to his own later testimony, pushed at the deputies meeting "to shut down or seriously restrict the flow of sensitive military technologies to Iraq."[60]

A plan was developed to strengthen U.S. and multilateral nonproliferation export controls. Working-level meetings of the Iraq PCC and its LWG (Chemical-Biological Warfare Export Licensing Working Group) proposed creating a "Country Group X" with controls even tighter than the existing multilateral Australia Group ones. Nations which had "used or threatened to use chemical or biological weapons" would be consigned to Country Group X. This at the moment meant one nation only: Iraq. A related proposal would have made it illegal "for a U.S. citizen to engage in activities with Iraqi chemical industries when there is a *reasonable* expectation that the enterprise will be used for chemical *warfare*."[61] A sense of urgency seemed evident in the two-week deadline established for the LWG to come up with its recommendations.

It also was around this time that British Customs made another intercept, this one of parts for the Super Gun. Just the previous month Super Gun inventor Gerald Bull had been mysteriously assassinated in Brussels. (Some suggested the Israeli Mossad.) As a result, the Super Gun was never completed, although it had been well on its way. One prototype already had been test-fired. Two others were well into development. After the Gulf War, fourteen tons of explosives would be found at the main Super Gun site.

Seizures of other military equipment bound for Iraq quickly followed in Greece, Turkey, Italy, West Germany, and Switzerland, as well as more in England.[62] But concerted export control tightening action was slow to follow. For all the position shifts, working groups tasked, and plans under development, the April 16 meeting ended with "nothing decided" in any definitive sense, according to a Commerce official. Key top foreign policy officials still were reluctant. A *Wall Street Journal* reporter quotes sources pointing to Deputy National Security Advisor Gates, who chaired the April 16 deputies meeting, as "leery about moving too quickly." A *Los Angeles Times* story citing the notes of participants in the meeting quotes both Under Secretary of State Kimmitt and a top NSC official as taking the position on export controls that "the President doesn't want to single out Iraq."[63] The approach that was agreed to, according to Under Secretary of State Kimmitt, was to "try to find a way to look at this issue on a global basis with particular focus on Iraq."[64]

The Bush administration also continued to oppose any and all congressional proposals for sanctions. It opposed one bill which would have imposed sanctions because of Iraqi human rights violations, even though part of the evidence establishing the "consistent pattern of gross violations of internationally recognized human rights" was drawn from the administration's own official human rights report. It opposed another bill as too "open-ended" in its sanctions.[65] Indeed, the Dole delegation in its meeting with Saddam assured him that President Bush likely would veto any sanctions bill passed by Congress.[66]

Nor had a final decision yet been made on the second CCC tranche. The USDA had sent an investigative team to Baghdad, but had been getting only limited cooperation at best from the Iraqi government. The Iraqis objected even to a USDA press release using the term "possible irregularities" in past CCC transactions to describe the purpose of the investigative trip. The USDA was also being pressured by Baker's aides not to use the term "suspend" when referring in public statements to the status of the second tranche, but rather to phrase it in terms of "the extension of any further guarantees awaiting resolution and additional information responding to the pending questions."[67]

The results of their investigations, though, were making USDA officials increasingly inclined to suspend the Iraqi CCC program. "All the worst fears were realized," one official stated. "Fraud and mismanagement, kickbacks, diversion of funds to the military."[68] The driving concern at the USDA was the fallout for CCC programs in general. Plagued would be too strong a word, but CCC was not without other controversies and allegations of mismanagement. The Iraqi market was important, but the priority for the USDA was becoming to prevent the Iraqi controversy from doing wide damage to other CCC programs.

The priority for the Bush White House, though, still seemed to be sustaining what remained of the NSD-26 strategy. On April 26 Assistant Secretary Kelly testified to the House Foreign Affairs Committee. He defined administration policy as still committed "to attempt to develop gradually a mutually beneficial relationship with Iraq in order to strengthen positive trends in Iraq's foreign and domestic policies." Congressman Tom Lantos (D-California) expressed his skepticism as to what those positive trends were. Their exchange:

> LANTOS: With all due respect, Mr. Secretary, I detect an Alice in Wonderland quality about your testimony. . . . You recite accurately a chamber of horrors. . . . You talk about Iraq using poison gas against its own people, diplomats engaging in murder plots in the United States, and the government smuggling nuclear trigger devices from here and from the U.K. and other places. . . . Then you express the hope, which boggles the mind, that somehow this will change and Iraq under Saddam Hussein will turn in the direction of being a responsible and civilized and peace loving and constructive member of the international community. At what point will the Administration recognize that this is not a nice guy?
>
> KELLY: We believe there is still a potentiality for positive alterations in Iraqi behavior.[69]

Similar strategizing rings through the cable sent by Ambassador Glaspie to help Kelly prepare for his testimony:

> Q: Why soft soap Saddam Hussein? Why not pull out of Baghdad? How can "business as usual" temper Iraqi excesses?
>
> A: Talking to Iraqis is in our national interest.
> —Iraq is too big and too dangerous to ignore.
> —We have little if any leverage (we supply no arms, no aid, no protection to Saddam); but we are a superpower and it is in Iraq's interest to listen to our views (jaw, jaw is better than war, war).
> —I believe in diplomacy.
> —Iraq has modified its behavior in large part because of our

diplomatic efforts and those of our allies. Example: The Iraqis are, at last, beginning a dialogue with Amnesty International.

Yet precisely on this "example" of Iraqi moderation, a month earlier congressional committees had received letters and reports from Amnesty and other human rights groups with such statements as "I can think of no clearer example of a country engaging in a consistent pattern of gross abuses of human rights." Quite a statement, given the company. And on the burn-Israel threat:

Q: Saddam threatened to incinerate Israel. What is the USG going to do about that?

A: No Iraqi leader can doubt that President Bush, this subcommittee and the American people find any threat of chemical warfare abhorrent ...

Don't forget Iraq has just come out of a searing eight-year war with Iran. With hundreds of thousands of casualties, tens of millions of dollars of war debt, and no certainty Iran wants peace, *Iraq is not spoiling to open a second front.*[70]

In May 1990 NSC aide Richard Haass went to Baghdad to convey Bush administration concerns, but he did so "in the context of Washington's desire to continue to seek friendship with Iraq."[71] There also was other evidence of this desire, such as the continuation of the intelligence-sharing relationship begun during the Iran-Iraq war. While scaled back, at least as late as the May 16, 1990, date of an administration memorandum, the United States was still providing Iraq "with limited information on Iranian military activity" that was significant enough that it "would be missed."[72]

In mid-May the USDA prepared to release its administrative review report and announce termination of the Iraqi CCC program because the possible irregularities had been found to be actual. A meeting was called by NSC staff to pressure the USDA not to cancel the CCC program so as not to "exacerbate the already strained foreign policy relations with Iraq."[73] National Security Advisor Brent Scowcroft personally phoned Agriculture Secretary Yeutter and asked him to euphemize this press release as well. Gone were the three-plus pages of details of the irregularities and the explicit language that "no further guarantees for Iraq will be made available." Instead the press release ran a single page, announced the purpose and scope of the review, but provided no details and made no mention of punitive action against Iraq. "With this press release," an NSC aide wrote USDA Under Secretary Richard Crowder, "the NSC has no objection to your releasing the report."[74]

On May 29 the Deputies Committee met again. This meeting, according to one participant, was "initiated by NSC staff because they want to prevent the CCC program from being canceled as it would exacerbate the already strained foreign policy relations with Iraq."[75] Again, the action taken was limited. The second CCC tranche remained suspended but still was not terminated. The announcement again was to cite the allegation of fraud and abuse but not make any linkage to foreign policy concerns. Export-Import Bank lending was to be made subject to project-by-project review, but the presidential waiver allowing any lending was left in place. Export controls were to be tightened but again not targeted at Iraq, rather as part of an effort to strengthen the multilateral nonproliferation regimes generally. The PCC again was tasked to develop these proposals.[76]

Yet at the same time that this latest further export control review was going on, the Bush administration gave approval to export the very glass-fiber technology about which it had urged caution to Western Europe and Japan the previous February. This was the technology with uses for commercial manufacturing but also for ballistic missiles and nuclear weapons. The exporter was none other than Matrix-Churchill; indeed, at $14 million this was Matrix-Churchill's biggest project. The original contract had been signed by the Nassr complex, identified in an intelligence report as "instrumental in Iraq's missile development effort" and precisely the suspected bad end-user for which our allies had been warned to watch out. When the export license was filed, the purchaser was listed as the Technical Corps for Special Projects (TECO), known to be a division of Nassr, and itself identified as having overall responsibility for Iraq's "highest priority military projects—chemical weapons, long-range missile programs, nuclear programs." Yet all Matrix-Churchill and the Iraqis were told they needed was a letter of assurance that the technology was to be used commercially and that it would not be transshipped to Communist countries or Libya. The letter was duly provided. The equipment was hurriedly shipped. A year later it would be found by U.N. inspectors as part of Iraq's nuclear weapons complex.[77]

Around the same time, an edition of *U.S. News and World Report* appeared on the stands with a cover photo of Saddam Hussein. "The Most Dangerous Man in the World," the headline read. "With billions to spend and help from the U.S., the Soviet Union and Europe, Saddam Hussein is amassing a truly terrifying arsenal."[78]

The *U.S. News* story also cited Saddam's ever more harsh rhetoric, most recently on display at an emergency Arab League summit meeting May 28–30 in Baghdad:

> There will be no concession on the liberation of Palestine. The United States has demonstrated that it is primarily responsible for the aggressive and expansionist policies of the Zionist entity against the Palestinian Arab people and the Arab nation. . . . It would not have been possible for the Zionist entity to engage in aggression and expansion at the Arab's expense if it did not possess the force and political cover provided by the United States—the main source of the Zionist entity's aggressive military force, and the main source of its financial resources. . . .
>
> Arab security and interests are on the receiving end of these American policies. We have to say as much to the United States without equivocation. We have to tell the United States that it cannot afford to pursue such policies and at the same time claim the friendship of the Arabs. . . .
>
> No Israeli aggression against the Arab nation can be isolated from the designs and the support of U.S. imperialism.[79]

Egyptian President Hosni Mubarak urged a more moderate approach. The "Arab message to the outside world," he said, "should be humane, logical, realist and consistent with the values and concepts of the age." But the final summit statement was a victory for Saddam's confrontational line. It explicitly criticized the United States, "the power which provides Israel with military capabilities, financial aid and political cover." It also denounced unspecified recent "aggressive threats, campaigns and measures" against Iraq, and affirmed Iraq's right to take all appropriate steps to protect its natural security.[80]

For all his invocation of pan-Arabism, Saddam also had some only slightly veiled threats for certain fellow Arab states. The economic grievances he had raised at the February ACC summit concerning forgiveness of Iraqi war debt and charges of oil quota cheating against Kuwait and other OPEC members had not been resolved. He used the full Arab League summit to raise them again, and to take them to another level.

> War takes place sometimes through soldiers and damage is inflicted by explosives, killings, or coup attempts. At other times, war is launched through economic means. To those who do not mean to wage war against Iraq, I say this is a kind of war against Iraq.

He didn't mention any country by name. But he also warned that Iraq was not going to tolerate "any more pressure."[81]

Meanwhile, while the Arab League summit was still in session, in the pre-dawn hours of May 30, Israeli forces intercepted a small flotilla of speedboats carrying armed terrorists toward the Israeli coast. The terrorist operation was targeted at the beaches near Tel-Aviv—beaches frequented by American and other tourists as well as Israelis—and also at the U.S. embassy.

Any doubt as to who was involved was removed when the Palestine Liberation Front (PLF) faction of Abu Abbas *from its Baghdad office* issued a communiqué proudly claiming responsibility. This was the same Abu Abbas who had been responsible for the *Achille Lauro* hijacking and the murder of Leon Klinghoffer in 1985, aided in his escape by Saddam Hussein. This time, as the State Department assessed it, "without state support it is doubtful that the May 30 attack could have come as close as it did to succeeding."[82] According to the surviving terrorists, their training and logistical support had come from Libya. The financing and planning were done by Iraq.[83]

Nor was it "just" Abu Abbas whose terrorism Saddam was aiding and abetting. The State Department cited "disturbing reports that Iraqi officials have been in contact with members of the notorious Abu Nidal organization . . . and a number of other Palestinian groups and factions which we believe have representatives in Iraq."[84] The *New York Times* had run a story earlier in May citing Arab diplomats as sources that Yasir Arafat had ordered "several thousand guerrillas" to relocate from Jordan and other Arab nations to Iraq.[85] By August, according to a report by the Rand Corporation, there would be some 1400 terrorists operating out of Iraq. Not only was this substantial as a raw number, it also amounted to about a 100 percent increase over the previous year.[86]

The State Department cable traffic shows that by late June a somewhat tougher line was being taken with Saddam on terrorism. On June 20, the same day that the Bush administration suspended its direct talks with the PLO, a State Department official urged Iraqi Ambassador Al-Mashat "to deny Abu Abbas all access to Iraq and close down any and all PLF offices in the country." The Iraqi ambassador held to the line that his country did not support Abu Abbas.[87] A week later a cable was sent from Washington to the American embassy in Baghdad:

> Since the May 30 seaborne attack on Israel, we have approached Iraq several items on its support for the Palestine Liberation Front of Abu Abbas without receiving a satisfactory response. . . .
> We want to put Iraq and others on notice that its actions are being watched carefully and will carry consequences in its relations with [the] U.S. and the West. Among other things we are . . . considering whether to put Iraq back on the terrorism list. . . .
> Ambassador should approach Foreign Minister or other appropriate senior official as soon as possible.[88]

Ambassador Glaspie met with Deputy Foreign Minister Hamdoon on June 27. "The potential for violence in the area is rising," Ambassador Glaspie expressed the U.S. concern, "and has been given a major boost by Abu Al-Abbas and others who seek through terrorism to polarize the region."

> It is because Iraq does not (repeat, not) support polarization and does want a genuine peace process (Hamdoon nodded vigorously) that the Ambassador's instructions are phrased on the assumption that Iraq will act positively. . . .
>
> Ambassador said that the GOI [government of Iraq] is well aware of our views about Abu-Al Abbas, Abu Nidal and their organizations. She asked Hamdoon to focus particularly on a third issue which she had not raised with the GOI before. We have become very concerned about other radical Palestinian groups we believe have representatives in Baghdad and with whom Iraq has had recent contact and does have influence. "What in the world are you talking about," Hamdoon asked. . . .
>
> As Ambassador Mashat has been informed, we are considering whether to place Iraq on our list of states who support terrorism and should new attacks be launched or supported by Iraq, our bilateral relations will be seriously affected. . . .
>
> Hamdoon had little to say other than he would convey all of this to Foreign Minister Aziz. . . . Hamdoon simply said wearily that "I know nothing about all these Palestinians."[89]

To have put Iraq back on the terrorism list would have had quite an effect. Nearly 85 percent of the exports licensed for Iraq since 1982 would not have been approved had it not been taken off the terrorism list.[90] But despite the demarches being delivered to Baghdad, there still was disagreement at high levels of the Bush administration "as to whether the evidence was sufficient to place Iraq on the list." Only after the invasion of Kuwait was such action finally taken. "I hereby determine that Iraq is a country which has *repeatedly* provided support for acts of international terrorism," the regulatory order signed by Acting Secretary of State Eagleburger on September 1 stated (emphasis added).[91]

July to August 2:
Crisis Mismanagement

In May 1990 two Rand Corporation analysts (one of whom was Zalmay Khalilzad, whose earlier "contain Iraq" memo written in September 1988 while a government official was cited in Chapter 2) circulated a draft paper assessing the threat posed by Saddam Hussein. It offered an "optimistic view" that Saddam "has learned his lesson from the Iran-Iraq war and would not return to his 'bad old days' of threatening Iraq's neighbors," and a "pessimistic view" that "historically, Saddam Hussein has been ambitious and ruthless" and that "given the current regional power balance—and the past pattern—Iraq is likely to use its power overtly or implicitly to achieve regional domination." The conclusion reached:

> At present the Iraqi policy direction appears closer to that seen in the pessimistic view than the optimistic one. Should Iraqi preponderance of relative power in the region continue, Iraq ambitions are likely to grow. . . . If, however, Iraqi power can be balanced without threatening Iraq's core interests, Saddam . . . might adopt policies more consistent with the optimistic perspective.[92]

This paper was the basis for a Rand workshop sponsored by the Pentagon. Participants included officers of the U.S. Central Command (CENTCOM) representing its commander General H. Norman Schwarzkopf, as well as officials of the Pentagon's Joint Staff, the CIA, the DIA, and the State Department. The workshop originally had been scheduled as a gaming exercise, "to experiment with political-military contingency analysis that would adamantly push ahead with 'But what if?' questions." As events had it, the first day of the workshop also turned out to be the day Saddam Hussein deployed the first contingents of what within two weeks would be 150,000 Iraqi troops along the Kuwaiti border. The what-if questions no longer were as hypothetical.[93]

On July 17, in his annual Ba'athist revolutionary day speech, Saddam accused certain states, unnamed but easily decipherable as Kuwait and the United Arab Emirates, of having stabbed Iraq in the back with "a poison dagger." The previous day Iraqi Foreign Minister Tariq Aziz had written a thirty-seven-page letter to the Arab League delineating the charges: $89 billion lost by Iraq from falling world oil prices, the principal cause of which was said to be Kuwaiti and UAE cheating on their OPEC quotas; $2.4 billion worth of oil "stolen" by Kuwait from the disputed border-area Rumaila oil field; Kuwaiti "intrusions" on Iraq's side of the border to set up military posts and other installations. Aziz set Iraqi demands as an increase in oil prices to $25 per barrel; cessation of Kuwaiti "theft" from the Rumaila oil field and restitution of the $2.4 billion "stolen"; a long-term lease on favorable terms on Bubiyan and Warbah islands with their oil facilities and Persian Gulf port access; a complete moratorium on Iraq's wartime debts; and an Arab version of the Marshall Plan " 'to compensate Iraq for some of the losses during the war.' " Saddam attributed these venal actions by Kuwait and the UAE to a plan "inspired by America." And he warned that if the Iraqi terms were not agreed to, "something effective must be done."[94]

The grievances and charges were not totally new. Saddam had raised them indirectly back at the February 1990 ACC summit and then again only slightly veiled at the late May Arab League summit. But now the grievances were being made into demands. And words were being backed by actions.

U.S. reconnaissance satellites had picked up the first Iraqi troop movements toward the Kuwaiti border the day before Saddam's speech. By July 19 an estimated 35,000 soldiers, over 300 tanks, and other equipment and supplies for three divisions had been amassed along the Kuwaiti border. The Kuwaiti government's initial reaction was that Saddam was only bluffing and posturing. The emir dismissed it as but a "summer cloud" which would soon blow away.[95] Protests were filed with the Arab League accusing Iraq of "extortion," and with the United Nations retorting that the Iraqi charges "falsified reality."[96] Kuwait, though, kept its distance from the United States. Even the

1987–88 reflagging operation had not altered Kuwait's traditional reticence about getting too close to the United States (or at least being perceived as such).

The UAE government actually was more concerned than the Kuwaiti government. It requested U.S. assistance for a joint air and naval exercise. The Bush administration agreed, sending two KC-135 aerial refueling tankers and six navy ships, in an effort to "lay down a marker for Saddam Hussein."[97]

It caught Saddam's attention, and without notice he called U.S. Ambassador Glaspie in. The problem, though, was that other more mixed signals were also being sent, most notably those from Ambassador Glaspie in this fateful meeting. This was Ambassador Glaspie's first private meeting with Saddam in the almost two years for which she had been at her post. It turned out to be the subject of enormous controversy.[98]

First impressions were shaped by a version of the meeting transcript released by Iraq about a month after the invasion of Kuwait. The meeting is depicted as having begun with bluster and threats from Saddam:

> The United States must have a better understanding of the situation and declare who it wants to have relations with and who its enemies are....
>
> We clearly understand America's statement that it wants an easy flow of oil. We understand America saying that it seeks friendship with the states in the region, and to encourage their joint interests. But we cannot understand the attempt to encourage some parties to harm Iraq's interests....
>
> If you use pressure, we will deploy pressure and force. We know that you can harm us although we do not threaten you. But we too can harm you. Everyone can cause pain according to their ability and their size. We cannot come all the way to you in the United States but individual Arabs may reach you.

Ambassador Glaspie was depicted as being quite conciliatory. She was said to have conveyed that "I have a direct instruction from the President to seek better relations with Iraq." On the Iraq-Kuwait dispute, she was said to have stated that "we have no opinion on the Arab-Arab conflicts, like your border disagreement with Kuwait." She is quoted as raising the issue of Iraqi troop deployments along the Kuwaiti border, but of couching it as a question asked "in the spirit of friendship—not in the spirit of confrontation—regarding your intentions."

Ambassador Glaspie later would call the Iraqi transcript "a fabrication, disinformation." Her claim was that it omitted what she characterized as "repeated and crystal clear warnings" that she had given Saddam at their meeting that "we would not countenance violence or in fact threat of intimidation." The account of her statement of no position on Arab-Arab disputes, she said, omitted the accompanying statement "that we would insist on settlements being made in a nonviolent manner, not by threats, not by intimidation, and certainly not by aggression."

But Ambassador Glaspie's own cable back to Washington after the meeting, as leaked in part to the press, does not wholly support her version. She titled it "Saddam's Message of Friendship for President Bush." And the tone is very reassuring. Saddam is described as "cordial, reasonable and even warm" in manner. His entreaty about his people's economic suffering is passed on at face value: "The financial situation is such that the pensions for widows and orphans will have to be cut. At this point, the interpreter and one of the note takers broke down and wept." Doubts are expressed as to whether negotiations will settle the Iraq-Kuwait dispute, but as to Saddam's intentions, "his emphasis that he wants peaceful settlement is surely sincere (Iraqis are sick of war)." Her cable also confirms the "spirit of friendship, not confrontation" couching of her question to Saddam about his intentions. Saddam's own sense is conveyed that further markers like the U.S.-UAE military exercise would be taken by Iraq as "public humiliations," and would leave it "no choice but to 'respond' however illogical and self-destructive that would prove." A call had come from Egyptian President Mubarak during their meeting and after a long conversation Saddam told Glaspie that he had agreed to negotiations with Kuwait to be held later in the week in Saudi Arabia. Saddam pledged to Mubarak that " 'nothing will happen until the meeting.' " Ambassador Glaspie indicated that "she was delighted to hear this good news." She recommended that "we would now be well-advised to ease off on public criticism of Iraq until we see how the negotiations develop."

The ambassador's cable does state that she did warn Saddam that "we can never excuse settlement of disputes by other than peaceful means." A statement of unwillingness to excuse nonpeaceful dispute settlement, though, is not quite the "crystal clear warning" claimed. The difference was brought out by Congressman Lee Hamilton when Ambassador Glaspie testified to his subcommittee:

MR. HAMILTON: Did you ever tell Saddam Hussein, "Mr. President, if you go across that line into Kuwait, we are going to fight"?

AMBASSADOR GLASPIE: No, I did not.[99]

Yet as the ambassador also testified, to have made such a statement would have been "a change in our policy." The day before the Glaspie-Saddam meeting State Department press secretary Margaret Tutwiler would only go so far as to affirm the U.S. commitment in principle "to supporting the individual and collective self-defense of our friends in the Gulf," while explicitly stating that "we do not have any defense treaties with Kuwait, and there are no special defense or security commitments to Kuwait."[100] A cable along the same lines went out also on July 24 from Secretary Baker to U.S. ambassadors in Europe and the Middle East for host government briefings, as well as to Ambassador Glaspie for presentation in Baghdad. Because the meeting with Saddam was called so abruptly, there was no time to request further instructions from Washington.

Two days after the Glaspie-Saddam meeting (July 27) OPEC ministers met in Geneva. Iraq made its demand for increasing oil prices from $18 to $25 per barrel. Only Libya supported it. But Kuwait, Saudi Arabia, and the others agreed to a compromise of $21, as well as to stricter enforcement against cheating on production quotas. This didn't settle all Iraq's economic grievances and Kuwait and Iraq were scheduled to meet August 1 in Saudi Arabia on the remaining issues, but it was enough for Saudi Ambassador Prince Bandar to assure JCS Chairman Colin Powell that Saddam wasn't going to invade. "Well, Colin, it looks good. Of course," the Saudi prince added, "if he does escalate this, you may have to come help us all."[101]

Meanwhile, in Washington, the Deputies Committee met to draft a personal message from President Bush to Saddam. Certain DOD officials objected to what one later called "this piece of pap." The tone once again was much more one of reassurance than deterrence: "Let me reassure you," the cable read, "that my administration continues to desire better relations with Iraq." The position was taken that "differences are best resolved by peaceful means"—"best," but not "must be." It was reaffirmed that "we still have fundamental concerns about certain Iraqi policies and activities," which would continue to be raised, but "in a spirit of friendship and candor." The goal remained "to build a more durable foundation for improving our relations." When they couldn't toughen it up, opponents tried to block the Bush message from being sent. They didn't succeed.[102]

On Capitol Hill the same day another sanctions bill came to a vote. The administration tried to strike another alliance with farm-state members of Congress. This time, though, it didn't work. The House passed a bill which included a provision seeking to mitigate the vested interest reverse leverage pressures by reallocating the CCC credits programmed for Iraq to the new democracies of Eastern Europe. In the Senate an administration-supported amendment sponsored by Senators Robert Dole and Phil Gramm, which would have gutted the bill, failed in a 57–38 vote. Among those voting against it was Senator Nancy Landon Kassebaum, Republican of wheat-producing Kansas. She stated her views on the floor of the Senate:

> Wheat from Kansas is certainly affected by this amendment, but I cannot believe that any farmer in this Nation would want to send his subsidized products, subsidized sales . . . to a country that has used chemical weapons and to a country that has tortured and injured their children. . . . There is no one who feels more strongly

than myself that food should not be used as a weapon. But as I said last night, there comes a time when I think we have to stand up and be counted.[103]

Controls were at least being tightened on dual-use technology exports. Finally. The latest intelligence agency reports had left little doubt about Saddam's weapons programs. One such report, entitled "Iraq's Growing Arsenal: Programs and Facilities," concluded that "many entities are false end users, passing the materials acquired from foreign suppliers directly to enterprises involved in military projects, including chemical and biological warfare." Another, "Beating Plowshares into Swords: Iraq's Defense Industrial Program," stated that "development of missiles and non-conventional weapons was Iraq's highest priority . . . Iraq's activities clearly presented tough problems for controlling U.S. dual use technologies that can easily be diverted."[104] Indeed, even the memo recommending that export controls now be tightened confirmed what critics long had been saying, that "licenses *were* granted for equipment with dual or not clearly stated uses for export to probably proliferation related end uses in Iraq."[105] One such case was the nuclear-suspect Consarc furnaces, for which the Bush administration had granted licenses in 1989. Now, at the last minute, and only after a story had broken in the press, the administration reversed its earlier licensing and seized the furnaces as they sat on the docks waiting to be shipped.[106]

Still, though, the Iraqi troop movement continued. DIA confirmed eight divisions, 100,000 troops along the Kuwaiti border. KH-III satellite reconnaissance photos now also were showing major movements of ammunition and supplies, what one senior Pentagon official later called "the logistics trail Iraq needed" for an invasion.[107]

On July 30, Pat Lang, the principal DIA analyst who had been following the Iraqi troop movements as closely as anyone in the U.S. government, sent an E-mail message to the agency director.

I have been looking at the pattern of reinforcement along the Kuwaiti border. There is some artillery and logistics moving; aircraft are moving. There is absolutely no reason for Saddam Hussein to do this, it doesn't make sense if his aim is to intimidate Kuwait. He has created the capability to overrun all of Kuwait and all of Eastern Saudi Arabia. If he attacks, given his disposition, we will have no warning.

I do not believe he is bluffing. I have looked at his personality profile. He doesn't know how to bluff. It is not in his past pattern of behavior....

In short, Saddam Hussein has moved a force disproportionate to the task at hand, if it is to bluff. Then there is only one answer: he intends to use it.[108]

Lieutenant General Harry E. Soyster, director of the DIA, disagreed, but passed Lang's assessment on. The CIA also had internal disagreement. Charles E. Allen, the national intelligence officer for warning, considered the case that Saddam was going to invade "convincing" as early as July 25.[109] His superiors would go only so far as to agree on the likelihood of a border crossing, but remained noncommital as to whether it would be a limited operation or full-scale invasion. General Powell still was not convinced. Neither was Defense Secretary Richard Cheney. Nor General Schwarzkopf.[110]

On July 31 Congressman Hamilton probed for a clarification of the U.S. position from Assistant Secretary of State Kelly:

MR. HAMILTON: What is precisely the nature of our commitment to supporting our friends in the Gulf?

MR. KELLY: We have no defense treaty relationship with any Gulf country. That is clear. We support the security and independence of friendly states in the region.... We are calling for a peaceful resolution of any differences in that area and we hope and trust and believe that the sovereignty of every state in the Gulf ought to be respected.

MR. HAMILTON: Do we have a commitment to our friends in the event that they are engaged in oil or territorial disputes with their neighbors?

MR. KELLY: As I said, Mr. Chairman, we have no defense treaty relationships with any of the countries. We have historically avoided taking a position on border disputes or on internal OPEC deliberations, but we have certainly, as have all administrations, resoundingly called for the peaceful settlement of disputes and differences in the area.

MR. HAMILTON: If Iraq, for example, charged across the border into Kuwait, for whatever reason, what would be our position with regard to the use of U.S. forces?

MR. KELLY: That, Mr. Chairman, is a hypothetical or a contingency the kind of which I can't get into. Suffice it to say we would be extremely concerned, but I cannot get into the realm of "what if" answers.

In his formal statement, Assistant Secretary Kelly added the "hope" that as a major power in the region Iraq would act in a manner showing that it understands that "power carries responsibility."[111]

On August 1 the Iraqi and Kuwaiti representatives met in Jiddah, Saudi Arabia. Versions vary as to who was the most intransigent. Kuwaiti officials already had backed off their commitment to abide by OPEC production quotas. The Iraqis accused them of being uncompromising and trying to humiliate Iraq. The Kuwaitis claimed they were willing to meet some of Iraq's economic demands, just not all of them. One version has it that the Iraqi negotiator even before he left Baghdad had been told by Saddam "to deliver a blunt message, stand up from the negotiating table, and walk out of the room."[112] That is what he did.

Senior Iraqi military officers captured during the war confessed that "the decision to invade had been made already [pre-Jiddah] in Baghdad." A Kuwaiti colonel stationed in Basra as a military attaché claimed to have been told by a Republican Guard officer on July 25—the same day as the Glaspie-Saddam meeting—that an invasion would occur *on August 2!*[113] There was other evidence of premeditation as well. Even before the Jiddah talks broke up, U.S. satellite pictures showed that the three Iraqi armored divisions had "uncoiled," hundreds of tanks evenly spaced along the four-lane highway leading into Kuwait. Some eighty helicopters had been moved close to the border, poised in an air-land assault posture.[114] The Pentagon's post–Gulf War report concluded that the rapidity with which the Iraqi troop buildup had proceeded "indicated the quality and extent of Iraqi staff planning."

> In retrospect, it appears Iraq probably never intended to come to terms with Kuwait through negotiation. Rather, it may well have been that, in Iraq's view, the late-July political maneuverings and 1 August talks in Jiddah were only a pretext to provide time for final preparation and to give an air of legitimacy to the coming invasion.[115]

General Schwarzkopf later pointed to invade-Kuwait computer simulations and war games that the Iraqi military had run. And there were other reports "that the Iraqis had been staging military exercises in preparation for the invasion for two years, including a mid-July rehearsal for a heliborne assault on Kuwait City."[116]

Assistant Secretary Kelly called the Iraqi ambassador in. He told him the situation was "extremely serious." The ambassador denied "any aggressive intent whatsoever." He added, "Any country has a sovereign right to deploy troops wherever it wants within its frontiers."[117]

On August 2, Iraq invaded Kuwait.

Lessons Beyond the Desert Storm Victory

Operations Desert Shield and Desert Storm proved to be George Bush's finest hour. Nearly 400,000 troops were deployed to protect Saudi Arabia (Desert Shield), and then employed to liberate Kuwait (Desert Storm). The military power displayed was truly formidable. The thirty-one-nation coalition assembled and the political support mobilized at the United Nations showed no less impressive diplomatic prowess. President Bush spoke of "a new world order" growing out of this crisis, "a new era—freer from the threat of terror, stronger in the pursuit of justice and more secure in the quest for peace, an era in which the nations of the world . . . can prosper and live in harmony."[118]

In the immediate afterglow of the overwhelming Gulf War victory, there were those who implied, and even those who openly argued, that this was a war which should not have been avoided, that American and world interests had been better served than if Saddam had not invaded Kuwait. Not to mention George Bush's political interests. His public opinion poll ratings broke all records. Some Democrats even only half-jokingly mused in mid-1991 that perhaps their party simply should second Bush's renomination and save the trouble of a full election campaign!

Things didn't quite turn out that way, though, in November 1992. The presidential campaign ended up not being a glorification of Desert Storm but rather about "the economy, stupid," and Bill Clinton won. Yet, interestingly, even the Iraq issue ended up problematic for Bush, as by mid-1992 the controversies involving the BNL affair and other aspects of "Iraq-gate" had intensified to the point that they were getting major media attention. A synergy developed between Iraq-gate and the latest revelations about Bush's role in Iran-Contra such that both his personal credulity and his foreign policy savvy, both supposed to be strong suits, ended up being widely questioned by voters.

Irrespective, though, of whatever scandals there may or may not have been, the crucial issue remains one of flawed foreign policy strategy. The euphoric better-off-than-before view of the Gulf War victory, at its best, was a coldly realpolitik calculus which too readily dismissed the death toll, other human suffering, the over $100 billion in economic costs, environmental destruction, and other consequences of the war.[119] Moreover, over time, even the realpolitik logic came into question. The conflicts with Iraq persisted. Saddam Hussein remained in power. Even with the unprecedented U.N. inspections and dismantling of Saddam's weapons complexes, CIA Director Robert

Gates had to concede that Iraq still would be a proliferation threat, that "the cadre of scientists and engineers trained for these programs will be able to reconstitute any dormant program quickly."[120] And the heralded "new world order" did not spring forth.

Along with the military lessons to be learned from how the war was fought, therefore, there are important lessons to be learned about why the war occurred.

Part II

ANALYSIS AND LESSONS

■

5

The Enemy of My Enemy May Still Be My Enemy, Too: Lessons for Foreign Policy Strategy

IN TESTIMONY AT A MAY 1992 CONGRESSIONAL HEARING, A TOP OFFICIAL of both the Reagan and Bush administrations defended the policy toward Iraq as "prudent at the time . . . a subtle leaning toward Iraq . . . seeking to probe, test and encourage the Iraqis while being wary of their intentions . . . to engage Iraq and to offer the Iraqis a mix of incentives and disincentives, but without any illusion."[1] Had the actual policy lived up to this self-characterization, it may well have been more successful. But it did not. And it was not.

Even though the United States and Iraq had common enemies, we didn't become friends. The alliance of convenience worked for a while, although not as well as was assumed at the time. The broader accommodation which the Reagan administration first began cultivating during the Iran-Iraq war and which the Bush administration kept pursuing right up to the eve of the invasion of Kuwait never took hold. In the end, the enemy of my enemy proved that he could still be my enemy, too.

Why did U.S. policy fail?

This question is posed conscious of the analytic distinction made by George Kennan and cited back in the introductory chapter between those factors which contribute to foreign policy failure but which are "outside the range of our influence" and those which are failings in "the concepts" and/or "the execution" of U.S. policy. No claim is made that the Iraqi invasion of Kuwait was solely and exclusively the consequence of failed U.S. policy. One always need be self-conscious about overattributing impact to the United States, be it as a matter of blame or credit. On one level, virtually all world events in the late 1980s in some way related back to the broader transformation of the international system brought on by the end of the cold war. On another level, there were at work the historical dynamics of what Walid Khalidi has called "the failure of the Arab political order as it has evolved since the end of World War II."[2] Then, too, there were the failings in the policies of other states, for example, of France and Germany, which provided the bulk of the nonconventional weapons technologies Iraq obtained, and of key Arab states such as Egypt and Kuwait which so misread their fellow Arab leader. And of course there was Saddam himself and his own characteristic mix of Machiavellianism and paranoia.

But to delimit must not be to deny.

Chapters 5 and 6 draw on the evidence presented in Part I of this book of what the Reagan-Bush strategy was so as to develop the analysis of why it failed. This chapter focuses on flaws in the basic strategy (the concepts), the next on the policy process (the execution). The intent is both to contribute to a better understanding of the dynamics of the U.S.-Iraqi case in itself and to draw more general lessons for the problem of relations with "rogue states"—a problem which clearly continues to be with us in the post–cold war era.

The argument is *not* that the idea itself of striking an alliance of convenience or even seeking an accommodation with Iraq was wrong. The United States did share with Iraq two major adversaries, Iran and the Soviet Union. This was especially true in the early 1980s, when Iran was winning the war with Iraq and when the Soviets were still widely considered "the evil empire." It still was true to a significant extent in the late 1980s: The Iran-Iraq war was over, but U.S.-Iranian relations remained highly adversarial; and the Soviets, for all their rapidly spiraling problems, had not yet lost their superpower status. My criticism, though, is of the particular strategy that the Reagan and Bush administrations pursued.

The essence of the argument goes to the most basic premise on which the Reagan-Bush strategy toward Iraq rested: "The enemy of my enemy is my friend." To be sure, there are situations, as with the walk-with-the-Devil World War II U.S.–Soviet Union alliance, in which the threat from the mutual enemy is of such immediacy and magnitude that former enemies do become fast friends. But such circumstances, as noted earlier, are more exceptional than typical—and even then, as with the "developing political problems" against which Kennan warned in 1944, there is no guarantee that an alliance of convenience will provide adequate basis for a broader and more enduring accommodation. One does not, however, have to revert to some purist pursuit of an absolute identity of interests to recognize that shared enemies may not always be a sufficient basis for anything more than a temporary and limited relationship between states which themselves have been adversaries in the past and which still have issues of tension and conflict between them.

But it cannot be assumed that the enemy of my enemy *is* my friend, only that he *may be* my friend. There is nothing automatic about the possibility of such a relationship working out. It requires a strategy which at once strikes a balance between attempting to entice the other state into improved relations, yet also guards against the risk of being exploited by it. Such a "mixed strategy" can be defined in terms of three key requisites, as derived from more general theories of international behavior:

1. *Reciprocity:* The threat of the mutual enemy can take priority, but except under the most extreme circumstances it must not be given exclusivity over the need for cooperation on issues of conflict and tension in the relationship.

2. *Proportionality:* Support should be sufficient to tilt the balance against the mutual enemy, but not of a type or magnitude to give the enemy-enemy-"friend" the military capabilities to pose its own threat to the balance of power.

3. *Deterrent Credibility:* The prospective friend must know both that cooperation has its rewards and that noncooperation has its consequences. Maintenance of a credible deterrence posture is complementary, not contradictory, to the achievement of a balanced and enduring accommodation.

These three requisites provide the framework both for analyzing the failings of the Reagan-Bush strategy and for drawing more general lessons for post–cold war U.S. foreign policy.

Reciprocity

The first requisite is the need, as is generally true for developing cooperation among nations in situations of conflict, to ensure *reciprocity*. While measures of reciprocity are often imprecise and somewhat subjective, the basic standard as set out by Robert Keohane is "rough equivalence" in the benefits derived by the respective partners to the relationship.[3] The enemy-enemy-friend calculus takes reciprocity as a given. However, the mutuality of enemies can be, but is not necessarily, sufficient to guarantee this rough equivalence.

Shared Enemies,
But Not Totally Shared Interests

Even when two states have a mutual enemy, their purposes and interests vis-à-vis the enemy may still diverge. This point was made in Chapter 1 in emphasizing that Saddam fought Iran for his own purposes, not as a surrogate for the United States. He wanted to defeat Iran because it was his rival, and he wanted to use this victory to lay claim to the mantle of Nasser as the new great leader of the Arab world. The fact that the United States also held Iran to be an enemy meant that Iraqi and American interests coincided. It did not, however, mean that they had converged. The limits of mutuality should have been all the more evident over the course of the Iran-Iraq war as Saddam engaged in military tactics that served Iraqi interests but threatened U.S. and Western ones (for example, widening the "tanker war" with the consequent shocks to Western economies from the oil price fluctuations, skyrocketing shipping insurance rates, and uncertainties of oil supply).

Similarly, the enemy-enemy-friend calculus with Iraq against the Soviet Union was too simplistic. Saddam was never interested in replacing one superpower patron with another—unlike Egypt under Sadat, for example. His strategy was a version of triangular diplomacy, not realignment, seeking to be the fulcrum point in the three-party relationship, playing off the Soviets and the Americans one against the other, and thus deriving greater independence of action than if he were the loyal client of one or the other. Indeed, Saddam used the initial U.S.-Iraqi opening in early 1982 to help convince the Soviets to cut back their arms shipments to Iran and increase them to Iraq. All told, the Soviets provided $23.5 billion in arms to Iraq between 1982 and 1989. And all the while Saddam also was receiving arms from France and other Western suppliers, including third-party indirect transfers of U.S. arms, as well as billions of dollars' worth of dual-use technology that the Soviet economy was ill equipped to offer.

It is true that the strategic bottom line remained the containment of Iran and the Soviet Union as our main adversaries. But the failure to grasp the extent to which U.S. and Iraqi interests against these shared enemies were not totally shared allowed the Iraqis to take advantage of this bottom line as something of an open account. They drew on this account to cover military excesses against Iran and diplomatic side deals with the Soviet Union, as well as "nonpayment" on a number of other issues on which the United States should have expected greater returns on its investment.

Terrorism and Middle East Peace:
Whither Iraqi Moderation?

As noted earlier, except under the most extreme circumstances, the threat of a mutual enemy can take priority but must not be given exclusivity over all other issues of conflict and tension in the relationship. To put the rest of the agenda aside is to invite the partner state to be a "free rider," quite rationally calculating that it can derive the benefits of security protection while still pursuing its own interests on other issues.[4] The free-rider problem often arises in alliance-type situations in which one party allows the other to reap the benefits of their mutual relationships ("free ride") without having to reciprocate comparably.

The Reagan and Bush administrations repeatedly contended that it was on such other issues on the foreign policy agenda like terrorism and Middle East peace that the reciprocation for U.S. support would come. In fact, though, on both terrorism and Middle East peace, Iraqi moderation was limited at best.

Under the immediate circumstances of early 1982, with Iraq genuinely near defeat, taking it off the state terrorism list as a means for making it eligible for U.S. economic assistance did have sound enemy-enemy-friend logic. But Iraq never seriously reciprocated with substantial lasting reductions in its support for terrorism. Nor was terrorism just a peripheral concern to the United States in these years. In the 1986 Chicago Council on Foreign Relations public opinion survey, terrorism ranked behind only the nuclear arms race as one of the biggest foreign policy problems.[5] President Reagan had declared "no rewards, no guarantees, no concessions, no deals" for terrorists. George Bush as vice-president chaired the administration's anti-terrorism task force. But it was not until September 1, 1990, a month after the invasion of Kuwait, that Iraq finally was put back on the terrorism list.

The point is not whether anti-terrorism was a more or less important security concern than averting an Iranian victory over Iraq. A more balanced strategy could have pursued both objectives together. It was one thing to make the initial concession of taking Iraq off the terrorism list. But especially given the asymmetry of the relationship, the United States should have been able to hold Iraq to its commitment not to threaten the interests of its new and vital supporter, if not as a precondition then at least as a follow-up reciprocal requisite. The economic benefits Iraq was reaping from being off the terrorism list were quite substantial: over $5 billion in agricultural credits on very favorable financial terms at a time when it was having trouble feeding its people; machinery and technology exports, 85 percent of which it would not have been eligible for had it been on the terrorism list. It should have been made clear to Saddam that the United States was serious about both objectives, and that if he valued the economic benefits Iraq was receiving, then he needed to take that into account in setting his priorities. Instead it was difficult for Saddam not to have concluded that the United States was so single-dimensionally fixated on the anti-Iran objective that it would not put him back on the terrorism list almost irrespective of what he did. So he went on with terrorism—and stayed off the list.

Another major issue on the agenda was the strong American interest in Iraqi support of the Arab-Israeli peace process. Yet here, too, tactical maneuvers were taken for strategic shifts of position. Saddam's support during the Lebanon war for the 1982 Arab League Fez peace plan and for the 1983 Israeli-Lebanon peace treaty was helpful to immediate U.S. interests. But in both of these instances, more than anything else, Saddam was pursuing Saddam's interests. He lined up behind the Fez plan in order to get the Arab League to more firmly line up behind him in his war against Iran. And he supported the Israel-Lebanon treaty as a maneuver in his inter-Arab rivalry with Syrian leader Hafez al-Assad, against whom the treaty was directed and with whom Saddam was locked in "the contemporary Arab version of England's fifteenth-century War of the Roses," an "undeclared intra-Ba'ath civil war."[6]

A similar assessment is warranted of the Reagan-Bush claim that Saddam's support for PLO Chairman Yasir Arafat's December 1988 decision to recognize Israel's right to exist was evidence that their policy was working. It is true that this was helpful to U.S. interests at the time in establishing a dialogue with the PLO. The question again, though, is over the interpretation of this as an indicator of a trend of Iraqi moderation. Saddam supported Arafat not because Saddam had moderated toward Israel but because Assad opposed Arafat. The same motivation also prompted Saddam to send arms to the Lebanese Christian general Michel Aoun, who was seeking to drive Syria out of Lebanon, a policy which the United States (and also France and the Arab League) strongly opposed.

When moderate positions toward Israel didn't serve such ulterior motives, Saddam didn't take them. Secretary Baker's October 1989 request for Iraqi cooperation was met with the curious claim from Foreign Minister Aziz, as recounted in Chapter 3, that it was Iraqi policy "to refrain from public statements on the peace process."[7] Yet Iraq hardly had so refrained in the past (such as its 1978 hosting of the Rejectionist Front denunciation of the Camp David Accords). Moreover, far from refraining, let alone supporting, it was in Baghdad that the PLO Central Council met to reject the Baker Plan and call for an escalation of the *intifada*. Saddam's interests still dictated support for the PLO, but they no longer coincided with support for the peace process. Indeed, it was his support for the May 30, 1990, Palestinian terrorist raid on Israel that led to the breakdown of the U.S.–PLO dialogue— that same dialogue of which his support supposedly was such a telling sign of his moderation. These weren't exactly mainstream, moderate, or reciprocating actions.

"The danger of mistaking a leader's tactically motivated good behavior as a sign of more fundamental change," as Alexander George observes, "is a familiar one in international relations."[8] Iraq was manipulating more than moderating, but the Reagan and Bush administrations failed to see the difference. On terrorism and Middle East peace, as toward Iran and the Soviet Union, Iraq was acting out of self-interest and self-interest only.

Trade But No Political Reciprocity

The main rationale cited by both the Reagan and Bush administrations for increasing trade with Iraq amounted to an assertion of political reciprocity. "Trade is the best key to political influence," Bush's transition team asserted. "Economic incentives," NSD-26 affirmed, were the best instrument the United States had for getting Iraq "to moderate its behavior and to increase our influence."

Yet at other times there were almost plaintive pleas as to how little political reciprocity we could expect in return. When anti-terrorism sanctions were proposed following the *Achille Lauro,* the Reagan administration opposed them for fear that they would be "resented in Baghdad." When the Senate overwhelmingly approved sanctions following the August 1988 chemical weapons attacks on the Kurds, the objection was that such action would "reduce" U.S. influence.[9] Nor were sanctions to be imposed during Saddam's 1990 "spring of bad behavior," including when he threatened to "make the fire eat up half of Israel." A Republican-led Senate delegation even assured Saddam that President Bush likely would veto any sanctions bill passed by Congress.

It is true that as a general rule, the political efficacy of economic sanctions often is overestimated. Sanctions tend to work best when the objective is limited and multilateral collaboration is broad.[10] Yet in this case all of the issues raised as "should haves" for Iraqi moderation—end to terrorism, support for Middle East peace, even ending the genocide against the Kurds—were objectives of relatively limited scope. And it was less that multilateral coalition formation had failed than that it had not been tried. Besides, as noted in Chapter 2, such considerations did not prevent these same administrations from imposing sanctions unilaterally and in pursuit of much more expansive objectives against the Soviet Union, Nicaragua, Panama, and Libya.

Moreover, the Iraqi economy had its vulnerabilities. Again, other policy experiences as well as the scholarly literature are sobering as to the difficulties in converting economic vulnerability to political influence.[11] But between talk of sanctions "bringing a country to its knees" and just writing off the sanctions strategy, there is plenty of middle ground for realistic assessments of vulnerability. An economy such as the Iraqi one, burdened by eight years of war debt, hampered in its reconstruction by low world oil prices, short on food, and tight on credit, can reasonably be put in this middle ground.

There thus was no objective basis for dismissing the sanctions option out of hand. Nor can the "quiet diplomacy" claim made by Reagan-Bush of being committed to exerting economic pressure but doing so through diplomatic channels and at their own discretion rather than through congressionally imposed mandates be accepted at face value. Quiet diplomacy works best when the target believes that the sender is discreet but serious, as opposed to trying to keep things quiet to prevent them from getting serious. Neither administration at any point in the relationship gave Saddam any reason to think that they disagreed only on the method of sanctions but were serious about even an implicit requirement of genuine political reciprocity in exchange for the economic benefits being proffered.

In effect, the Reagan and Bush administrations were trying to have it both ways. They argued that we should increase trade because it would bring leverage over Iraqi political behavior, but then, when moderated Iraqi political behavior was not forthcoming, insisted that we had too little leverage to do anything about it. When policy needed to be justified, leverage was invoked. But when we needed to use leverage, we were said not to have it.

There were, to be sure, economic benefits for American farmers and firms from the newly booming trade with Iraq. This was part of the *reverse leverage* paradox, most evident in the 1988 controversy over the chemical warfare sanctions and which will be discussed further in Chapter 6. Here the key point is that it would have been less contradictory to simply have made the case for trade in terms of mutual economic gains. Trade for trade. But political reciprocity is what the Reagan and Bush administrations advertised—falsely.

Summary

Measuring by the very standards and objectives set by the Reagan and Bush administrations, there was no rough equivalence in the gains made and goals served by the relationship. Iran was contained—but even on this shared interest, the difference was not insignificant between Iraq being a party to the war and having its very survival threatened and the United States having important interests but not its direct security at stake. Soviet influence was countered—but in a way that allowed Iraq to be the key fulcrum point in the three-party triangle, and play the Soviets off without having to become a U.S. client. And on the Middle East regional agenda, Iraqi moderation was exceedingly limited, and mostly tactical maneuver. Fundamentally, Iraq was supposed to have become a positive, constructive force for an Arab-Israeli peace. *It didn't.* Iraq was supposed to have stopped supporting terrorism. *It didn't.* Iraq was supposed to have been a force for regional stability. *It surely wasn't.*

Proportionality

A second problem with the simple enemy-enemy-friend calculus is that it risks being too static. The essence of its logic is that conditions warrant a particular relationship which would not be warranted without those conditions. It is the existence of the mutual threat that brings the enemy-enemy-friends together. What, therefore, if these conditions change? What if the mutual enemy is defeated or its threat otherwise reduced, and the two states are then left again with their own relationship without the extenuating overlay?

One possibility is that major preexisting conflicts have been eliminated or at least manageably reduced and that the two states now have a basis beyond just the mutual enemy to deepen the alliance of convenience into an enduring accommodation. This, however, as Kennan observed about the U.S.-Soviet World War II alliance, is more often a dashed hope than a fulfilled one. It therefore is more realistic and prudent to assume that *(a)* the conditions which created the mutual enemy will change and *(b)* the likelihood of the basis for accommodation continuing is a possibility but not a probability. This means that even while the enemy-enemy-friend calculus still holds, there are risks in providing assistance, in particular military assistance, of a type or magnitude which could enhance the partner state's capabilities in ways which could be turned against you at a later point in time. While this also must be a consideration in any relationship, it should be an especially salient one in relationships with allies so much of convenience.

It is necessary therefore for there to be a degree of *proportionality* between the support provided to the enemy-enemy-friend and the threat faced. Support should be sufficient to tilt the balance against the mutual enemy, but not of a type or magnitude as to give the enemy-enemy-"friend" the military capabilities to pose its own threat to the balance of power. So long as other major conflicts and tensions remain, the relationship must be viewed as a tactical maneuver and modulated as such.

The Reagan-Bush strategy failed to abide by this need to maintain proportionality in the type and magnitude of support provided to Iraq.

Military Assistance Against Iran

It is true that the United States never actually sold Iraq arms. It did, however, provide Iraq with substantial military assistance of other types and in other ways during Iraq's war with Iran.

First, there were the "nods and winks" toward third-party arms sales to Iraq, including transfers of U.S. arms by Egypt, Jordan, Saudi Arabia, and Kuwait. Under the exigencies of the war and given that these largely were conventional and defensive arms, this in itself did not violate the tenet of proportionality as I've defined it. It is, though, important to establish that a simple arms-sales/no-arms-sales distinction doesn't hold up.

Second, both the Reagan and the Bush administrations did sell dual-use equipment and technology to the Iraqi military. Records show at least eighty such direct U.S. exports to the Iraqi military. Many of these, especially those exported while the Iran-Iraq war was still going on, also could be justified as proportional to the mutual threat against which they were to serve. There were, however, cases such as the helicopters sold to the Iraqi air force ostensibly for search-and-rescue missions but used for search-and-destroy chemical weapons attacks on the Kurds.

A third form of U.S. military assistance was the intelligence-sharing operation. Overall this, too, can be deemed proportional to the objective at hand, helping, according to one Reagan official, "save the Iraqis from being overrun in several key battles."[12] Yet here, too, some qualification is necessary. The original hope that the intelligence sharing would be an exchange and the United States would gain access to Iraqi intelligence on Soviet weaponry and on terrorists was never fulfilled—"useless junk" was the characterization by one expert of what the Iraqis were willing to share. Also, the U.S. side of the sharing continued at least as late as mid-May 1990, well after the end of the war, and at a level that, while more limited, was said to be significant enough that it "would be missed."[13]

Dual-Use Exports and Iraqi
Nonconventional Weapons Programs

What far exceeded any reasonable construction of proportionality were the dual-use exports that went to the Iraqi military-industrial complex, during as well as after the Iran-Iraq war, and which contributed to Iraqi nuclear, chemical, and biological weapons and ballistic missile programs. Examples have been detailed throughout this book. Exact counts vary: Congressman Henry Gonzalez cites two of every seven U.S. nonagricultural exports to Iraq between 1985 and 1990 as having gone to its military-industrial complex; Douglas Frantz and Murray Waas of the *Los Angeles Times* say export licenses were approved in 410 of 526 cases with potential nuclear applications, though Congressman Sam Gejdenson puts this figure at 162.[14]

Yet when pressed during the 1992 presidential campaign, George Bush unequivocally claimed that "we did not . . . enhance his [Saddam's] nuclear, biological or chemical capabilities."[15] Nor was it just campaign trail statements. In the fall of 1991 President Bush had provided formal certification to Congress that the United States had not contributed to Iraqi nonconventional weapons programs. But the United Nations Special Commission on Iraq (UNSCOM) and International Atomic Energy Agency (IAEA) inspection teams that went into Iraq after the war found on-the-ground evidence quite to the contrary. "The simple answer to the question of whether U.S. produced equipment and technology has been found to be part of the Iraqi nuclear weapons program," the head U.N./IAEA inspector stated, "is *yes.*"[16]

It is true that exports of American origin were much less than from other Western sources, notably France and Germany. It also is true that the Reagan and Bush administrations did take some steps both unilaterally and multilaterally to tighten export controls and strengthen the nonproliferation regimes. But the fact remains that, contrary to President Bush's assertions, the United States *did* contribute to Saddam Hussein's development of nuclear and other weapons of mass destruction. The very efforts the Bush administration finally made in late July 1990 to tighten export controls, while better late than never, implicitly amounted to a recognition of the excessive looseness of policies as they had existed up to that point. Indeed, the administration's own internal review acknowledged seventy-three cases of exports "to probably proliferation-related end users in Iraq." While less than the counts of others, it was much more than the zero to which George Bush tried to hold.[17]

In November 1990, as he sought to build public support for converting Desert Shield to Desert Storm, Bush increasingly emphasized the Iraqi nuclear threat as the ultimate stakes for the United States, beyond just the liberation of Kuwait. "No one knows precisely when this dictator may acquire nuclear weapons," Bush warned, "or exactly who they may be aimed at down the road. But we do know this for sure: He has never possessed a weapon that he didn't use."[18] This *was* part of the dilemma which ultimately made Desert Storm necessary. But it also had been Bush's own policies, as well as those of the Reagan administration, which had helped create this dilemma separate from and before Saddam invaded Kuwait. It was one thing to feed the Iraqi population while it was at war with Iran, or to provide some industrial equipment, or even to share military intelligence and to bolster Iraqi defensive military capabilities. It was quite another to have loosened export controls on dual-use technology and equipment so much that Iraq was able to develop its offensive military capabilities, and especially its nuclear, biological, and chemical weapons capabilities, far beyond the needs of its war with Iran—indeed, *to the point where it became the principal threat to the regional balance of power and to U.S. interests in the region.* Indeed, even after the heavy attacks of Desert Storm and despite the dismantling and inspections mandated by the United Nations, few experts felt assured that the genie could be put back in the bottle. Bush's own CIA director, Robert Gates, stated in January 1992 that the Iraqis hid much of their biological weapons equipment during the war, and could begin producing biological agents "in a matter of weeks." As to chemical weapons, Gates said they could begin producing at least some quantities "almost immediately," and would need only about a year to regain prewar capability.[19] Some U.N. inspectors believed that at whatever point the embargo was lifted, it would take Saddam only five to seven years to have a nuclear weapon.[20]

In his 1989 inaugural address, George Bush had proclaimed that "the spread of nuclear weapons must be stopped. Our diplomacy must work every day against the proliferation of nuclear weapons." His diplomacy toward Iraq failed to meet his own standard until it was almost too late—and still may have been.

Deterrent Credibility

In the end, Saddam Hussein calculated, as a distinguished bipartisan study group put it, "both that the regional balance of power stood in his favor and that local and outside powers would not react vigorously."[21] U.S. policy was not the only factor in such a calculation. It was, however, a critical one. The United States lacked deterrent credibility in the eyes of Saddam Hussein.

One of the falsest of the false dichotomies which have plagued American foreign policy in both theory and practice is that between deterrence and cooperation. A "viable theory of deterrence," as Alexander George and Richard Smoke have argued now for over twenty years, requires less of an "exclusive preoccupation with threats of punishment" as the sole means for influencing an adversary's behavior, and more of "a broader theory of processes by which nations influence each other, one that encompasses the utility of positive inducements as well as, or in lieu of, threats of negative sanctions."[22] The falseness of the dichotomy works in the other direction as well—that is, against theories of cooperation which focus too exclusively on positive inducements and fail to encompass the utility that threats and negative actions can have for building cooperation. Nor is this true only with respect to American foreign policy. "The record demonstrates," British diplomat and scholar Evan Luard wrote in 1967 with more general historical reference, "that neither a policy of conciliation nor deterrence can ever be successful if conducted in isolation from the other."[23]

This pertains to an extent even for efforts to forge cooperation among states which on the whole are allies. It especially holds for efforts at accommodation between states which have been adversaries and still have significant conflicts and tensions in their relationship. Even within the limits defined by the requisites of reciprocity and proportionality, the positive inducements for cooperation are there: a mutual enemy against which security is being enhanced; trade and other economic benefits flowing; military assistance, even if limited to conventional weaponry and largely defensive purposes, still quite significant. But as long as reasonable doubt remains about the prospective new friend's intentions, the leader of that state must know both that cooperation has its benefits *and* that noncooperation has its consequences. In sending the latter message, and affecting cost-benefit calculations accordingly, the deterrent component can serve as its own inducement, while also guarding against the possibility that the accommodation strategy will fail.

This amounts to what might be called a "flexible-but-firm" accommodation strategy, analogous to the "firm-but-flexible" deterrence strategy shown by Paul Huth and others to be quite effective in the prevention of war.[24] The firm-but-flexible strategy is distinguished from harder-line deterrence strategies by its keeping the door open to cooperation while still maintaining a credible deterrent. The flexible-but-firm strategy analogously differs from softer-line accommodation strategies in pursuing cooperation but also maintaining the credibility of its deterrent posture to convey a willingness and ability to slam the door shut, if necessary.

Deterrent credibility thus is the third crucial requisite for a strategy of accommodation. But on this count as well, U.S. policy toward Iraq fell short, both during the immediate pre-invasion crisis period and as a matter of more general standing deterrence posture tracing back through the 1980s.

Failings as Crisis Deterrence

Once nations are enmeshed in a crisis, deterrence requires that there be careful yet clear communication of what constitutes unacceptable action, supported by a credible retaliatory threat.[25] The statements and actions of the Bush administration, as detailed in Chapter 4, fell well short of these standards.

It would be going too far to say that as of July 17, when Saddam made his initial direct threats against Kuwait and started mobilizing troops along the border, the Bush administration should have assessed an invasion to be probable. But as the threats intensified and the troop mobilization escalated on an almost daily basis, the prospect of an invasion no longer should have been taken to be as improbable as it was. Numerous general statements were made of principles and expected behavior, but not once during the crisis period did a Bush administration official unequivocally state that the United States would defend Kuwait if attacked.

By July 25, the evidence that Iraq was planning to invade Kuwait was considered "convincing" by the CIA's chief national intelligence officer (NIO) for warnings.[26] While others in the intelligence community disagreed, this should have been a credible enough level of warning to have prompted at least a hedging of bets with a firming up of the deterrence posture to go along with the reassurances still being extended. Yet July 25 was the same day that Ambassador Glaspie met with Saddam and delivered her "direct instruction from the President to seek better relations with Iraq."

The total available record of the Glaspie-Saddam meeting—not just the Iraqi transcript but also including the ambassador's congressional testimony, the cables leaked to the press, and statements by other administration officials—indicates that her warnings were not as "crystal clear" as claimed. Three days after the Glaspie-Saddam meeting, President Bush cabled his own less-than-firm personal message to Saddam. Some within the administration first tried to toughen the message up, and then to block it, but failed on both counts. Some of these officials had participated in the Rand crisis simulation group originally scheduled to play out a scenario based on an imaginary Iraqi threat against Kuwait, but which coincidentally convened the same day that Saddam began his actual troop buildup. The Rand group had concluded "that the only way to forestall such a situation would be to get the President of the United States to warn Saddam that if he stepped over the border, the United States was going to come get him."[27] But President Bush's message stopped well short of such firmness and clarity.

Nor had American actions since the Iraqi troop buildup done much to firm up the deterrent. Secretary of State Baker later would stress two major signals supposedly sent to Iraq during the crisis period. "Signal No. 1," Baker said, "was to slap foreign policy export controls on exports to Iraq." Yet while tighter than before, export controls still were loose enough that some dual-use export licenses were being granted even in these last pre-invasion days. "Signal No. 2 was to cancel or suspend the CCC program."[28] Yet this, too, was very little very late, especially since at this same time the Bush administration again was opposing an economic sanctions bill Congress was seeking to pass.

The constraints, both international and domestic, that the Bush administration was operating under during the crisis period do have to be recognized. "The basic principle is not to make threats you can't deliver on," one official said, with reference to doubts about support for a firmer stand from both Arab allies and the American public.[29] No Arab leader demanded tougher U.S. actions or even indicated he would support such actions. The emir of Kuwait was still rather blasé ("summer cloud"); President Mubarak, King Hussein, and King Fahd were still taking their fellow Arab leader at his word. And at home, the American public was basking in the fall of communism in Eastern Europe and focusing on the budget deficit and other domestic problems.

There is a big difference, however, between options being constrained, which the Bush administration's were, and options being precluded, which was not the case. It surely was not standard practice either in its Middle East diplomacy or more generally for the Bush administration to automatically take the views of allies as fixed and not subject to U.S. influence and persuasion. We thus can't really know whether Arab reluctance was a surmountable constraint because the Bush administration made little effort to surmount it. Indeed, there may even have been a self-feeding cycle at work with the Arab reluctance to take a firmer stand a function in part of "doubts about our own intentions and credibility" and thus itself potentially changeable through "a more decisive and unambiguous [U.S.] approach."[30]

Similarly, the American public on a number of issues involving the use of military force in the 1980s had shown itself to have become less strictly opposed to a muscular foreign policy than during the earlier post-Vietnam period. Elsewhere I have characterized the pattern as a continued reluctance to get involved in civil wars and other intrastate conflicts, but a greater willingness to threaten and even use military force to impose restraint on international aggressors.[31] This included, for example, the 1987–88 reflagging operation defending

Kuwait against Iranian aggression, which despite its rather substantial risks had averaged 55.5 percent support in public opinion polls. When Iraq finally did invade Kuwait and the American public responded with upwards of 80 percent support for Operation Desert Shield despite the tremendous risks and uncertainties associated with this most rapid buildup of U.S. forces since World War II and largest overseas commitment since Vietnam, it was because this was such a clear case of aggression threatening vital U.S. interests.[32]

By most accounts (including the Pentagon's post–Gulf War studies), Saddam had already made the decision to invade Kuwait before the Jiddah talks on August 1. The collapse of these talks was more pretext than precipitant. Saddam's accusation of an economic "dagger in the back" leaving no other choice but to take what Kuwait would not give, and more, was but a cover story, and a transparent one at that. There *were* other options. Saddam could have continued to try to coerce Kuwait. Or he could have seized just the Rumaila oil field and Bubiyan and Warbah islands (which he may well have gotten away with). He also could have cut his huge military spending, which was eating up 42 percent of his oil revenues. But the Iraqi military already had run its computer simulations and war games. Military exercises, even including a dress rehearsal for a heliborne assault on Kuwait City, had been staged. And on August 2, Saddam moved.

Failings as Standing Deterrence

The deterrence posture cast by a state as perceived by another state is not just based on crisis period maneuvers. It is also a matter of "standing credibility," of the reputation the state has developed in another's eyes over the course of their past relations. The need to deter Iraq did not just crop up in July 1990. There were numerous and substantial long-standing indicators of potential aggressive will and capabilities: that Saddam never demobilized his military after the Iran-Iraq war, maintaining a million-man army with over 50 divisions and 5800 main battle tanks; that his rhetoric toward Kuwait had turned coercive almost immediately after the Iran-Iraq war; that he had been showing other "aggressive tendencies"; that we knew he was pursuing nuclear weapons and ballistic missile delivery systems.[33] *But the record of actions taken and not taken, of statements made and not made by the Bush and Reagan administrations, in the years and months leading up to the crisis in key respects was lacking in the firmness necessary to establish standing credibility in the eyes of a rogue-state leader like Saddam Hussein.*

It was in this respect, as but one example, that much more was at stake in the no-sanctions response to the August 1988 Iraqi chemical weapons attacks on the Kurds than the immediate issue itself. What was a dictator like Saddam to have thought when even the use of chemical weapons fell within the bounds of behavior which the United States considered undesirable but nevertheless for which it still would show some flexibility? If the United States was not prepared to be firm on chemical warfare, especially now that the Iran-Iraq war was over, then on what else might it not be firm?

The point was made earlier that Saddam also appeared to have understood much better than Reagan and Bush that the tactical coinciding of U.S. and Iraqi interests on certain issues and at certain points in Middle East regional politics was not the same thing as a strategic convergence. It could not have done much for U.S. credibility for Saddam to have seen how he could diplomatically outmaneuver the United States by supporting PLO moderation toward Israel when it was a useful means to his own anti-Syria ends and then supporting PLO radicalism when it served his interests. And with terrorism: Perhaps Saddam understood, even respected, the original realpolitik rationale for the United States taking him off its state terrorist list in 1982. But he also knew very well what support he was still giving to the various factions of Palestinian terrorists. He knew that they still had bases and camps in Iraq, that they were broadcasting on Iraqi radio, that their attacks were being planned and launched from within his borders.

Similarly, the dual-use equipment and technology Saddam was diverting to his weapons programs not only had its direct military value but also carried its own credibility-damaging messages. Saddam knew that when MIMI or Nassr or Sa'ad 16 or his other military-industrial complexes stated "civilian uses" for the American export licensing paperwork, they (and he) had nothing of the sort in mind. Saddam also knew about his BNL connection, and, apparently, the diversion of CCC financing to military purchases. But Secretary Baker and others kept showing themselves willing to not take the charges being made all that seriously. How seriously, then, was the United States to be taken by Saddam?

From December 1989 on, NSD-26 notwithstanding, Saddam's statements and actions grew more antagonistic both directly toward the United States and more generally to U.S. interests in the region. When Saddam tested new and longer-range ballistic missiles, the Bush administration dismissed the data on the missile tests as "still sketchy," refused to put stock in "recent rehashing of allegations" regarding Iraqi nuclear weapons, and even went ahead in January 1990 with a presidential order for a waiver of the Export-Import Bank credit restrictions recently imposed by Congress.[34] Saddam's call in his February 1990 ACC speech to all "good" Arabs to oppose U.S. efforts to "govern" the Gulf region was dismissed at the time as just a retort for the VOA editorial criticizing Saddam's dictatorial rule. The VOA editorial itself was considered an unfortunate misunderstanding for which the Bush administration offered regrets and apology. The burn-half-of-Israel threat in April did elicit a denunciation by President Bush himself and did prompt a policy review, but only limited concrete actions. The same day as Saddam's even more vitriolic May 29 Arab League speech, the Bush NSC again declined to cancel the CCC program, again only partially tightened export controls, again stopped short of a firm posture.

Later, when the first stories broke in the press about the Glaspie-Saddam meeting, the Bush administration gave the embattled ambassador little support. There even were statements attributed to anonymous senior officials confirming the general accuracy of the Iraqi transcript of the meeting. The Bush administration seemed prepared, if not eager, to have a scapegoat. It need be borne in mind, however, that ambassadors carry out policy, they do not make it. The message delivered by Ambassador Glaspie was an affirmation of, not an aberration from, existing policy. And not just policy during the immediate crisis, but of a broader and more deeply rooted pattern of a lack of firmness in the Reagan-Bush posture over the preceding eight-year period which gave Saddam ample reason to doubt U.S. credibility.

The "Un-Deterrability" Counterargument

A very different argument has been made, not only by Bush administration officials but also by a number of scholars and journalists, that deterrence was less a failed than an "impossible task."[35] This "un-deterrability" thesis rests on a view of Saddam as so convinced that the United States was an intractable enemy bent on dominating the Persian Gulf region and even undermining his regime that any additional firmness would only have antagonized him further.

Supporting evidence is based heavily on an assessment of Saddam's motivations as imputed from his rhetoric and from statements by top aides such as Foreign Minister Aziz. But while there was plenty of such verbiage, the key analytic question is how reliably motivations can be imputed from rhetoric. In interpreting the meaning of a leader's statements, a distinction between *expressive* and *instrumental* uses of rhetoric is critical. When a leader such as Saddam Hussein makes statements about the United States as the enemy, is he expressing genuine beliefs and perceptions? Or might he be consciously using such statements for any number of purposes, such as arousing the Iraqi people to distract them from their own domestic plight and xenophobically legitimize his own brutal rule, and/or another effort at Nasserite casting of himself as the defender of the Arab world, and/or as a tacit bargaining strategy to intimidate an American administration concerned about demonstrating its bona fides into further concessions on issues in their bilateral relations? It is at least as plausible to argue that Saddam's rhetoric was purposive in nature, another instrument being used to pursue his objectives, as to accept it strictly at face value as expressive of his "true beliefs."

It is true that by his own political experiences and what we know of his personality, Saddam had strong tendencies toward paranoic views of enemies in general. This was his upbringing in Iraqi politics and part of how he sustained his own rule. Compared to other Arab leaders, he also had had much less contact with the United States and the West in general. And, as it is said, even paranoids have some real enemies.

But this was almost a decade into his relationship with the United States. The relationship had been less than pure harmony, but it also had been much more than old-time hostility. Billions of dollars in U.S. trade assistance had flowed to Iraq. Vital intelligence had been supplied during the war with Iran. The United States even engaged its own naval forces on Iraq's side for the last year of the war.

Moreover, this belief that the United States was an intractable enemy is said to date to "late 1989."[36] Yet this was the high point of Bush administration offerings to Saddam. President Bush had just signed NSD-26. Secretary Baker had just pushed the new CCC credit guarantees through, and had sent "the good news" to Foreign Minister Aziz. A U.S. diplomat conveyed the reassurance that Baker considered the BNL-related allegations against Iraq to be "baseless."[37] The president bucked Congress to exempt Iraq from the newly legislated Export-Import Bank lending restrictions. Iraqi scientists had recently been invited to the Department of Energy's nuclear research symposium. U.S. reaction to the December long-range ballistic missile tests was muted.

It is one thing for an initial attempt at accommodation to be discounted because of the psychological barriers of the image of the enemy. But when cooperative actions are numerous, there is no inherent psychological reason why they cannot overcome a view of them as the design of an intractable enemy. If they are so viewed anyway, if amidst such carrots and goodwill Saddam still could not overcome a deeply entrenched view of America as the enemy, then the Bush administration should have drawn its own conclusions *right then* about Iraq's intractability and the consequent very limited prospects for a meaningful accommodation beyond the alliance of convenience of the Iran-Iraq war period, and adjusted policy accordingly.

A further consideration is that some of the Iraqi rhetoric from which the paranoic un-deterrability has been imputed could well have been quite simply intentional misrepresentation and fabrication. Milton Viorst, writing in *The New Yorker,* in particular puts a great deal of credence on his 1991 interview with Tariq Aziz. Yet this is the same loyal foreign minister who in September 1988 flatly denied that Iraq had used chemical weapons against the Kurds; who held that Iraq did nothing wrong in the BNL affair; who claimed that the British journalist Farzad Bazoft received a fair trial; who claimed that the only reason Iraq was still buying arms was because the cease-fire with Iran might break down; and who as late as June 1990—after the Iraq-assisted PLO terrorist raid on Israel, amidst Saddam's mounting denunciations of the United States, in the face of all the intelligence reports on Iraqi nuclear and other nonconventional weapons programs—still insisted that "we committed no acts against American interests."[38] It also would be Aziz who in Geneva in early January 1991 would rebuff Secretary Baker's final efforts to avert war. On what basis can his statements that Iraq acted strictly out of justified conviction that the United States was an intractable enemy be accepted as reliable and valid?

Further, if one is to make evidentiary use of quotations, the question is which ones. The day of the invasion, for example, the Iraqi press issued a dismissive statement that "we know that Washington's threats are those of a paper tiger. . . . No American official, be it even George Bush, would dare to do anything serious against the Arab nation."[39] And to Ambassador Glaspie, Saddam had brashly said, "Yours is a society which cannot accept 10,000 dead in one battle." Back in his February 1990 ACC speech, he was even more contemptuous:

[T]he weakness of a big body lies in its bulkiness. . . . We saw that the United States as a superpower departed Lebanon immediately when some Marines were killed, the very men who are considered to be the most prominent symbol of its arrogance. . . . The United States has been defeated in some combat areas for all the forces it possesses and it has displayed signs of fatigue, frustration and hesitation.[40]

While Desert Storm proved how much Saddam had underestimated American capabilities and resolve, the pertinent point here is that these statements don't sound like someone convinced that the United States was an intractable enemy, determined "to undermine his regime."[41] They sound much more like someone convinced that the United States, whether or not an enemy, was not to be feared.

Moreover, there is the past pattern of Iraqi behavior. In 1961 Iraq tried to seize Kuwait as it was getting independence from Britain, but backed down when Britain deployed troops and naval forces to defend Kuwait. In 1973 (when Saddam was not officially in charge but was the power behind the scenes) Iraq seized a Kuwaiti border post and announced plans to annex a strip of Kuwaiti territory, but withdrew when Saudi Arabia, with Arab League backing, supported Kuwait. In 1980 Saddam calculated that the internal weakness and international unpopularity of Iran made it ripe for attack. This time he did attack. But here, too, when he met with more resistance from Iran and initially less support from the international community than anticipated, as early as 1982 he began suing for peace.

In sum, the pattern was of Iraq being quite prepared to "throw its weight around," but also being "deterred when faced with superior countervailing regional or international military power."[42] Prince Bandar, the Saudi ambassador to the United States, even speculated that Saddam manipulated the April 1990 assurances from the United States and Israel in response to his fire-eat-half-of-Israel threat that Israel would not attack Iraq as protection on "his western flank . . . freeing him to do what he wanted on the east with Kuwait." Bandar retrospectively concluded, according to Bob Woodward, "that he and the Bush administration had been set up."[43]

There is nothing inherently un-deterrable about such a pattern of behavior. It is only too normal among nation-states with aggressive aspirations—analytically speaking, quite rational behavior. When convinced of the threat of resistance or retaliation from other powers, Iraq has not been internationally aggressive. When not so convinced, it has. It indeed has a history of needing to be deterred—but of being deterrable.

Lessons for the Post–Cold War Era

In an important recent book, Alexander George stresses the need for "bridging the gap" between theory and practice in U.S. foreign policy. "The most promising way to bridge the gap," George writes, "is to focus on the relationship between knowledge and action in the conduct of foreign policy."[44] Action, or *statecraft*, is the business of leaders, policymakers, diplomats—statesmen. The "essential task" of statecraft, simply put, is "to develop and manage relationships with other states that will protect and enhance one's security." Simply put, but an enormously complex undertaking requiring "that policymakers clearly define their own state interests, differentiate these interests in terms of relative importance, and make prudent judgments as to acceptable costs and risks of pursuing them." When possible, this involves efforts "to recognize and seek out common interests and to develop policies for promoting them." When necessary, it involves efforts to "try to narrow and manage the disputed issues in ways that reduce the potential for destructive conflicts and contamination of the entire relationship." And when all else fails, it may also mean threatening or actually using military force.[45]

One of the key contributions scholarly analysis can make is to help with the "conceptualization of strategies." Such analysis, while abstract and not itself in an operational form, "identifies the critical variables of that strategy and the general logic that is associated with [its] successful use." It "is not itself a strategy," but it is "the starting point for constructing a strategy."[46] It must be combined with other types of knowledge, especially specific understanding of the particular situation and actor at hand. It also must be both reasoned and presented in a manner and form sensitive to policymakers' skepticism about academic overtheorizing. But it also can provide an extremely valuable framework for putting a particular situation and strategy in the type of broader context which can facilitate the design and implementation of effective strategies.

This was done quite extensively during the cold war with respect to strategic deterrence and nuclear arms control. The theoretical work of a number of scholars and think tank analysts (in particular at Rand) directly and indirectly provided much of the conceptual basis for U.S. nuclear strategy toward the Soviet Union.[47] But the gaps have been much less bridged in other areas of foreign policy strategy, including the need for the type of mixed strategies for dealing with rogue states as delineated herein. Helping to bridge this gap is a central purpose of this book, a purpose crucial to learning about and learning from U.S.-Iraqi relations in the 1982–90 period.

It is, to be sure, easier to lay out requisites for a strategy in the abstract than to apply them to a particular policy situation. But given the already evident instabilities of the post–cold war world, it is especially crucial to do so. Far from a "new world order," this is a world in which alliances are more shifting than fixed, in which regional balances of power are highly unstable, in which domestic instability may be even more pervasive and violent than in the past, and in which the roster of rogue states grows longer while these states become better armed. Regions which long have been unstable—the Middle East and the Persian Gulf, South Asia (India-Pakistan), Southeast Asia, Northeast Asia (the Korean peninsula)—remain so. Other regions—the Balkans, former Soviet Eurasia—are now more unstable than during the cold war. And the likes of Iraq, Iran, Libya, and North Korea already have been joined by Serbia on the rogue-state roster, with others undoubtedly to follow.

The need in such a world for the United States to choose friends carefully and strike alliances strategically could not be greater. For as the U.S.-Iraqi case shows, there is nothing automatic about the enemies of enemies becoming friends. This venerable axiom of realist orthodoxy in fact is not quite realistic enough. There *are* critical variables which must be identified, there *is* a general logic which must be followed, if this strategy is to be used successfully.

Reciprocity

First, other than under the most extreme exigencies, the threat of a mutual enemy can take priority but should not be given exclusivity over all other issues and tensions in the relationship.

•*Coinciding vs. Converging Interests:* Even when two states have a mutual enemy, their purposes and interests vis-à-vis that enemy may still diverge. The defeat or containment of the mutual enemy may be a common means intended to serve quite different ends. Tactical maneuvers leading to the coinciding of interests are not to be taken for strategic shifts making for the genuine convergence of interests.

•*Free Riders:* Even if one were to assume that shared enemies more fully equated with shared interests, the "rough equivalence" standard for reciprocity is not met if both states share the benefits of gains made against the mutual enemy but other actions of one state are significantly detrimental to the interests of the other on other issues of conflict and tension in their bilateral relationship. To accept such inequivalence other than under extreme circumstances of mutual threat is to allow the partner state to be a free rider and have accommodation on its own terms.

•*Reverse Leverage Paradox:* Political influence can be gained from extending trade and other economic benefits only if the reverse leverage paradox can be averted. A strategy cannot be based on the utility of trade as leverage over another state if when it comes time to exert that leverage, the domestic political pressures from groups which have developed interests in the continuation of that trade are likely to be so great as to be constraining if not prohibitive.

A variety of strategies for meeting the reciprocity requisite—including "tit-for-tat," "GRIT" (graduated reciprocation in tension-reduction), and "conditional reciprocity"—can be devised. Each has its strengths and weaknesses, advantages and disadvantages given particular situations, issues, and actors.[48] All, however, as Robert Axelrod writes of tit-for-tat, must be both "forgiving" and "retaliating." Perfect behavior and self-effacing concessions need not be required. Linkages need not be explicit or specific. But there must be a standard, there must be some conditions, there must be certain parameters for expected reciprocity so that a willingness to accommodate is not equated with an accession to appeasement.[49]

Proportionality

Second, military aid and trade must abide by a degree of proportionality in the nature and extent to which the enemy-enemy-"friend"'s military capabilities are enhanced.

•*Priority of Nonproliferation:* In particular, long-term interests in nonproliferation should not be given short shrift because of geopolitical concerns of the moment. The dynamics of geopolitics are prone to shift. When they do and the extenuating overlay for military assistance is gone, there is no getting back whatever already has been provided. In particular, it is exceedingly difficult to put nonconventional weaponry genies back into their bottles—even when, as in Iraq, the international community can actually go into a country and destroy its military-industrial complexes, seize its weapons and weapons technology, and maintain an international embargo.

•*Better Intelligence on Front Companies:* Global front company networks such as the one set up by Iraq need to be made a much higher priority focus for intelligence agencies. Iraq was neither the first nor the last rogue state to seek to acquire nuclear and other nonconventional weaponry through a global front company network. There is no reason why intelligence agencies which penetrated the KGB should not be able to penetrate rogue-state front companies.

•*Technology Transfer:* Selling the technology to produce weaponry is even more potentially threatening than selling the weaponry itself. Weapons sales, at least in theory, can be cut off. But acquisition of the weapons-producing technology, including dual-use technologies, can lead to military self-sufficiency. Concerns about proportionality thus bear particularly on militarily relevant technology exports.

It is sobering to realize that had he not overextended himself with the invasion of Kuwait—or, for that matter, had he just waited a year or two—Saddam Hussein might well have had nuclear weapons. We may not be so lucky next time. Moreover, only time will fully tell what lessons other aspiring proliferators may have drawn from the willingness of the United States and other Western countries to opt for the short-term geopolitical gambit over long-term nonproliferation commitments.

Deterrent Credibility

Third, deterrent credibility must be maintained at the same time that other efforts are being made to develop positive bases for the relationship.

• *Tilt, Don't Lunge:* The kind of reflexive balancing which ends up lunging, not just tilting, toward one state because of antagonisms with another is to be avoided. The balance-of-power game, when played at all, requires calibration and nuance. Maintaining credibility in the eyes of the prospective ally should not be ignored in the name of maximizing credibility in the eyes of the immediate adversary. Moreover, in regions like the Persian Gulf where both major powers pose threats to U.S. interests, both may need to be contained rather than tilting toward either.

• *Flexible-but-Firm Strategy:* Deterrence and cooperation can be reinforcing and not necessarily mutually exclusive tracks. Strategies of cooperation which too exclusively focus on positive inducements have the mirror-image flaws of strategies of deterrence which too exclusively draw on threats and coercion. A constructive accommodation can only be achieved with a rogue state if the strategy is both flexible enough to indicate that cooperation has its benefits and firm enough to continue to convey that noncooperation has its consequences.

It is only logical that mixed relationships require mixed strategies. The prospective partner is welcome and even encouraged to join the family of nations. And with that come certain rights. But so, too, are there responsibilities which must be met, and which will be supported, affirmed, and enforced.

"Identity of interests," Thucydides wrote centuries ago, "is the surest bond, whether between states or individuals."[50] The surest of bonds, perhaps, but not the most common. Indeed, in those rare instances when alliances are based not just on mutual threats but also on close societal affinities and shared interests (for example, the United States and Great Britain), we call them "special relationships." The semantics are telling.

It is much more often the case that "alliances are against, and only derivatively for, someone or something."[51] Yet we need bear in mind that the enemy of my enemy may be my friend—but he also may still be my enemy. Without effective statecraft, the latter is more likely to be the result. Otherwise, with friends like these . . .

Premises, Processes, and Politics: Lessons for Foreign Policy Making

IT WAS ONLY "WITH THE BENEFIT OF 20/20 HINDSIGHT," SECRETARY OF State Baker asserted, that there were "some things that we might have done differently if we had known that this was going to happen." During the 1992 presidential campaign, amidst the rising controversy over "Iraq-gate," President Bush ratcheted up the requirement to "90/90 hindsight."[1]

In fact, though, as traced throughout Part I of this book, warnings were sounded early, and they were sounded often. They were issued while the Iran-Iraq war alliance of convenience was being built and maintained; in the wake of the August 1988 chemical weapons attacks on the Kurds; in 1989 amidst the formulation of NSD-26; during the 1990 "spring of bad behavior"; and as the crisis over Kuwait built up. They came both from within the Reagan and Bush administrations and from Congress, foreign policy analysts, journalists, and other governments. They were about Saddam's actions as well as his rhetoric, his capabilities as well as his ambitions. Indeed, this was not simply a matter of *some* things that *might* have been done differently *if* only Saddam Hussein's true colors *could* have been known. Rather there were *many* things which *should* have been done differently based on information and analysis that *were* available at the time.

This is not to deny the inherent uncertainties of all international affairs, and that the information available to policymakers was somewhat imperfect and ambiguous, less than definitive. Yet how often before have we looked back on a key foreign policy decision and asked how could we have done what we did, how could we have not known? For example, the Bay of Pigs, 1961, with its assumptions about the ease of success and the dysfunctional decision-group dynamics in the Kennedy White House.[2] Vietnam, 1965, when the Johnson administration made the first major commitments of American ground troops, in a decision process distorted by stacked-deck assessments of policy options, inaccurate intelligence, misguided political calculations, and the impact of the president's own personality.[3] The 1978–79 fall of the Shah of Iran, the warning signs of which were ignored for so long and then, once realized, decisive decisions were precluded by the deep divisions among the Carter administration's foreign policy principals.[4] Lebanon, 1982–84, when the Reagan administration sent American troops into war-torn Beirut under peacetime rules of engagement and assumptions of a "benign" environment on a mission the internal contradictions of which were in part evaded and in part ignored by policymakers.[5]

In all these cases (and others) the foreign policy failures have been attributed at least as much to flaws in the making, or "execution," of American foreign policy as to flaws in the strategy/concepts. Thus, a second level of explanation and a second set of lessons in the U.S. pre–Gulf War Iraqi policy case concern the failings in the processes by which that policy was made.

There are, of course, those schools of thought in international relations theory that doubt whether such domestic-level analysis really matters.[6] Traditional "realist" theorists deride studies of the foreign policy making process as of descriptive interest but as more trivial than causal in their explanatory value. We are told instead to stay concentrated on abstractions like the structure of the international system as creating imperatives to which states merely respond.[7] Or, as even more of an innate matter, reference still is often made to Hans

Morgenthau's claim of an objective law with roots in human nature that "statesmen think and act in terms of interest defined as power."[8]

This is not the place for a full review of the counterarguments. Two basic points, however, need to be made. First, from a comparative foreign policy perspective, there are both strong theoretical arguments and ample empirical evidence that all states which occupy the same systemic position do *not* behave the same way. Second, with American foreign policy particularly in mind, it also has been amply shown that the same state faced with comparable situations at different times will *not* always take the same or even comparable actions. For even when international structures and the external environment impose their pressures, and notwithstanding whatever professions policymakers make to the tenet of interest defined as power, interpretations of those systemic "imperatives" and definitions of how interests translate to power are subject to variations in individual perceptions, bureaucratic processes, and political pressures.

A different critique is made by rational-choice theorists, notably by game theorists and expected-utility theorists.[9] Here the central argument is less that foreign policy making is trivial than that it is predictable. Decision-makers are said to have more of a domain of choice than systemic and power imperative theories allow, but to operate still according to objectively determined preference orderings ("payoff structures," "expected utility calculations").

However, even if we accept the notion that decision-makers seek to be rational maximizers, the key point is that they are doing so not according to some objective reality but rather within their own particular construing of reality. How preferences are ordered and how expected utility is calculated are affected by who is doing the deciding, and through which processes and under what pressures it is being done. Further, as attested to by the very complexity of the models used by rational-choice theorists, these calculations are hardly simple single-factor assessments. Quite to the contrary, they involve a multitude of variables, including but not limited to assessments of one's own capabilities, the adversary's intentions, the adversary's capabilities, the intentions and capabilities of prospective third parties, and so on. Calculations such as these are neither objective nor self-evident;

rather, they are subjective estimations. As such, they constitute all the more reason for not leaving foreign policy process as an unopened black box.

Even among those who do open the black box, though, there are varying approaches over which part to focus on. Some studies look primarily at top-level decision-makers; others at the bureaucratic politics more widely in the executive branch; others at the influence of interest groups; others at executive-legislative relations. In some cases, when the principal dynamics of the foreign policy process are in fact rather concentrated within one of these dimensions, such narrowing is appropriate. But when the dynamics spread more broadly across these dimensions—which, in fact, is more often the case than not—it is important to be more encompassing in our conception of the foreign policy process. The Reagan-Bush Iraqi policy is such a case.

I thus approach the analysis of foreign policy making in this case, and as a more general domestic-level framework, with a three-dimensional analysis: (1) high-level decision-making, with particular emphasis on the *premises* held by key decision-makers and the persistent power these have in shaping policy; (2) bureaucratic *processes,* within and among executive branch agencies in both the formulation and implementation of policy; and (3) the *politics* of relations with Congress, both as a matter of Republican-Democrat partisanship and more inherent executive-legislative institutional competition and of interest group pressures.

Decision-Making:
The Power of Premises

In trying to understand how they could have been so wrong about Saddam for so long and amidst so many warnings, one Bush administration official acknowledged the prevalence of a "mind-set" which was more the manifestation of a set of premises than the product of analytic assessments. This is a common problem in foreign policy decision-making. No decision-maker is a *tabula rasa,* free of preconceptions or paradigms or other perceptual lenses. It is "often impossible," one noted scholar observes, "to explain crucial decisions and policies without reference to the decision-makers' beliefs about the world and their images of others."[10] The problem arises when such beliefs are taken too strictly as premises to be accepted rather than hypotheses to be tested. Premises are presumed to be true, not requiring confirmation and thus inclining decision-makers to dismiss dissonant information. Indeed, prominent on a list of the causes of policymakers being caught by surprise are "above all, the premises and preconceptions of policy-makers."[11]

The power that premises have not only affects initial decisions that are made but also the ongoing capacity for assessment and adjustment. It is critical for high-level policymakers to "maintain receptivity to indications that current plans are not working out well so that policy adjustments can be made."[12] But strongly held premises foster both an overconfidence in the policies to which the decision-maker already stands committed and an insensitivity to information critical of those policies or otherwise outside the mind-set.[13] The result is a constraining, distorting, self-perpetuating operational tautology: We know the policy is working because we believe it is the right policy; we believe it is the right policy because we know it is working.

This was very much the dynamic of the decision-making process on Iraq. The Reagan-Bush mind-set was characterized by two principal premises. One, as one official conceded shortly after the invasion of Kuwait, was that "we were obsessed with Iran."[14] It was one thing to recognize the extent to which Iran remained a threat throughout this period. It did. Indeed, the strategy of reaching out to Iranian moderates which underlay the 1985–86 arms-for-hostages gambit was not just illegal, it was poorly reasoned. But the problem was that even policy proposals like the September 1988 Khalilzad State Department paper were so tarred with the soft-on-Iran brush that the arguments this paper had to make and evidence it had to present on the increasing threats being posed by Iraq were dismissed more than refuted. The proposal didn't get a hearing so much as the large "No" angrily written on its cover page by Secretary of State Shultz. The obsession with one enemy complicated knowing the other.

The corollary premise to the absoluteness of the Iranian threat was the "Saddam is changing" one. We saw this at the time diplomatic relations were normalized in 1984, when Reagan administration officials confidently stated that "Iraq no longer regarded itself as a 'front-line Arab state,' " and that Saddam now believed that a Middle East peace "should include peace for Israel."[15] It also was manifested in the March 1988 State Department "deeper-into-the-mainstream" intelligence assessment, and in NSD-26.

To be sure, the Reagan and Bush administrations were not alone in holding this positive view of Saddam. Endorsements of diplomatic normalization could be found on the editorial pages of the *New York Times* and *Washington Post*. When the Reagan administration initially was reluctant to go ahead with reflagging, the pro-Israel *The New Republic* ran an article proclaiming Iraq "now the de facto protector of the regional status quo," ostensibly even willing to make peace with Israel. In Chapter 2, various regional experts were quoted on how by the end of the war with Iran Saddam himself had changed in "fundamental and enduring ways," how he was "a popular leader . . . young, energetic, alert to the needs of his people," how he even had come around to being "much concerned about democracy. . . . He thinks that it is healthy."[16] Indeed, even as Iraqi troops mobilized on the Kuwaiti border, regional leaders from Egyptian President Hosni Mubarak to Kings Fahd of Saudi Arabia and Hussein of Jordan personally reassured President Bush that Saddam would not invade.

That others made the same mistake hardly amounts to a justification, especially given the available evidence. Consider what was knowable about Saddam well before he invaded Kuwait:

1. Even as Dictators Go, Saddam Was Brutal

This was a man who began his political career as the hit man in the 1959 Ba'athist coup attempt. His rise to power had left a "trail of blood" marking his path. The stories were legion even once he was in power of his penchant for personally participating in killings and other political violence. He even shot his own son in the hand and nearly pistol-whipped him to death for the high crime of interfering with Saddam's relationship with one of his mistresses.[17] He created in Iraq, as Samir al-Khalil titled his 1989 book, "a republic of fear." Biographers Efraim Karsh and Inauri Rautsi attribute to Saddam the transformation of Iraq from "just" an "autocracy ruled by successive short-lived military regimes, into a totalitarian state, with its tentacles permeating every aspect of society, and with the omnipotent presence of the supreme leader towering over the nation."[18] When unrest began increasing during the Iran-Iraq war, Saddam met it with intensified repression and propagation of his personality cult. After the war, despite the huge debts and enormous economic problems with which the country was left, Saddam ordered so many monuments built to the struggle against Iran and especially his role in it that a British journalist described Baghdad as taking on a "Stalinesque feel."[19] He even reached back to the glory days of Babylon, reconstructing the ruins with yellow bricked walls bearing the inscription "the Babylon of Nebuchadnezzar was rebuilt in the era of Saddam Hussein."[20]

At the same time he continued to live up to his self-selected sobriquet as "the Butcher of Baghdad." Amnesty International stated in its appeal to the U.N. Commission on Human Rights that "we can think of [no other violation of human rights] which cries out more for international attention and action."[21] The State Department Human Rights Bureau continued to make similar findings and points in its 1986 report and 1987 report and 1988 report and 1989 report ...

Saddam's brutalities thus were there to be known, they just were given little weight in the setting of policy.

2. This Was a Man Who Repeatedly Had Used Chemical Weapons

The 1925 Geneva Protocol Banning the Use of Chemical Weapons in War stood as one of the more successful international efforts to establish rules and norms even for warfare. The world had experienced the horrors of chemical weapons in World War I and concurred on prohibiting a recurrence. Adherence was not perfect; the Soviets appeared to have used chemical weapons in Afghanistan, the Vietnamese possibly in Cambodia/Kampuchea. But over the past sixty to seventy years it is only Saddam Hussein who has used chemical weapons so repeatedly and extensively.

The United Nations documented at least four instances of Iraqi chemical weapons attacks on Iranian forces. (Iran also used chemical weapons, but in retaliation for the Iraqi attacks.) His forces were facing defeat, and so he resorted to whatever means were available. This is a logic which, while coldly explicable in its most basic tactical calculus, is no less revealing of an amoral disregard for international norms and willingness to do whatever he deems necessary to pursue his interests. Nor did Saddam use chemical weapons just against foreign military forces, as tragically witnessed the Kurds. Eyewitness reports on the March 1988 Halabja attacks appeared in the *Washington Post* and other newspapers. A U.S. Senate investigative team issued a report on the August 1988 attacks on the Kurds. The Reagan administration even had intercepted communications between Iraqi pilots dropping some of the chemical bombs.

George Bush later would say, as he sought to raise the fear that Saddam was building nuclear weapons in an effort to build the case for going to war following the invasion of Kuwait, that this was a man who "has never possessed a weapon that he didn't use."[22] This was a new discovery?

3. He Was Seeking to Build a Massive Military Arsenal, Including Nuclear Weapons and Ballistic Missiles

With all due credit to Saddam's skillful, clandestine, intricate web of front companies, the warnings of his military buildup were ample and repeated, as summarized in the accompanying table. It is quite a list.

THE PATTERN OF WARNING ON SADDAM'S PURSUIT OF NUCLEAR WEAPONS, BALLISTIC MISSILES, AND OTHER WEAPONRY

DATE	WARNING
1970s	U.S. intelligence aware of Iraqi efforts to recruit scientists for incipient nuclear weapons program.
June 1981	After Israeli attack on Osirak, Saddam issues call to "all peace-loving nations" to help Arab world "in one way or another to obtain the nuclear bomb," and declares "no power can stop Iraq from acquiring technological and scientific know-how to serve its national objectives."
March, July 1985	Assistant Defense Secretary Perle warns that Iraq "continues to actively pursue an interest in nuclear weapons . . . and that in the past, Iraq has been somewhat less than honest in regard to the intended end-use of high technology equipment."
November 1986	Sa'ad 16 identified as main site for Condor II and other missile development programs, not university research unit and industrial facility.
March 1988	Energy Department report documents Iraqi efforts to gain illegal access to "export controlled information critical to nuclear weapons technology" from DOE national weapons laboratories.
June 1988	Customs Service sting "Operation Ali Baba" intercepts Condor II ballistic missile technology and other illegal exports.

(continued)

DATE	WARNING
July 1988	Nassr State Establishment for Mechanical Industries tagged as a "bad end-user," but the dual-use export then under consideration licensed anyway.
September 1988	Customs Service launches Operation Quarry, based on tip from company approached by Iraqi agents about selling equipment usable as nuclear triggers.
	Saddam boasts of new super weapon, which when completed would "put Iraq among only two other countries in the world."
November 1988	CIA National Intelligence Officer for Warnings expresses concern that Iraq still has not demobilized despite end of the war with Iran.
December 1988	DOE intelligence briefing that Iraq "highly motivated to pursue nuclear weapons," that it "probably can command the resources to constitute a serious effort," and that it "deserve[s] special attention."
January 1989	News stories about Iraqi biological weapons development, confirmed by U.S. government sources and independent analysts but denied by Iraqi ambassador to the United States, who claimed small village identified as main site was but honeymooners' riverside resort.

DATE	WARNING
February, March 1989	Testimony to Congress by CIA Director William H. Webster about Iraqi pursuit of technological self-sufficiency for its chemical weapons programs, and from Director of Naval Intelligence that Iraq was "actively pursuing a capability" for nuclear weapons.
April 1989	Mid-level DOE officials propose NSC review of "recent evidence indicating that Iraq has a major effort underway to produce nuclear weapons," but fail to win support from their superiors who contend that Iraq is still "10 years away" from a nuclear bomb. Consarc Corporation, approached by Iraqi agents with a $10 million order for its high-technology industrial "skull" furnaces ostensibly for manufacturing prosthetic limbs, requests advisory opinion from Bush administration because of concern that equipment could be diverted to nuclear weapons production, but is advised to go ahead with the export. At the First Baghdad International Exhibition for Military Production, Iraq parades weapons including a prototype for the Super Gun and at least 10 different Iraqi-built ballistic missiles.

(continued)

DATE	WARNING
May 1989	Hussein Kamil, Saddam's son-in-law and head of MIMI, declares goal of "implementing a defense industrial program to cover all its [Iraq's] armed forces needs for weapons and equipment by 1991."
June 1989	Export-Import Bank staff report links Iraqi creditworthiness problems to military spending constituting 39% of the gross domestic product and 60% of the government budget, and military imports consuming 42% of oil revenues.
	DIA report specifically cites Matrix-Churchill Ltd. (British based) and Matrix-Churchill Corporation (its U.S. subsidiary) as key to global front company network, yet this wasn't even first such awareness as British intelligence had been running an agent inside Matrix-Churchill since 1987 and had been sharing at least some of the intelligence with U.S.
June–September 1989	Series of CIA and DIA reports provide extensive evidence of extent of Iraqi global front company network across Europe and in U.S., and of priority efforts for nuclear weapons development.
August 1989	FBI raid on BNL-Atlanta, and evidence of over $4 billion in illegal loans to Iraq, including many for sensitive nonconventional weapons technology purchases.

DATE	WARNING
November 1989	Report by interagency Subcommittee on Nuclear Export Control (SNEC) concludes that "Iraq is acquiring nuclear related equipment and materials without regard for immediate need."
December 1989	Iraqi tests two new ballistic missiles with enhanced range and payload capacity. DOE task force established to track intelligence reports on Iraqi nuclear weapons development "died of neglect."
February 1990	U.S. intelligence detects construction of five SCUD-type fixed missile launcher complexes in western Iraq. Cable instructs American embassies to warn Western European and Japanese governments of Iraqi efforts to obtain glass-fiber technology, yet three months later same technology licensed for export by American company.
March 1990	Operation Quarry comes to fruition with intercept of shipment of 95 krytrons (nuclear triggers) crated at London's Heathrow Airport as "air conditioning parts."

(continued)

DATE	WARNING
April 1990	Saddam threatens to "make the fire eat half of Israel" and states that he now possesses binary chemical weapons.
	Parts shipments for the Super Gun intercepted in Britain, and other military equipment bound for Iraq seized in Greece, Turkey, Italy, West Germany, and Switzerland.

Sources: R. Jeffrey Smith and Glenn Frankel, "Saddam's Nuclear Weapons Dream: A Lingering Nightmare," *Washington Post,* October 13, 1991, p. A45; Defense Department memorandum, "Subject: High Technology Dual Use Exports to Iraq," July 1, 1985; U.S. Congress, House of Representatives, Committee on Energy and Commerce, *Nuclear Nonproliferation,* hearing before the Subcommittee on Oversight and Investigations, 102nd Congress, 1st Session, April 24, 1991, pp. 37–38, 48–49, 353, 476–90; *Congressional Record,* July 21, 1992, pp. H6338–46; "President Says Iraq Working on Secret New Super Weapon," *Washington Post,* September 29, 1988, p. A35; U.S. Congress, Senate, Committee on Foreign Relations, *Chemical and Biological Weapons Threat: The Urgent Need for Remedies,* Hearings, 101st Congress, 1st Session, March 1, 1989, pp. 27–45; U.S. Congress, House of Representatives, Committee on Armed Services, *HR 2461: Department of Defense Authorization for Appropriations for Fiscal Year 1990—Title I,* hearings before the Subcommittee on Seapower and Strategic and Critical Materials, 101st Congress, 1st Session, February 22, 1989, pp. 39–41. See also Glenn Frankel, "Iraq Said Developing A-Weapons," *Washington Post,* March 31, 1989, pp. A1, A32, citing Israeli sources; *Congressional Record,* August 10, 1992, p. H7873; Ruth Sinai, "Administration's Support for Iraq Ignored Multiple Early Warnings," Associated Press wire story, June 4, 1992; *FBIS-NES,* April 3, 1990, pp. 32–37.

Yet despite all these warnings, on the eve of the Iraqi invasion of Kuwait the Bush administration still maintained that "Iraq is a long-standing adherent to the NPT [Nuclear Non-Proliferation Treaty] whose nuclear energy program seems to be in full compliance with IAEA safeguards."[23]

4. *The Evidence that Saddam Was Prepared to Be a Force for Regional Peace and Security Was Well Less than Reassuring*

Saddam Hussein, George Bush declared within days of the invasion of Kuwait, was nothing short of a new Adolf Hitler. Yet while the invasion of Kuwait definitely did provide a significant new piece of data, quite a bit had been available all along. Saddam's aspirations to regional hegemony should not have been such a shock. He long had spoken of Iraq's "destiny in the Arab world" and the duty of the Iraqi army to "remain strong to defend the honor of all Arabs."[24] His war with Iran, as discussed earlier, was much more opportunistic than defensive. Similarly, as analyzed in Chapter 5, much of Saddam's ostensible moderation on Arab-Israeli peace issues had more to do with tactical maneuvering against his other regional rival, Syria, than with any substantive shift toward accepting Israel. His rhetoric still flailed against "hostile, aggressive and usurpist Zionism," and he threatened to "make the fire eat half of Israel."

Nor was he behaving moderately toward other Arab brethren. He demanded from his fellow Arab states a moratorium on his $40 billion debt, $30 billion in new economic assistance, and reallocation and stricter enforcement of OPEC quotas. "Let the Gulf regimes know," he told President Mubarak and King Hussein, "that if they do not give me this money, I will know how to get it."[25] He further escalated these demands at the May Arab League summit, and then on July 17 presented his thirty-seven-page "economic dagger in the back" letter to the Arab League, with Kuwait especially and also the United Arab Emirates singled out.

Summary

It is true that for all these warnings, there was not one which unequivocally gave date, time, or even absolute certainty of action by Saddam to invade Kuwait. But they were numerous, they were recurring, they were timely, they were credible. And they formed a pattern. Yet the Reagan and Bush administrations stayed their chosen courses.

If policymakers are so set on holding to their premises that it takes a sure-bet warning to make those premises open to question, there is something wrong with the policy process. "Sometimes we tell the policy level things that don't correspond with actual policy initiatives or thinking," a top CIA official who had been trying to shake the premises about Iraq lamented.[26] Nor was it a matter of the warnings not reaching key decision-makers. They did reach them: for example, the June 1989 DIA analysis which reportedly reached "high level Administration officials"; the September 3, 1989, CIA report to "38 Administration officials, including 7 at the National Security Council and 10 at the State Department"; the September 4, 1989, CIA report written in "stronger and more definitive language" to Secretary Baker and others.[27]

We thus must distinguish between the impossibility of perfect predictability of leaders or events and the failure to know that which is knowable. There was some failure *of* intelligence in this case. But there also was failure to use the intelligence that was available.[28]

Moreover, the available warnings and intelligence fit and provided at least initial corroboration for quite plausible alternative views of Saddam. There is, for example, much in the general international relations literature about the need dictators have for external enemies as a source of domestic legitimation. This was the essence of Mr. "X" 's analysis of "the sources of Soviet conduct."[29] It also was part of the "Third World security problematic" as more generally identified, in which concerns about internal challenges to their rule often lead Third World leaders "to become enmeshed in and, not infrequently, to generate interstate conflict."[30] One Arab scholar specifically cited Saddam as an example "of an Arab leader who used foreign policy to broaden his base of mass support." Another author observed how Saddam had used the war with Iran "to extend his own personal control and to assert his right to absolute obedience," and how internal political challenges—tensions within the armed forces, attempted coups, restiveness among the Kurds—emerged soon after the war with Iran was over.[31] Saddam himself in an April 1990 conversation with Prince Bandar of Saudi Arabia mentioned his concern that the Iraqi people needed to be "whipped up into a sort of frenzy or emotional mobilization so they will be ready for whatever happens."[32]

There also were alternative plausibilities to the "exhaustion thesis" view that economic problems would make Saddam more receptive to U.S. economic incentives. Like other authoritarian leaders, Saddam could not draw on "legitimacy based on political institutions," and thus had to base any such claim on "a capability to 'deliver the goods.'"[33] In the 1970s he had used his windfall oil wealth to pay for numerous social welfare and modernization programs. But the tremendous toll of the war with Iran had left him much less able to deliver what were far fewer goods. The U.S. economic carrots were small pickings compared to other economic benefits he could seek to obtain, and without necessarily moderating his political behavior—through his global front company network, for example, and even by seizing his neighbor Kuwait. Moreover, precisely because of key economic problems, Saddam might need the distraction of external enemies all the more. (That, for example, was a big part of the motivation of the Argentinean generals for starting the Falklands War.)

The point is not that any one of these alternative hypotheses should automatically have been accepted in place of the dominant premises, but that the Saddam-is-changing view should not have been automatically accepted. Whether the war with Iran had left Saddam consigned to turn inward or needing again to move outward should have been subjected to reality testing—both could have been true, but one was presumed to be. Only when Saddam went to the extreme of invading his neighboring country, about as unmistakable a sign of failure as there can be, were the premises seriously questioned. Until then the premise-based assumption that the policy was working did not change despite the signs, the warnings, the evidence to the contrary.

Nor was it that there were no other viable policy options. This was not strictly a pro-Saddam/anti-Saddam policy dichotomy, the only other alternative being reversion to strict antagonism. Indeed, both the alternative strategies cited as proposed from within the Reagan and Bush administrations and the reciprocity/proportionality/deterrent credibility strategy laid out in Chapter 5 offered middle-ground positions of scaling back but not abandoning efforts at accommodation. Had these been refuted on the basis of counteranalysis and deliberation, the Reagan-Bush policy could have been considered just a mistake. But they were less refuted on the merits than dismissed out of hand. Premises can be very powerful.

To be sure, policymakers cannot be expected to somehow cleanse themselves of their beliefs, values, and perceptual lenses. That is both unrealistic and undesirable. Beliefs will always be there. And they should be, as it is the core beliefs about the nature of the international system and the purposes of American power that can give coherence to American foreign policy. But there must be a greater self-consciousness about the need to subject premises to analysis and to be open to even (or, arguably, especially) dissonant information. The key is for policymakers to maintain a stronger sense of how their premises can distort their decision-making and make what could have been seen with foresight knowable only in hindsight.

The Flaws in Bureaucratic Processes

Any cognitive-level analysis, as Ole Holsti has observed, needs to be "embedded in a broader context," particularly one which addresses "the behavior of groups and organizations."[34] A second dimension to the analysis of foreign policy making thus involves the intra–executive branch ("bureaucratic") processes by which policy was formulated and implemented. It is not just what premises and perceptions decision-makers hold in their heads that shape policy, but also the processes by which they make decisions and carry the policy out.

President Bush's Foreign Policy Making Style

As with all complex organizations, the executive branch takes its principal cue from the decision-making and policy style of its "CEO," the president. George Bush generally has been given lots of credit for his foreign policy skills. Much of this was deserved. But in this case three of the flaws in his decision-making style were evident.

First, Bush tended to be "reactive, not quite passive, [but] anything but proactive," as one "seasoned" Washington political analyst put it.

> His instinct when it comes to issues is to say: "Let's let things germinate." Not, there's a problem, we better solve it; or, there might be a problem, let's do something before it becomes a problem. . . . Maybe the problem will go away. Maybe it will turn out to be less severe than we thought. If it does turn out to be worse and the time has come to act, then I'm perfectly comfortable looking at the alternatives and making a decision.[35]

This surely has advantages over impulsive decision-making, and Desert Storms can go a long way toward rectifying things. But even then there was the toll of the war as well as the realization that even such an overwhelming military victory did not resolve all the problems or undo all the gains Saddam had made during the years in which the accommodationist policy was allowed to continue on its course. There are costs that are incurred, time that is lost, options that are narrowed, opportunities that are missed when presidents are too slow to adjust the course of their policies. Indeed, similar criticisms were made of Bush's overly reactive stance toward the fall of communism in the Soviet Union and Eastern Europe, where and when he consistently seemed to be a step behind: slow to accept Gorbachev as being "for real"; pushing for NATO to stick to its "first-use" doctrine when the Warsaw Pact had ceased to exist in anything other than name; dismissing as naive the proposals for economic aid to the Soviet Union when made by German Chancellor Helmut Kohl and House Majority Leader Richard Gephardt, only to put forward his own later the same year; and, finally, slow to acknowledge Gorbachev's political weakness and to accept Yeltsin as the legitimate alternative.

Second, there were drawbacks to the "buddy system" which characterized the inner circle of foreign policy advisors on which he relied so heavily.[36] The professionalism and cohesiveness of the Bush foreign policy team in many respects were a welcome change from the infighting, and in some instances outright questions of competence, which caused such controversy during the Reagan years. Baker, Cheney, Scowcroft, Powell—all were highly respected, and all had worked with George Bush before. Questions were raised, though, as to whether this team was too tightly drawn and too homogeneous in its basic world view. Bush was quoted on how he used his close friends/top advisors as "a catalyst for decision making or bull session-ing." But the less positive view, as expressed by presidential scholar James David Barber, was that "Bush wants twins around him and that can be dangerous." William Safire similarly remarked on the "absence of creative tension [which] has generated little excitement or innova-tion . . . as a result of the Bush emphasis on the appearance of unanimity, we miss the Rooseveltian [Franklin] turbulence that often leads to original thinking."

Again there were other cases in which this criticism was made (such as Bush's policy toward China). In the Iraq case, it helps explain the pattern of unheeded warnings in two respects. One is the difficulty of getting the warnings to the attention of high-level decision-makers. Second is that when the warnings did reach top decision-makers, as with the June–September 1989 CIA and DIA reports, the elements of "groupthink" facilitated a collective minimization and even shutting out of their significance. As I have shown elsewhere involving other presidents and other cases, top-level advisors have the greatest poten-tial to mediate the premises and beliefs presidents hold.[37] But to the extent that a president's advisors hold to the same basic premises and beliefs as he does, the opportunity for constructive and broadening dissenting input is lost.

Third was Bush's predilection for leader-to-leader diplomacy, what often was referred to as his "Rolodex" diplomacy. This also had two aspects. One was his overreliance on the advice given during the July 1990 crisis period by fellow leaders King Hussein, King Fahd, and President Mubarak. There is a logic to listening to how the leaders of other Arab countries assessed Saddam's plans. They were, after all, of the same culture, and had dealt with one another longer and more closely. Yet Bush never asked whether their assessments reflected their own perspectives and agendas in ways that might affect the confidence level the United States should put in them. Might not their views of Saddam have been a function of their own premise that Arab leaders just don't invade each other? Or the interests each had in maintaining good relations with Iraq that even implicitly and not conspiratorially could have led to wishful thinking more than hard analysis?[38] Yet Bush did not ask any such probing questions; instead he automatically accepted the results of his Rolodex consultations on the basis of his inherent faith in leader-to-leader contacts as superior to the analyses even of his own intelligence agencies, which were less sanguine about Saddam's intentions.

The other aspect was Bush's belief that in the end, like other world leaders, Saddam Hussein would respond to George Bush's personal diplomacy. The July 28 cable was supposed to accomplish this. Reasonable men could reason with each other. Indeed it may well be that the extreme to which Bush went after the Kuwait invasion of equating Saddam to Hitler was a reaction to this sense of having been personally let down. While there's little doubt as to Saddam's venality, even he does not really approach Hitler, who fed millions of people into gas chambers and ovens. Ironically, Bush's personalization of diplomacy led him to stick for too long to too positive a view of what his policy could achieve with Saddam, and then to go to the other extreme in so personalizing the conflict when his expectations were dashed.

Baker's Role and Management Style

Secretary of State Baker played an enormously influential role, especially in the critical October–November 1989 die-casting decisions on NSD-26 and approval of the fiscal year 1990 $1 billion CCC package.

As traced in Chapter 3, it was through Baker's personal intervention and the intervention of his deputies in his name that intra-administration opposition to approval of the full $1 billion CCC package even in two tranches was overcome. When the Agriculture Department started to back off its own CCC program based on initial reports from the U.S. Attorney's Office in Atlanta investigating the BNL case, Baker ordered his staff to pressure the USDA "to get it back on the table . . . to 'get on with the programs.' " Yet the State official dispatched to the USDA came back with his warning about BNL as potentially "a four alarm blaze." Baker was said to have received this memo but to have reacted not with caution but by intensifying his efforts to get the CCC program approved. He personally called Agriculture Secretary Yeutter ("Done. CY: 'I think we're seeing it the same way you guys are.' JAB III"). Deputy Secretary Eagleburger pressed Treasury Deputy Secretary Robson to overcome his department's economic risk-based opposition by stressing the overriding "foreign policy grounds" and, as the ultimate rationale, that CCC was consistent with the mandate "ordered by the President in NSD-26." And then in January 1990, as concerns of others mounted, an envoy still assured the Iraqi minister of trade that "the Secretary has personally satisfied himself that no evidence has been offered imputing the Iraqi program."[39] Also, with respect to Export-Import Bank financing for Iraq, it was Baker who proposed the national interest waiver to overcome the congressional ban. And when the VOA incident occurred in February 1990, Baker readily apologized to Saddam, punished VOA by requiring his prior approval of its future editorials, and accepted the explanation that Saddam's anti-American speech at the ACC summit later that month needed to be interpreted in this hurt-feelings context, as evidence that we needed to be more intent on providing reassurances.

A second problem was Baker's style of managing the State Department. Baker operated largely through a very small circle of top aides and advisors. His predecessor, Secretary of State George Shultz, had drawn on career foreign service officers and other experts to a much greater extent than any secretary of state in recent memory. Baker's approach, however, was almost the other extreme. Deputy Secretary Lawrence Eagleburger, Under Secretaries Robert Kimmitt and Robert Zoellick, Policy Planning Director Dennis Ross, and Assistant Secretary Margaret Tutwiler were the inner circle—the "Baker half dozen," as they were called within the State Department—on which

Baker drew to a much greater and more exclusive extent than most other secretaries.

One consequence of this was the "full-plate" problem of top aides having so many issues to deal with that they simply could not give some the attention they deserved. This has been a problem for other administrations—for example, with the fall of the Shah in 1978–79 when the Carter administration was too absorbed in the Camp David negotiations and SALT II to focus adequately and in a timely manner on events in Iran.[40] For all the other advantages of America's global reach, the United States must be conscious of the inherent problem that "with its global horizons, it is difficult for a superpower to pay equal attention to all regions, whereas regional powers with their horizons restricted to their immediate neighbors have a more intense interest in calculating the regional balance of power correctly."[41] Indeed, the world Baker and Bush were faced with in 1989–90 was in a state of almost unprecedented flux. The changes in the Soviet Union and Europe received (and deserved) primary attention. "In another administration," two close observers remarked, "more junior officials might have been able to seize control of the issue and force the Secretary of State to concentrate on it. But that was not possible in Baker's State Department."[42] The same top aide, Dennis Ross, the director of policy planning, was holding the Soviet, European, Arab-Israeli, and Persian Gulf portfolios. Even under normal circumstances such a range of portfolios would have been quite substantial. Amidst the nearly unprecedented rapidity of global change that thrust itself upon American foreign policy in 1989–90, it was virtually impossible for any individual on whom a secretary of state relied so heavily to give all these regions the attention they required. As but one example, Saddam's May 28, 1990, Arab League summit speech with its threats against Kuwait and anti-American diatribe was given the same day as Soviet President Mikhail Gorbachev arrived in Washington, D.C., for a summit. The very fact that Ross is as widely respected as he is yet even he ran into the limits of a full plate makes the point even more.

Moreover, even among those working on the Middle East, Iraq was not a top priority. They knew, as one official put it, that "to the extent that he [Baker] worried about the Middle East at all, it was about how you could get peace talks going between Israel and the Palestinians."[43] The Near East Bureau still at this time was also responsible for South Asia, and, as it was later revealed, in May 1990 India and Pakistan had slid to the edge of a dangerous conflict which according to some reports risked becoming a nuclear war.[44]

It is these aspects that make Baker's "20/20 hindsight" claim so disturbing and disingenuous. To the extent that he didn't have the foresight to see the need for adjustment in U.S. policy, it was not because it was not possible to do so. Indeed, at least as much as any other single individual, James Baker bears responsibility for the failure of U.S. policy toward Iraq.

Bureaucratic Malfunction

The Iraqi case also was full of the kinds of malfunctions which give bureaucracy a bad name.

It in particular exemplified the problems which have plagued export control policy. Some have criticized the system for too often controlling what it shouldn't. Others have criticized it for too often not controlling what it should. Both are right, as the Iraqi case demonstrates but by no means exhausts.

American exporters long have complained about too many regulations, too many government agencies, too many delays in the export control system. This was, for example, a major issue in the 1970s when as part of détente there were efforts both to liberalize the scope of controls on exports to the Soviet Union and to streamline the licensing process to generally reduce the delays and other inefficiencies. In the 1979 version of the Export Administration Act, for example, six of the nine declarations in the preamble were statements about the importance of exports to the American economy—for example, "it is the policy of the United States that export trade by United States citizens be given a high priority." Yet still in 1991 a National Academy of Sciences study found that "export controls can, in some circumstances, impose significant burdens on the [U.S.] economy." A House Government Operations Committee report the same year cited cases in which "U.S. companies have waited years to obtain a license while interagency groups—or even the President—have struggled to resolve interagency disputes over the disposition of their application."[45]

On the other hand, quite a few exports were reaching adversaries like Iraq which shouldn't have. Part of the reason for this was the increasingly anachronistic design of a system geared primarily against the cold war threat of Soviet acquisition of dual-use technologies at a time when the Soviet threat was on the decline yet new security threats such as rogue-state proliferators like Iraq were on the rise. Some anti-proliferation controls had been adopted, such as the MTCR (ballistic missiles), Nuclear Referral (nuclear weapons), and Australia Group (chemical weapons) lists. Even these, however, still left a broad range of dual-use technologies which had potential nuclear and other nonconventional weaponry applications, but for which there were inadequate statutory bases for control. The main basis for control still was the risk of diversion to the Soviet Union. But with countries like Iraq, while this risk was low, the risk of its own use for its own military programs was high. This was the issue raised by Assistant Defense Secretary Perle in March 1985 when, as recounted in Chapter 1, he proposed that Iraq be required to give its own non-nuclear assurance. It also was raised in a 1988 export licensing case discussed in Chapter 2 involving the "bad end-user" (DOD quote) NASSR state complex but in which a Commerce official held that even the fact that NASSR was "under the Military Industry Commission is not grounds for denial."[46] The problem was addressed more generally in 1991 congressional testimony by Defense Deputy Under Secretary for Trade Security Policy William N. Rudman, under questioning by House Foreign Affairs International Economic Policy Subcommittee Chairman Sam Gejdenson:

MR. GEJDENSON: Let's go to the export dual-use issue. From 1985 to 1990, the U.S. Government approved 771 licenses to Iraq. Of the 771, the Department of Defense reviewed 487 pursuant to a 1985 national security directive.... Didn't the Department of Defense concur in all but 11 of these licenses?

MR. RUDMAN: Yes, but you need a further explanation, sir. It is important to remember that our role was limited to review based on the risk of diversion to the Soviet Union or other proscribed destinations.

MR. GEJDENSON: So your hands were tied also?

MR. RUDMAN: The review was limited, sir.

MR. GEJDENSON: Your review was limited because there were no foreign policy controls to deal with Iraq or other countries of that nature?

MR. RUDMAN: It was based on an Administration decision back in 1985, sir.

MR. GEJDENSON: Didn't Defense have the opportunity to pursue all of the 11 to high levels within the Administration how they wanted to?

MR. RUDMAN: Well, again, it is a question of—we had no legal authority once it was determined that there was no threat of diversion.[47]

One basis for broader authority was a country being on the state terrorism list. But Iraq had been taken off the list in 1982.

Another part of the problem being manifested was the tension between the competing policy priorities of export promotion and nonproliferation. On the one hand, exports to Iraq were to be promoted for both the political and the economic gains to be made from trade. There was the war effort with Iran to be buttressed, political influence to be gained, markets to be tapped. These priorities inclined toward a narrow range of controls: when in doubt, don't control; set the threshold of potential military significance high. On the other hand, there were the concerns about proliferation, which inclined toward controlling when in doubt according to a lower threshold for military significance. The tension between these priorities was strongly reflected in the November 1989 interagency Subcommittee on Nuclear Export Control (SNEC) memo cited in Chapter 4, expressing frustration over how to fulfill the NSD-26 mandate of "improving relations with Iraq, including trade" while abiding by standing SNEC policy "not to approve exports for Iraq's nuclear program."[48]

The old adage of bureaucratic politics that "where you stand depends on where you sit" was quite evident in the different positions taken by different executive branch actors on Iraqi policy.[49] It was, for example, DOD which most consistently raised objections about proliferation and other military significance of dual-use exports. Yet often these positions were written off by others within the executive branch as "typical" DOD overconcern with potential military applications, as for example with the reaction to Assistant Defense Secretary Perle's concerns as simply using the anti-proliferation argument as "quite convenient" and his real agenda being "to block any high-tech sales to Iraq."[50] The Commerce Department, in contrast, often took a very narrow view of potential military significance, as in the glass-fiber factory and Consarc furnace cases, which it licensed without even referring them to DOD. Commerce has within its jurisdiction both export promotion and export control responsibilities. Its strong tendency, irrespective of a Republican or Democrat administration, has been to give higher priority to the former than the latter.

Similar patterns played out on the CCC credit guarantees. The USDA's top priority was the well-being of its CCC program. Initially this meant pushing for the full fiscal year 1990 $1 billion. When it began backing off the proposal and had to be pressured to stand by it by Secretary of State Baker, brandishing the NSD-26 mandate, it was because by then the BNL investigations had raised concerns of a "HUD-or-S&L-type scandal" which risked extremely damaging fallout for other CCC programs. Then in May 1990 the NSC staff, also having the NSD-26 objective of improving relations still in mind, had to pressure the USDA not to issue a tough report on Iraqi abuses of the CCC program. The Federal Reserve and the Treasury, both of which are key players in NAC, equally predictably were the strongest voices expressing concern about the economic risks of further lending to Iraq. It took high-level intervention to finally bring Treasury around, and even then it was with obvious reluctance.

This process is more natural than sinister. Whether it is traced to an instrumental defending of the interests to which a department or agency is most closely connected, or more a matter of premises and perspectives at the bureaucratic level, the problem that results is one of capacity to aggregate the national interest. It is, of course, ideal when policy priorities are complementary and can be equally served by a particular policy option. The ideal, however, tends to be more the exception than the rule. Indeed, one of the dilemmas of the post–cold war world is that both the threat of proliferation and the importance of export competitiveness and aggressiveness are increasing. Iraq, Iran, Libya, North Korea: The threats posed by rogue-state proliferators keep increasing. Yet in a world in which economic competition has intensified and the American economy has become more export dependent than even before, economic trade-offs in the name of security objectives are not so readily absorbed.

A further part of the bureaucratic problem is one of coordination. Even to the extent that common priorities are held and common objectives are set during the policy formulation stage, there often are problems of coordination among the numerous executive branch departments and agencies in the implementation of policy.

There again were numerous examples in the Iraq case of this lack of coordination within the executive branch. Perhaps the most glaring was the Iran arms-for-hostages affair. Here was a clandestine operation being run out of the Reagan White House, providing Iran within substantial weaponry, right at a time in the Iran-Iraq war when State Department officials warned about Iranian military victories and trends in the war raising the specter of an Iraqi defeat, precisely the outcome U.S. policy was intended to avert. Here were Secretaries Shultz and Weinberger pressuring allies to cooperate with the Operation Staunch arms embargo against Iran, yet Oliver North et al. were personally delivering weapons to the Iranians. North even promised his Iranian interlocutors to help get rid of Saddam Hussein, a goal which, whatever merit it may have been argued to have, was not particularly well coordinated with the rest of U.S. policy. And while in this instance the lack of coordination was intentional, it proved to be no less of a problem at the time, and especially later on.

Another major example involved the CIA and the Justice Department with respect to the BNL-Atlanta case.[51] One of the key questions in the BNL case concerned what the Bush administration knew about the $4 billion worth of illegal lending to Iraq prior to the actual August 1989 bank raid. As the trial proceeded, it was revealed that the CIA had withheld information from the Atlanta prosecutors and the presiding judge, Federal District Court Judge Marvin Shoob. The CIA then claimed that it had done so only under pressure from a senior Justice Department official. The charge was denied by Justice. The charges and countercharges were highly public and, at minimum, showed huge intra-administration problems in getting their stories in sync. Others, such as Judge Shoob, saw "grave questions" being raised as to whether "decisions were made at the top levels of the United States Justice Department, State Department, and within the intelligence community to shape this case."[52]

And there were other instances as well of failed coordination:

- the Iraqi scientists invited to the August 1989 Department of Energy symposium at which numerous papers were presented on nuclear explosive technologies, despite their institute having previously been identified by U.S. intelligence agencies as part of the Iraqi nuclear weapons complex;
- the Customs Service, which had front-line responsibility for export control enforcement, not receiving the intelligence agencies' reports on Matrix-Churchill until after the invasion of Kuwait;
- the glass-fiber technology case, in which the Bush State Department beseeched allies to block its potential export, but the Bush Commerce Department approved the same export by an American company in a deal brokered by Matrix-Churchill;

- the various separate investigations of the BNL affair by the Agriculture Department, the Customs Service, the Justice Department, the Federal Reserve, the Treasury Department, and others.

Again one need not assume sinister motives to explain this policy process failing. But whatever the explanation, the consequences of such poor policy coordination are numerous. Information that could contribute to successful decisions and implementation is not effectively utilized. Parts of the same government can find themselves working at cross purposes. Credibility is damaged in the eyes of allies who perceive the U.S. position as do-as-I-say-not-as-I-do.

Summary

Many critiques have been made of the bureaucratic politics and other organizational process literature. Some of the theories and paradigms do overreach in their broad claims of explanatory power. But the fact remains that even under that ideal set of policymakers, bereft of flawed premises and other cognitive distortions, process still would matter.

Some of the process problems in the Iraq policy case were traceable to particular characteristics of the Reagan and Bush administrations. The picture painted herein especially of President Bush and Secretary of State Baker is rather different from that yielded by Operations Desert Shield and Desert Storm and other foreign policy successes. My point is not to seek to refute that dominant image of foreign policy skillfulness—but it is, as a matter of historical assessment, to fill it out and appropriately qualify it.

The bureaucratic malfunction problems had their particular manifestations in this case but hardly were unique to it or to these administrations. In this respect, they have even greater significance for our thinking about foreign policy making. How are competing economic and security objectives like export promotion and nonproliferation to be balanced? Interagency processes can be structured and refined to ensure that a range of views are heard as policy is formulated. But redrawing organizational charts is one thing, making them work is another.

Similarly with the coordination problem. The executive branch is truly a mammoth entity, with difficulties of coordination even within departments let alone on an interagency basis. Even when the will is there, the coordination problem is a formidable one. There also are times when, for turf protection and other reasons, the will is not there.

And all this is even without the additional complexities of the politics of working under pressures from interest groups and with Congress.

The Politics of Interest Group Pressures and Divided Government

It has been quite a while since politics "stopped at the water's edge." Whether for better or worse can be debated, but the reality is that foreign policy has become more and more a part of American politics. There still are situations in which the nation "rallies round the flag," but such consensus is far from the norm. Foreign policy politics often are no less about "who gets what, where, when, why, and how" than are domestic policy politics. It thus is hardly unnatural that interests groups bring their pressure to bear, and that presidents and the Congress compete and conflict.

Interest Groups and the Reverse Leverage Paradox

While the level of interest group activity on Iraq policy was less than on many foreign policy issues, interest groups still had their impact. The anti-sanctions lobbying against the 1988 chemical weapons sanctions bill, as discussed in Chapter 2, was the most striking example. Both agricultural and manufacturing groups mobilized to oppose the sanctions, and had substantial impact on the House's watering down of the tough Senate sanctions bill and the eventual defeat of any sanctions bill. Group pressure also was brought to bear every other time sanctions were considered, including on the eve of the Iraqi invasion of Kuwait.

The paradoxical result was that the trade relations which were supposed to bring increased political influence ended up as a further influence-reducing constraint. The assumption was that Iraq wanted and needed the trade so badly that it would make political concessions (be they explicit or tacit) to get it and then keep it. But such an assumption omitted the U.S. domestic groups who also directly benefited from the trade, and who would want to get and keep it at least as much as the Iraqis. This was the essence of the reverse leverage paradox, in which political influence arguably *decreased* as trade expanded. Indeed, a state which boasts or threatens about the power that it has ("trade is our most important source of influence over Iraq"), but then is unwilling and/or unable to exercise any such power at points of conflict, can be worse off than if the boast/threat had never been made. As Bruce Russett and Harvey Starr argue in a more general context, when domestic pressures "prevent a government from pursuing certain policies or using certain capabilities, the credibility of that government declines in the eyes of the other states. Its ability to influence them declines as its reputation as a 'bluffer' grows."[53]

It need be said that there was nothing inherently negative or abnormal about U.S. interest groups defending their interests. It is the way of American politics. But that, too, is the point. A strategy cannot be based on the utility of trade as leverage over another state if, when it comes time to exert that leverage, the domestic political pressures from groups which have developed interests in the continuation of that trade are likely to be so great as to be constraining, if not prohibitive.

It should also be noted how many instances there were in which American companies which had been offered lucrative but suspicious export contracts looked beyond their own particularistic benefits and took the initiative to notify federal officials about their military diversion concerns. This was the origin of the Operation Quarry sting which led to the March 1990 intercept of the krytrons shipment (nuclear triggers). The Consarc furnace case also developed only after Consarc executives had raised their concerns about nuclear weapons applications of their products, concerns which were dismissed by Bush administration officials. We thus should resist any simplistic equating of corporate political behavior with corporate economic interests.

Pennsylvania Avenue Diplomacy

Neither the Reagan nor the Bush administration took a particularly positive view of Congress's role in foreign affairs. The Reagan administration was especially confrontational, with the bitter battles over Nicaragua and South Africa as memorable examples.[54] Even in general when Ronald Reagan called for "bipartisanship," for "Republicans and Democrats standing united in patriotism and speaking with one voice," the one voice was meant to be his, with Congress merely joining in at the refrains. George Bush pledged in his inaugural address to change all this with "the age of the offered hand."[55] He also moved quickly to forge bipartisan compromises to defuse the Nicaragua and South Africa political albatross carryover issues. But Bush proved to be no less a jealous guardian of executive prerogatives, vetoing numerous foreign policy bills, in part on policy grounds and in part, as he put it in one veto message, for "intrud[ing] into areas entrusted by the Constitution exclusively to the executive."[56]

Ironically, had Reagan and Bush been more open to a congressional role in their Iraq policy, the policy would have benefited greatly. It was Congress which wanted to hold Saddam to the standards of being off the state terrorism list, so that there would have been a greater degree of reciprocity between what we got in return for what we gave. But it was told repeatedly, as in the 1985 letter from Secretary of State Shultz to Congressman Berman (Chapter 1), that to do so legislatively would excessively hamper presidential discretion, and that "I assure you" the executive will take care of it on our own.[57] It was Congress which sought economic sanctions to hold Saddam accountable for gassing the Kurds, but was told that its methods would be "counterproductive."[58] It was Congress that was much more concerned with the proliferation risks of dual-use technology exports, but was told that it was unduly worried. It was Congress which again sought to impose sanctions in late July 1990, when Saddam's troops were poised to invade Kuwait, but which was told that even these sanctions would get in the president's way. Indeed, George Bush even vetoed a chemical weapons sanctions bill after the Iraqi invasion of Kuwait in the midst of the Desert Shield buildup in part on the grounds that its mandatory nature would unduly constrain presidential authority.[59]

Nor was it only the overt conflicts that soured relations with Congress. Worse in many respects were the breaches of trust. The most egregious was Iran-Contra. The institutional ill will left by Iran-Contra cannot be underestimated.[60] Part of Congress's reluctance to support the 1987–88 Kuwaiti reflagging mission was a reaction to what it saw as an effort to recoup the damage done to U.S. regional interests by Iran-Contra. What was the Reagan administration up to now, could it be trusted to consult and be truthful, would Congress again be deceived? Trust in a political relationship is no less crucial, and no less difficult to repair once violated, than in personal relationships.

There also were other trust-breaching incidents, less profound but still sketching a pattern. The 1985 Shultz to Berman letter claimed that Iraq "had effectively disassociated itself from international terrorism," yet the administration's own internal study called the shifts in Iraqi policy "painfully slow."[61] In February 1990 Agriculture Secretary Clayton Yeutter assured Senate Agriculture Committee Chairman Patrick Leahy (D-Virginia) that foreign policy considerations were not affecting USDA willingness to continue the CCC program for Iraq despite the BNL scandal and other allegations. Yet, at the November 8, 1989, NAC meeting, his own deputy had cited foreign policy considerations as the main reason for USDA support for the fiscal year 1990 $1 billion package. Still another example, this one even censured by the department's own inspector-general, was the Commerce Department's alteration of export license records subpoenaed by a congressional committee in an attempt to conceal the military significance of the exports.

When all is said and done, it is trust that is key to presidential-congressional relations.[62] A Congress that trusts a president is more likely to grant him a greater degree of discretion. For its part, Congress must restrain the other incentives that too often lead it into micromanagement. Interbranch conflict needs to be limited and managed as well as possible, but we must shed the myth that it is a systemic malfunction. This myth grew out of the so-called golden age of bipartisanship, during the early cold war, when presidents and Congresses shared a foreign policy consensus across party lines. But while the proximity of this period made it seem the norm, in the long sweep of American history it appears much more the exception than the rule. From the 1797 Jay Treaty to the 1919 Versailles Treaty, from the 1840s Mexican War to the 1930s Neutrality Acts, presidents and Congresses repeatedly have vied with each other to fill in the details of that blueprint. Only during wartime do we see more of a consistent historical pattern of presidential-congressional consensus. It was the unique circumstances of the early cold war as being seen as the functional and moral equivalent of war, combined with the more general post-FDR "cult of the presidency" glorifying presidential power, that caused such a departure from the more typical conflictual peacetime foreign policy politics. Indeed, no less a later critic of "the imperial Presidency" than Senator J. William Fulbright still as late as 1961 reflected on whether, because of the exigencies we faced, "we must give the Executive a measure of power in the conduct of our foreign affairs that we have hitherto jealously withheld."[63] To be sure, the deep and bitter conflicts of the Vietnam era were worse than normal. But ultimately we come back to Edward Corwin's classic analysis of the Constitution as "an invitation to struggle for the privilege of directing American foreign policy," or to Louis Henkin's more recent assessment of it as a "starkly incomplete, indeed skimpy . . . blueprint for the governance of our foreign affairs."[64] In the early days of the Clinton administration it already was clear that even with a president and Congress of the same political party for the first time in twelve years, they still were going to have their share of foreign policy conflicts.

A second myth is that presidential-congressional conflict on foreign policy is inherently a negative thing. It definitely can be, and we have at times shown ourselves to be "our own worst enemy."[65] But, as a starting point, it is to be recognized that the "golden age" was not as purely golden as often depicted. It did, after all, include the visceral experience of McCarthyism. The country also learned the hard way, in Vietnam and elsewhere, the risks of bipartisanship and congressional deference when it means blank checks of discretionary authority for presidents. Moreover, there have been numerous instances in which interbranch conflict has led to "constructive compromises" around policies which turned out to be more in the national interest than either of the original alternatives being pushed (such as U.S. policy toward the Philippines in the 1980s).[66] In some instances policy and ideological differences are so sharp that political conflict is intense and policy compromise difficult. But often the difference is a matter of how both presidents and congressional leaders approach the process, whether they seek principally to win politically and thus intentionally emphasize ideological rifts and exacerbate antagonisms, or whether there is a basic recognition at both ends of Pennsylvania Avenue of the value and legitimacy of the other's institutional role. These roles are fundamentally different, and presidents always should have the stronger and dominant foreign policy role. But it must be taken as a given that Congress will play a substantial foreign policy role. The challenge, therefore, is one of making the conflict inherent in this institutional power sharing as constructive as possible.

Lessons: Diplomacy Begins at Home

I have never subscribed to the view of democracy, and American democracy in particular, espoused by Alexis de Tocqueville as inherently ill suited for foreign policy. "Foreign policy demands scarcely any of those qualities which are peculiar to a democracy," de Tocqueville wrote. "They require, on the contrary, the perfect use of almost all those in which it is deficient." Were this true, of course, we should wonder why the fostering and promotion of such ill-suited forms of government has been such a priority goal of American foreign policy for most of this century!

On the other hand, there is the now-heralded Kantian view that "democracies do not fight each other" and that therefore the more democracies there are in the world, the less likely war becomes.[67] The process may be messy, but the product can't be all bad if it works against war. Indeed, the messiness of the process itself has been reassessed by a number of scholars, who have shown how democracy can and has had positive effects on U.S. foreign policy.[68]

Analyses such as in this book of failings in foreign policy making thus should prompt reform rather than despair. The problems of process are difficult, but they are not unchangeable. One of the qualms often expressed about foreign policy strategies such as the mixed reciprocity/proportionality/deterrence credibility strategy developed herein is whether it is too nuanced for the American foreign policy process to handle. But if a strategy is substantively sound, the question needs to become how can the process be improved so as to be able to execute that set of policy options most in the national interest.

Recognition of the distorting effects of premises on decision-making would not only improve one's capacity to deal with rogue states like Iraq, it would improve foreign policy making more generally. The problem is not unique to Republican or Democrat administrations. All top policymakers bring to their positions arrays of beliefs, assumptions, hypotheses, and hunches about how best to pursue American interests, who our friends are, what our policies should be. No one could function in such demanding and complex positions without such a framework. The key is to be able to discern premises from postulates, to be sensitive to the distinction between that which can be taken as a given and that which needs to be tested against reality. While some procedural mechanisms likely could be developed to facilitate this process, ultimately it is a matter of self-consciousness by top policymakers of the power their premises can have over them.

As to bureaucratic process, we again need to be realistic in the sense of acknowledging the inherence of the problems yet also in affirming the essential importance of making process better serve policy. Each president and secretary of state brings his own decision-making style to his office. But while that sets the basic approach, it does not necessarily have to be taken as immutable. If a president or secretary of state draws too narrow a circle, the president in the White House and the secretary of state within his own department, they can be advised to widen it in a manner and to a degree which do not take them to an artificial or uncomfortable extreme. Similarly, it is one thing to recognize the difficulties of making "the bureaucracy" function well, but quite another to concede that nothing can be done. When turf battles and parochialism run rampant, foreign policy suffers. That is adequate rationale in itself for bureaucratic reform.

So, too, with the politics of foreign policy, which will not stop at the water's edge much in the future either. When the United States confronts a clear and present danger, threatening its own security or its vital interests, the public, the Congress, and the president are best able to forge consensus. But in other instances—that is, in most of foreign policy—the politics more and more resemble those of domestic policy. Different groups have different interests at stake and bring pressure to bear. Even when the same political party controls both ends of Pennsylvania Avenue, Congress and the president still have institutional power sharing and political competition to work out.

Diplomacy needs to begin at home. When it does not, as it did not in the Iraqi case, we see the results.

American policy toward Iraq from 1982 to 1990 failed. It failed because it was flawed in both its concepts and its execution. But it didn't have to fail. And there are lessons to be derived from why it failed, so that we *do* learn from history and are *not* condemned to repeat it.

Notes

Introduction: "The Enemy of My Enemy . . ."

1. National Security Directive (NSD) 26, declassified version, signed by President Bush on October 2, 1989.
2. See Saddam Hussein, "Speech to ACC Summit," February 24, 1990, *Foreign Broadcast Information Service—Near East Section (FBIS—NES)*, February 27, 1990, pp. 1–5; Saddam Hussein, "Speech to Arab Summit in Baghdad," May 28, 1990, *FBIS—NES*, May 29, 1990, pp. 2–7.
3. For an early initial raising of these questions, see Larry Berman and Bruce W. Jentleson, "Bush and the Post–Cold War World: New Challenges for American Leadership," in Colin Campbell and Bert A. Rockman, eds., *The Bush Presidency: First Appraisals* (Chatham, N J: Chatham House Publishers, 1991), pp. 118–21.
4. Transcript of the third 1992 presidential campaign debate, *New York Times*, October 20, 1992, p. A24.
5. This is not in any way to lend credence to the attempts by such critics as Ramsey Clark to blame the United States primarily and even exclusively for the costs of the war. The "blame America always and especially" ideology of such leftism is no more genuinely analytic than the "blame America never" ideology of many ardent conservatives. See, for example, the commentary of Jim Hoagland, "Ramsey Clark: Wrong Again," *Washington Post*, March 23, 1993, p. A21.
6. Baker's statement on October 29, 1990, cited in Thomas L. Friedman, "Baker Seen as Balancing Bush's Urge to Fight Iraq," *New York Times*, No-

vember 3, 1990, p. 6; Bush statement during the third presidential debate, *New York Times,* October 20, 1992, p. A24.

7. Defense Department memorandum, "Subject: High Technology Dual Use Export to Iraq," July 1, 1985.

8. State Department memorandum, "Meeting with Iraqi Under Secretary Hamdoon," March 23, 1989.

9. Friedman, "Baker Seen as Balancing Bush's Urge to Fight Iraq."

10. Janice Gross Stein, "Deterrence and Compellence in the Gulf, 1990–91: A Failed or Impossible Task?," *International Security,* 17 (Fall 1992), pp. 147–79; Lawrence Freedman and Efraim Karsh, *The Gulf Conflict, 1990–1991: Diplomacy and War in the New World Order* (London: Faber and Faber, 1993), pp. 42–63; Milton Viorst, "Report from Baghdad," *The New Yorker,* June 24, 1991, pp. 55–73.

11. *Restoring the Balance: U.S. Strategy and the Gulf Crisis,* Initial Report of the Washington Institute's Strategic Study Group (Washington, D.C.: Washington Institute for Near East Policy, 1991), p. 13 (emphasis added).

12. Paul K. Davis and John Arquilla, *Deterring or Coercing Opponents in Crisis: Lessons from the War with Saddam Hussein* (Santa Monica, CA: Rand Corporation, 1991), R-4111-JS, p. 6 (1991 was the publication date of the unclassified version of the study).

13. Tutwiler statement on July 24, cited in *New York Times,* September 23, 1990, p. 18; Kelly testimony in U.S. Congress, House of Representatives, *Developments in the Middle East, July 1990,* hearing before the Subcommittee on Europe and the Middle East of the Committee on Foreign Affairs, 101st Congress, 2nd Session, July 31, 1990, pp. 6, 14; Bush July 28 cable in *Washington Post,* October 21, 1992, p. A17.

14. George F. Kennan, *American Diplomacy, 1900–1950* (Chicago: University of Chicago Press, 1951), p. vii.

15. Stephen M. Walt, *The Origins of Alliances* (Ithaca, NY: Cornell University Press, 1987); Kenneth Waltz, *Theory of International Politics* (Reading, MA: Addison-Wesley, 1979); Hans. J. Morgenthau, *Politics Among Nations,* 5th edition (New York: Alfred A. Knopf, 1985); F. H. Hinsley, *Power and the Pursuit of Peace; Theory and Practice in the History of Relations between States* (Cambridge: Cambridge University Press, 1963).

16. State Department memorandum, "Iraq's Foreign Policy: Deeper into the Mainstream," March 3, 1988.

17. Winston Churchill put it in very similar terms: "If Hitler invaded Hell, I should at least make a favorable reference to the Devil in the House of Commons"; Walt, *The Origins of Alliances,* p. 38.

18. Kennan, *American Diplomacy,* p. 86.

19. Alexander L. George, *Bridging the Gap: Theory and Practice in Foreign Policy* (Washington, D.C.: U.S. Institute of Peace, 1993), pp. 117–18.

20. Unnamed source, quoted in Don Oberdorfer, "Missed Signals in the Middle East," *Washington Post Magazine*, March 17, 1991, p. 40.

1: Reagan, Saddam, and the Iran-Iraq War, 1982–88

1. The other members were Turkey, Pakistan, Iran, and Britain. The United States was not a formal member.
2. U.S. Department of Defense, *Conduct of the Persian Gulf War*, Final Report to Congress Pursuant to Title V of the Persian Gulf Conflict Supplemental Authorization and Personnel Benefits Act of 1991 (PL 101-25), Chapters I–VII, p. 6. See also Dilip Hiro, *Desert Shield to Desert Storm: The Second Gulf War* (London: HarperCollins, 1992), Chapter 1.
3. Efraim Karsh and Inauri Rautsi, *Saddam Hussein: A Political Biography* (New York: Free Press, 1991), pp. 64–65.
4. Judith Miller and Laurie Mylroie, *Saddam Hussein and the Crisis in the Gulf* (New York: Times Books, 1990), pp. 141–42.
5. Oles M. Smolansky, with Bettie M. Smolansky, *The USSR and Iraq: The Soviet Quest for Influence* (Durham, NC: Duke University Press, 1991), pp. 17–19.
6. James A. Bill, *The Eagle and the Lion: The Tragedy of American-Iranian Relations* (New Haven: Yale University Press, 1988); Barry Rubin, *Paved with Good Intentions: The American Experience and Iran* (Hammondsworth, England: Penguin Books, 1980).
7. 1982 letter to members of Congress from Kenneth Duberstein, Reagan administration chief of congressional relations, cited in "Congress and Iraq: A Chronology," *Congressional Quarterly Weekly Report*, April 27, 1992, p. 1070.
8. Former Assistant Secretary of Defense Noel Koch, quoted in Guy Gugliotta et al., "At War, Iraq Courted U.S. into Economic Embrace," *Washington Post*, September 16, 1990, p. A34.
9. John E. Rielly, ed., *American Public Opinion and U.S. Foreign Policy, 1983* (Chicago: Chicago Council on Foreign Relations, 1983), p. 19.
10. Quoted in "An Open Eye on Baghdad," editorial, *New York Times*, May 5, 1980, p. A18.
11. Jimmy Carter, *Keeping Faith: Memoirs of a President* (New York: Bantam Books, 1982), p. 506.
12. Quoted in Kenneth R. Timmerman, *The Death Lobby: How the West Armed Iraq* (Boston: Houghton Mifflin, 1991), pp. 76–77.
13. John Bulloch and Harvey Morris, *Saddam's War: The Origins of the Kuwait Conflict and the International Response* (London: Faber and Faber, 1991), pp. 75–76.
14. Carter, *Keeping Faith*, pp. 558–59.
15. Ibid., p. 559.

16. Gary Sick, *All Fall Down: America's Tragic Encounter with Iran* (New York: Penguin Books, 1986), pp. 368–70; Zbigniew Brzezinski, *Power and Principle: Memoirs of the National Security Advisor, 1977–1981* (New York: Farrar, Strauss and Giroux, 1983), p. 504.

17. Sick, *All Fall Down*, p. 370.

18. Brzezinski, *Power and Principle*, pp. 452–53.

19. Carter, *Keeping Faith*, p. 559.

20. Brzezinski, *Power and Principle*, p. 506.

21. Cited in Lawrence Freedman and Efraim Karsh, *The Gulf Conflict: Diplomacy and War in the New World Order* (London: Faber and Faber, 1993), p. 7.

22. Joseph J. Sisco, "Middle East: Progress or Lost Opportunities?," *Foreign Affairs*, 61 (America and the World 1982), pp. 611–40. The Iranian threat was a key factor prompting Saudi Arabia, Kuwait, Oman, Bahrain, Qatar, and the United Arab Emirates to create a new regional alliance, the Gulf Cooperation Council (GCC), in February 1982.

23. Cited in Timmerman, *The Death Lobby*, p. 57; see also Richard K. Herrmann, *Perceptions and Behavior in Soviet Foreign Policy* (Pittsburgh: University of Pittsburgh Press, 1985), pp. 148–49, 153–54.

24. Amazia Baram, "Iraq: Between East and West," in Efraim Karsh, ed., *The Iran-Iraq War: Impact and Implications* (New York: St. Martin's, 1989), p. 78; Adeed Dawisha, "Iraq: The West's Opportunity," *Foreign Policy*, 41 (Winter 1980–81), p. 138.

25. Baram, "Iraq: Between East and West," p. 79.

26. Stephen R. Grummon, *The Iran-Iraq War: Islam Embattled* (New York: Praeger, 1982), p. 60.

27. In his January 23, 1980, State of the Union speech, President Carter declared that "any attempt by an outside force to gain control of the Persian Gulf will be regarded as an assault on the vital interests of the United States of America and such an assault will be repelled by any means necessary, including military force."

28. Both cited in Smolansky, *The USSR and Iraq*, p. 232.

29. *Pravda*, October 11, 1980, cited in Karen Dawisha, "Moscow and the Gulf War," *The World Today* (January 1981), p. 13.

30. Smolansky, *The USSR and Iraq*, p. 233. Smolansky also sees the Israeli bombing of the Iraqi Osirak nuclear reactor/nuclear weapons plant, which occurred in June 1981, as a factor.

31. Ibid., p. 237.

32. "Chronology 1982," *Foreign Affairs*, 61 (America and the World 1982), p. 726.

33. Karsh and Rautsi, *Saddam Hussein: A Political Biography*, p. 4.

34. Ibid.

35. Bulloch and Morris, *Saddam's War*, p. 27; see also Samir al-Khalil, *Republic*

of Fear: The Inside Story of Saddam's Iraq (Berkeley: University of California Press, 1989).

36. Adeed Dawisha, *The Arab Radicals* (New York: Council on Foreign Relations, 1986), p. 30.

37. A. Dawisha, "Iraq: The West's Opportunity," p. 150.

38. Alan R. Taylor, "Political Currents in the Arab World Before the Iraqi Invasion of Kuwait," in Robert F. Helms II and Robert H. Dorf, eds. *The Persian Gulf Crisis: Power in the Post–Cold War World* (Westport, CT: Praeger, 1993), p. 86.

39. Elaine Sciolino, *The Outlaw State: Saddam Hussein's Quest for Power and the Gulf Crisis* (New York: John Wiley and Sons, 1991), p. 140.

40. Christine Moss Helms, *Iraq: Eastern Flank of the Arab World* (Washington, D.C.: Brookings Institution, 1984), p. 23. Many holy Shi'ite shrines are within Iraq, in such cities as Karbala, Samara, Najaf, and also Baghdad.

41. For this view see A. Dawisha, "Iraq: The West's Opportunity," and Freedman and Karsh, *The Gulf Conflict,* pp. 19–22. For a strong refutation, see Richard W. Cottam, "Levels of Conflict in the Middle East," in Joseph Coffey and Gianni Bonvicini, eds., *The Atlantic Alliance and the Middle East* (Pittsburgh: University of Pittsburgh Press, 1989), pp. 30–36.

42. This also is the conclusion reached by the Pentagon in its post–Desert Storm assessments. Saddam started the war when he did because he believed that his "troops could defeat the Iranian armed forces, badly disintegrated by the Iranian revolution." Department of Defense, *Conduct of the Persian Gulf War*, p. 10.

43. Howard Teicher and Gayle Radley Teicher, *Twin Pillars to Desert Storm: America's Flawed Vision in the Middle East from Nixon to Bush* (New York: William Morrow, 1993), pp. 65–66.

44. Letter dated December 24, 1983 (copy obtained by author).

45. Cited in *Congressional Record,* February 24, 1992, p. H517.

46. March 8, 1984, telex from U.S. Interests Section in Baghdad to the Secretary of State, cited in *Congressional Record,* February 24, 1992, p. H517.

47. State Department memorandum for Mr. Donald P. Gregg (national security advisor to Vice-President Bush), "Eximbank Financing for Iraqi Export Pipeline," June 12, 1984.

48. The Aqaba pipeline never actually was built, primarily because the rest of the financing could not be satisfactorily arranged. The irony, of course, is that had it been built, the economic sanctions imposed against Iraq in 1990 following its invasion of Kuwait would have been even more difficult to enforce, given Jordan's support for Saddam and noncooperation with the sanctions.

49. U.S. Congress, House of Representatives, Committee on Government

Operations, *U.S. Government Controls on Sales to Iraq,* hearing before the Commerce, Consumer, and Monetary Affairs Subcommittee, 101st Congress, 2nd Session, September 27, 1990, p. 306.

50. Cited in R. Jeffrey Smith, "Selling to Scoundrels: Why We Won't Stop," *Washington Post,* November 15, 1992, pp. C1, C4.

51. Howard Teicher, quoted in Douglas Frantz and Murray Waas, "Secret Effort by Bush in '89 Helped Hussein Build Iraq's War Machine," *Los Angeles Times,* February 24, 1992, p. A6.

52. Sciolino, *The Outlaw State,* p. 166.

53. Smolansky, *The USSR and Iraq,* pp. 24, 29–30; Anthony H. Cordesman, *The Iran-Iraq War and Western Security, 1984–87: Implications and Policy Options* (London: Jane's Publishing, 1987), pp. 24–25; Natalie J. Goldring, *Arms Transfers to the Middle East* (Washington, D.C.: Defense Budget Project, April 25, 1991), Tables 2–4; Sciolino, *The Outlaw State,* p. 148.

54. Alan Friedman, *Spider's Web: The Secret History of How the White House Illegally Armed Iraq* (New York: Bantam Books, 1993), p. 82.

55. Frantz and Waas, "Secret Effort by Bush in '89 Helped Hussein Build Iraq's War Machine," p. A6.

56. In one case, some concerned Reagan administration officials admonished that "whatever the explanation for this transfer, we are required by the Arms Export Control Act to report promptly—repeat promptly—to Congress." While the intention was stated to send such notification to Congress, congressional records found no evidence of any notification. See Murray Waas and Douglas Frantz, "Saudi Arms Link to Iraq Allowed," *Los Angeles Times,* April 18, 1992, pp. A1, A14.

57. Seymour M. Hersh, "U.S. Secretly Gave Aid to Iraq Early in Its War Against Iran," *New York Times,* January 26, 1992, pp. 1, 12; Elaine Sciolino, "U.S. Documents Raise Questions Over Iraq," *New York Times,* June 7, 1992, pp. 1, 16; Douglas Frantz and Murray Waas, "Italian Report Suggests U.S. Knew of Bank's Loans for Iraqi Military," *Los Angeles Times,* April 18, 1992, p. 1, 14.

58. Timmerman, *The Death Lobby,* pp. 191–92, 212–13; House Government Operations Committee, *U.S. Government Controls on Sales to Iraq,* pp. 300–306; Hersh, "U.S. Secretly Gave Aid to Iraq Early in Its War Against Iran."

59. Teicher and Teicher, *Twin Pillars to Desert Storm,* p. 207.

60. Friedman, *Spider's Web,* p. 167; U.S. Senate, Select Committee on Intelligence, *Nomination of Robert M. Gates to be Director of Central Intelligence,* Executive Report 102–19, 102nd Congress, 1st Session, October 24, 1991, pp. 179–80.

61. Bob Woodward, *Veil: The Secret Wars of the CIA* (New York: Simon & Schuster, 1987), pp. 439, 480; statement by Congressman Henry Gonzalez,

Congressional Record, March 9, 1992, pp. H1107–12; Jim Hoagland, "America's Frankenstein Monster," *Washington Post,* February 7, 1991, p. A19.

62. Frantz and Waas, "Secret Effort by Bush in '89 Helped Hussein Build Iraq's War Machine," p. A6; Timmerman, *The Death Lobby,* pp. 122–24.

63. Miller and Mylroie, *Saddam Hussein and the Crisis in the Gulf,* p. 145; Elaine Sciolino, "Iraq's Nuclear Program Shows the Holes in U.S. Intelligence," *New York Times,* October 20, 1991, p. E5.

64. The total number of attacks on Persian Gulf shipping during the first three years of the Iran-Iraq war was 43. In 1984 there were 71 attacks. U.S. Congress, Congressional Research Service, "Ship Attacks in the Persian Gulf, 1981–March 1987," June 1987.

65. All 43 of the 1981–83 attacks on shipping were by Iraq. In the 1984 escalation, 53 were by Iraq, 18 by Iran. Ibid.

66. Gerald F. Seib, "Reagan Orders Secret Plan to Shield Other Gulf States as Iran Presses War," *Wall Street Journal,* April 11, 1989, p. 2.

67. Timmerman, *The Death Lobby,* p. 185; Dusko Doder, "Soviet-Iraqi Ties Said to Improve Amid Reports of Credits for Arms," *Washington Post,* April 28, 1984, p. A25.

68. State Department memorandum, "Letter to Secretary Weinberger on U.S.-Iraqi Relations and Advanced Technology Exports to Iraq," April 29, 1985.

69. Teicher and Teicher, *Twin Pillars to Desert Storm,* pp. 277, 286–88.

70. Bernard Gwertzman, "U.S. and Iraq Reported Ready to Renew Ties After 17 Years," *New York Times,* November 13, 1984, p. 14; Bernard Gwertzman, "U.S. Restores Full Ties with Iraq But Cites Neutrality in Gulf War," November 27, 1984, p. 1; Timmerman, *The Death Lobby,* p. 193.

71. Helms, *Iraq: Eastern Flank of Arab World,* pp. 194, 206–207.

72. Nizar Hamdoon, "Ambassador's Diary: How to Survive in Washington," *Washington Post,* August 30, 1987, pp. C1, C4.

73. George P. Shultz, *Turmoil and Triumph: My Years as Secretary of State* (New York: Charles Scribner's Sons, 1993), p. 238.

74. United Nations, Security Council, Document S/16433, "Report of the Specialists Appointed by the Secretary General to Investigate Allegations by the Islamic Republic of Iran Concerning Use of Chemical Weapons," March 26, 1984.

75. al-Khalil, *Republic of Fear,* pp. 283–84; Department of Defense, *Conduct of the Persian Gulf War,* p. 18.

76. Lally Weymouth, "Despite Improving Ties, Iraqi Leader Assails U.S.," *Washington Post,* May 13, 1984, pp. A31, A36; "Is Baghdad Using Poison Gas?," *Newsweek,* March 19, 1984, pp. 39–40.

77. Based on an intelligence analysis which Secretary of State Shultz says he was "stunned to read"; see *Turmoil and Triumph,* p. 239.

78. Weymouth, "Despite Improving Ties, Iraqi Leader Assails U.S.," pp. A31, A36.

79. U.S. Congress, House, Committee on Foreign Affairs, *Country Reports on Human Rights Practices for 1985,* submitted by the Department of State, 99th Congress, 2nd Session, February 1986, p. 1246.

80. Frederick W. Axelgard, *A New Iraq? The Gulf War and Implications for U.S. Policy* (New York: Praeger, 1988), p. 41.

81. Ibid., p. 45.

82. R. Jeffrey Smith and Glenn Frankel, "Saddam's Nuclear Weapons Dream: A Lingering Nightmare," *Washington Post,* October 13, 1991, p. A45.

83. Timmerman, *The Death Lobby,* p. 202.

84. Murray Waas and Craig Unger, "In the Loop: Bush's Secret Mission," *The New Yorker,* November 2, 1992, p. 70.

85. Defense Department memorandum, "Subject: Computers for Iraq," March 10, 1985.

86. Defense Department memorandum, "Subject: High Technology Dual Use Exports to Iraq," July 1, 1985.

87. State Department memorandum, "Computers for Iraq: DOD's Proliferation Concerns," April 3, 1986.

88. Timmerman, *The Death Lobby,* p. 241.

89. International Institute for Strategic Studies, *Strategic Survey 1985–86* (London: IISS, 1986), p. 19.

90. State Department memorandum, "Iraq's Retreat from International Terrorism," July 1, 1986.

91. Ian Black, "Israeli's Assailant Said to be Iraqi Agent," *Washington Post,* March 8, 1983, p. A10; Ian Black, "Iraqi Colonel Led Terrorists in London," *The Guardian,* March 13, 1983, p. 4; Teicher and Teicher, *Twin Pillars to Desert Storm,* p. 196.

92. Scott MacLeod, "The Terrorist's Terrorist," *New York Review of Books,* May 28, 1992, pp. 9–10. See also Ze'ev Schiff and Ehud Ya'ari, *Israel's Lebanon War* (New York: Simon and Schuster, 1984), pp. 99–100; Dilip Hiro, *The Longest War: The Iran-Iraq Military Conflict* (London: Grafton Books, 1989), p. 63.

93. Patrick Seale, *Abu Nidal: Gun for Hire* (New York: Random House, 1992), p. 111.

94. "Iraq Supplies PLO Army Units," *Washington Times,* February 8, 1985.

95. Abu Abbas's escape route also took him through Yugoslavia. However, as Secretary Shultz stated at a press conference, "with respect to Yugoslavia, he [Abbas] passed through. With respect to Iraq, he seems to have been welcomed there. That is different and it constitutes more of a problem." Shultz, *Turmoil and Triumph,* p. 676.

96. State Department, "Chronology: October 4 through December 6, 1985," p. 1.

97. Letter dated June 20, 1985, from Secretary of State George Shultz to Congressman Howard L. Berman (D-California); U.S. Congress, House Committee on Foreign Affairs, *U.S. Exports of Sensitive Technology to Iraq,* hearing before the Subcommittee on International Economic Policy and Trade, 102nd Congress, 1st Session, April 8 and May 22, 1991, p. 22.

98. Letter dated January 2, 1986, from Assistant Secretary of State for Legislative and Intergovernmental Affairs William L. Ball III to Congressman Howard L. Berman (D-California).

99. State Department memorandum, "Iraq's Retreat from International Terrorism."

100. Letter to Congressman Howard Berman from Carl F. Schwensen, executive vice-president of the National Association of Wheat Growers, June 24, 1985.

101. Timmerman, *The Death Lobby,* p. 227.

102. Murray Waas and Douglas Frantz, "Bush Had Long Supported Aid for Iraq," *Los Angeles Times,* February 24, 1992, p. A7.

103. State Department memorandum, "Iraq: CPPG Meeting of Wednesday July 23" (1986).

104. Waas and Unger, "In the Loop," pp. 66–67. Israel reportedly went ahead anyway, including sales of some U.S. arms. Brzezinski says that he and President Carter learned of this later and "much to our dismay," as it may have weakened simultaneous U.S. efforts to bargain for release of the hostages with the stockpile of arms purchased by the Shah; see *Power and Principle,* p. 504.

105. Waas and Unger, "In the Loop," p. 67.

106. Seymour M. Hersh, "U.S. Said to Have Allowed Israel to Sell Arms to Iran," *New York Times,* December 8, 1991, pp. 1, 16.

107. U.S. Congress, Senate, Select Committee on Secret Military Assistance to Iran and the Nicaraguan Opposition, and House, Select Committee to Investigate Covert Arms Transactions with Iran, *Iran-Contra Affair,* Report No. 100-216, 100th Congress, 1st Session, November 1987, p. 159.

108. Caspar Weinberger, *Fighting for Peace: Seven Critical Years in the Pentagon* (New York: Warner Books, 1990), pp. 421–24.

109. Senate and House Select Committees, *Iran-Contra Affair,* pp. 160–61.

110. Walter Pincus and George Lardner, Jr., "Iran-Contra Data, Disclosures Shed Light on What Bush Hasn't Told," *Washington Post,* October 22, 1992, p. A4.

111. Waas and Unger, "In the Loop," pp. 74–80.

112. "Transcription of Meetings with Albert Hakim, Richard Secord, Oliver

North and Iranian Intermediaries in Mainz," *The Iran-Contra Affair: The Making of a Scandal, 1983–1988* (Alexandria, VA: Chadwyck-Healey, 1990), Document #03563. North later acknowledged having concurred with the Iranians that "there is a need for a non-hostile regime in Baghdad" and led them to believe that "we can bring our influence to bear with certain friendly Arab nations" to get rid of Saddam; Christopher Hitchens, "Realpolitik in the Gulf: A Game Gone Tilt," in Micah L. Sifry and Christopher Cerf, eds., *The Gulf War Reader: History, Documents, Opinions* (New York: Times Books, 1991), p. 114.

113. State Department memorandum, "U.S.-Iraqi Relations: Picking Up the Pieces," December 3, 1986.

114. Letter dated December 12, 1986.

115. State Department memorandum for Mr. Donald P. Gregg (assistant to the vice-president for national security affairs), "The Vice President's March 2 Meeting with Iraqi Ambassador Nizar Hamdoon," February 26, 1987.

116. Export-Import Bank memorandum, "Interagency Review of Iraq," April 17, 1987.

117. Weinberger, *Fighting for Peace,* p. 387. Such evidence of mounting Iranian aggression and military threats was one of the reasons Weinberger viewed the North et al. search for Iranian moderates by providing them with arms as "one of the more absurd proposals" (p. 363) he had ever heard.

118. Iranian attacks on Persian Gulf shipping increased from 14 in 1985 to 41 in 1986 and 22 in the first three months of 1987. As earlier in the war, this was part of an escalatory cycle in which Iraqi attacks still were greater: 33 in 1985, 66 in 1986, and 24 in the first three months of 1987. Congressional Research Service, "Ship Attacks in the Persian Gulf." See Chapter 5 for further discussion of the Iraqi strategy in the tanker war.

119. Michael A. Palmer, *Guardians of the Gulf: A History of America's Expanding Role in the Persian Gulf, 1833–1992* (New York: Free Press, 1992), pp. 122–23.

120. On doubts as to how accidental the attack on the U.S.S. *Stark* may have been, see Baram, "Iraq: Between East and West," p. 86; Sciolino, *The Outlaw State,* pp. 169–70.

121. U.S. Congress, Senate, Committee on Foreign Relations, *War in the Persian Gulf: The U.S. Takes Sides,* Committee Print 100-60, 100th Congress, 1st Session, November 1987, p. 37.

122. Janice Gross Stein, "The Wrong Strategy in the Right Place," *International Security,* 14 (Winter 1988/89), pp. 148–49.

123. Palmer, *Guardians of the Gulf,* p. 125.

124. Commerce Department memorandum, "The NSC and Iraq," May 27, 1991.

125. U.S. Congress, House of Representatives, Committee on Banking, Finance, and Urban Affairs, *Banca Nazionale del Lavoro (BNL)*, Hearing, 102nd Congress, 1st Session, April 9, 1991, p. 79.

126. "Approved Licenses to Iraq, 1985–1990," U.S. Department of Commerce; U.S. Congress, House of Representatives, Committee on Government Operations, *Strengthening the Export Licensing System*, Report 102-137, 102nd Congress, 1st Session, July 2, 1991; Gary Milhollin, "Licensing Mass Destruction: U.S. Exports to Iraq, 1985–1990" (Washington, D.C.: Wisconsin Project on Nuclear Arms Control, 1991).

127. Friedman, *Spider's Web*, p. 156; Timmerman, *The Death Lobby*, pp. 157–60, 207; Sciolino, *The Outlaw State*, p. 142.

128. Congressman Henry Gonzalez (D-Texas) provides a great deal of detail in his statement in the *Congressional Record*, August 10, 1992, pp. H7871–82.

129. Statement by Congressman Gonzalez, *Congressional Record*, July 21, 1992, pp. H6338–46.

130. State Department memorandum, "Application (Iraq)," September 21, 1987.

131. Robert D. Shuey et al., *Missile Proliferation: Survey of Emerging Missile Forces* (Washington, D.C.: Congressional Research Service), Report 88-642F, October 3, 1988.

132. Timmerman, *The Death Lobby*, pp. 235–37, 301–304.

133. Defense Intelligence Agency, "Assessment of the Activities of Abdul Kader Helmy, et al., and the Egyptian/Iraqi Condor Missile Program," September 19, 1989, filed with the U.S. Attorney, Eastern District of California, U.S. Courthouse, Sacramento, California.

134. U.S. Congress, House of Representatives, Committee on Energy and Commerce, *Nuclear Nonproliferation*, hearing before the Subcommittee on Oversight and Investigations, 102nd Congress, 1st Session, April 24, 1991, pp. 37–38, 48–49.

135. Bruce W. Jentleson, "The Reagan Administration and Coercive Diplomacy: Restraining More than Remaking Governments," *Political Science Quarterly*, 106 (Spring 1991), pp. 57–82.

136. Stein, "The Wrong Strategy in the Right Place," p. 148.

2: Saddam Gasses the Kurds: Why No U.S. Sanctions?

1. Eyewitness accounts, recounted to staff of the Senate Foreign Relations Committee, in U.S. Congress, Senate, Committee on Foreign Relations, *Chemical Weapons Use in Kurdistan: Iraq's Final Offensive*, S. Rpt. 100-148, 100th Congress, 2nd Session, October 1988, p. 12.

2. Ibid., p. 13.

3. The Genocide Convention defines genocide as "any of the following acts committed with intent to destroy, in whole or in part, a national, ethnical, racial or religious group as such: (a) killing members of the group; (b) causing serious bodily or mental harm to members of the group; (c) deliberately inflicting on the group conditions of life calculated to being about its physical destruction in whole or in part."

4. George P. Shultz, *Turmoil and Triumph: My Years as Secretary of State* (New York: Charles Scribner's Sons, 1993), p. 241; Pamela Fessler, "Congress' Record on Saddam: Decade of Talk, Not Action," *Congressional Quarterly Weekly Report*, April 27, 1991, p. 1072; Douglas Frantz and Murray Waas, "Bush Secretly Helped Iraq Build Its War Machine," *Los Angeles Times*, February 23, 1992, p. A12; State Department memorandum, "Administration Policy on Proposed Iraq Sanctions," October 18, 1988.

5. David B. Ottaway, "Iraqi Army Flies U.S.-Made Civilian Helicopters," *Washington Post*, October 6, 1988, p. A45; Stuart Auerbach, "$1.5 Billion in U.S. Sales to Iraq," *Washington Post*, March 11, 1991, p. A16.

6. Laurie Mylroie, *The Future of Iraq* (Washington, D.C.: Washington Institute for Near East Policy, 1991), Policy Papers, Number 24, pp. 24–25; Senate Foreign Relations Committee, *Chemical Weapons Use in Kurdistan*, pp. 6–8.

7. Barry Rubin, *Paved with Good Intentions: The American Experience and Iran* (Hammondsworth, England: Penguin Books, 1980); James A. Bill, *The Eagle and the Lion: The Tragedy of American-Iranian Relations* (New York: Yale University Press, 1988); Henry A. Kissinger, *White House Years* (Boston: Little, Brown, 1979).

8. Raymond Garthoff, *Detente and Confrontation: American-Soviet Relations from Nixon to Reagan* (Washington, D.C.: Brookings Institution, 1985); Alexander L. George, ed., *Managing U.S.-Soviet Rivalry: Problems of Crisis Prevention* (Boulder, CO: Westview Press, 1983); Kissinger, *White House Years*.

9. Safire wrote numerous columns on the Kurds. See, for example, the collection of columns from 1976 to 1979 in his book *Safire's Washington* (New York: Times Books, 1980), pp. 82–88, 330–36.

10. Walter Isaacson, *Kissinger: A Biography* (New York: Simon and Schuster, 1992), p. 564.

11. Cited in Bill, *The Eagle and the Lion*, pp. 205–206. The Pike Committee report was never officially released. It was made public in news leaks to Daniel Schorr, then of CBS and the *Village Voice*.

12. Samir al-Khalil, *Republic of Fear: The Inside Story of Saddam's Iraq* (Berkeley: University of California Press, 1989), p. 23.

13. William Safire, "Son of 'Secret Sellout,'" *New York Times*, February 12, 1976, p. 31.

14. Ibid.

15. Cited in Bill, *The Eagle and the Lion,* pp. 206–208.

16. In the first volume of his memoirs, *White House Years,* Henry Kissinger disparages what he calls "the excited polemics published on this subject." He devotes one paragraph and one footnote to the Kurdish issue (p. 1265), promising to provide further discussions in the second volume of his memoirs. However, one does not even find "Kurds" in the index of *Years of Upheaval.* Finally, in a newspaper column after the 1991 Gulf War and amidst the Bush administration's abandonment of the Kurds, Kissinger acknowledged his 1975 decision to abandon the Kurds as "painful, even heartbreaking"; see Isaacson, *Kissinger,* p. 564.

17. Frederick W. Axelgard, *A New Iraq? The Gulf War and Implications for U.S. Policy* (New York: Praeger, 1988), pp. 29–33.

18. U.S. Congress, Senate, Committee on Foreign Relations, *War in the Persian Gulf: The U.S. Takes Sides,* Staff Report 100-60, 100th Congress, 1st Session, 1987, p. 16.

19. The name "al-Anfal" is taken from a verse in the Koran said to legitimize the plundering of the property (and women) of infidels—in this instance, the Kurds (their Sunni Moslem identity notwithstanding).

20. Fourteen tons of secret police documents were captured by the Kurds during their 1991 post–Desert Storm uprising. In April 1992 they entrusted the records to the U.S. Senate Foreign Relations Committee. Peter W. Galbraith, then a senior staff member, played the key role in making the transfer. The examples that follow are drawn from his report, *Saddam's Documents* (U.S. Congress, Senate, Report to the Senate Foreign Relations Committee, S. Rpt. 102-111, 102nd Congress, 2nd Session, May 1992). See also Judith Miller, "Iraq Accused: A Case of Genocide," *New York Times Magazine,* January 3, 1993.

21. Patrick Tyler, "Poison Gas Attacks Kill Hundreds," *Washington Post,* March 24, 1988, pp. A1, A36; Senate Foreign Relations Committee, *Chemical Weapons Use in Kurdistan,* p. 30.

22. Seth Carus, *The Genie Unleashed: Iraq's Chemical Weapons and Biological Weapons Production* (Washington, D.C.: Washington Institute for Near East Policy, 1989), Policy Paper Number 14, pp. 7–9.

23. R. Jeffrey Smith and Marc Fisher, "German Firms Primed Iraq's War Machine," *Washington Post,* July 23, 1992, pp. A1, A26. There also was the involvement of figures like Anton Eyerle, a fifty-seven-year-old trading company executive who was a veteran of Göring's Luftwaffe and still a Hitler worshiper. Saddam Hussein was " 'a strong man for whom it is worth fighting.' The Iraqis were 'people who still had character.' ... 'This is as it was in my youth,' " he said. Kenneth R. Timmerman, *The Death Lobby: How the West Armed Iraq* (Boston: Houghton Mifflin, 1991), p. 105.

24. Timmerman, *The Death Lobby,* p. 35.

25. Senate Foreign Relations Committee, *Chemical Weapons Use in Kurdistan,* pp. 30–31. Anthony Cordesman claims that Iraq actually began using chemical weapons against Iranian troops as early as December 1982, as well as during the July 1983 Iranian Val Fajr 2 offensive and October 1983 Iranian offensive at Panjwin. See his article, "Creating Weapons of Mass Destruction," *Armed Forces Journal,* January/February 1989, p. 56.

26. Eight precursor chemicals were under special controls applicable only to Iraq and Iran, in addition to forty others under more general controls; State Department memorandum, "Curbing Proliferation of Chemical Weapons," June 10, 1985.

27. U.S. Congress, Senate, Committee on Foreign Relations, *Civil War in Iraq,* Staff Report (S. Rpt. 102-27), 102nd Congress, 1st Session, May 1991, p. 13.

28. U.S. Congress, Senate, Committee on Foreign Relations, *United States Policy Toward Iraq: Human Rights, Weapons Proliferation and International Law,* Hearing, 101st Congress, 2nd Session, June 15, 1990, p. 60.

29. Michael Eisenstadt traces a pattern of decreasingly discriminating use from an initial core of counterattacks against Iranian troop advances, to more offensive "pre-assault preparations of Iranian positions," to late in the war actual delegation of chemical weapons use decisions to divisional commanders as a tactical matter; see *"The Sword of the Arabs": Iraq's Strategic Weapons* (Washington, D.C.: Washington Institute for Near East Policy, 1990), Policy Paper Number 21, p. 6. And then came the attacks on the civilian population in Halabja, and then the attacks on cities and villages across Kurdistan.

30. *Congressional Record,* September 9, 1988, pp. S12136–37.

31. John Felton, "A Rebuke of Iraq," *Congressional Quarterly Weekly Report,* September 10, 1988, p. 2528.

32. Shultz, *Turmoil and Triumph,* p. 242; Thomas L. McNaugher, "Ballistic Missiles and Chemical Weapons: The Legacy of the Iran-Iraq War," *International Security,* 15 (Fall 1990), pp. 21–22.

33. Letter from J. Edward Fox, Assistant Secretary of State for Legislative Affairs, to Congressman Dante B. Fascell, Chairman of the House Foreign Affairs Committee, September 13, 1988; letter from the Acting Secretary of State to Congressman David Obey, Chairman of the House Appropriations Subcommittee on Foreign Operations, September 30, 1988.

34. *Congressional Record,* September 9, 1988, p. S12136.

35. Shultz, *Turmoil and Triumph,* pp. 239–41.

36. Aziz statement cited in a letter from the Iraqi ambassador to the United States, Abdul-Amir Al-Anbari to Congressman Dante Fascell, September 21, 1988; Khairallah quotation in Clyde Haberman, "Iraq's Right to Chemical Arms Upheld by Official," *New York Times,* September 16, 1988, A11.

37. Jim Hoagland, "Iraq Is One Place Where Sanctions Might Work," *Washington Post,* September 15, 1988, p. A25.

38. Patrick Tyler, "Iraq Denies Using Chemical Weapons on Kurds," *Washington Post,* September 16, 1988, p. A20.

39. Elaine Sciolino, *The Outlaw State: Saddam Hussein's Quest for Power and the Gulf Crisis* (New York: John Wiley and Sons, 1991), p. 105.

40. Export-Import Bank, "Country Report: Iraq," April 24, 1989, Appendices 1 and 2.

41. U.S. Congress, General Accounting Office, *Iraq's Participation in U.S. Agricultural Export Programs,* GAO/NSIAD-91-76, November 1990.

42. U.S. Department of Energy, "Petroleum Supply Annual," Energy Information Administration, Office of Oil and Gas, 1981–90; "Discount Prices on Imports of Iraqi Oil, 1988–1990," document provided by U.S. Congress, House of Representatives, Committee on Energy and Commerce, Subcommittee on Energy and Power.

43. When Secretary of Agriculture John Block, upon signing the agreement, condemned the 1980 grain embargo as a "distasteful chapter" in American-Soviet relations, Zbigniew Brzezinski, former Carter national security advisor, retorted, "What is truly distasteful is Secretary Block crawling on his knees to Moscow." *New York Times,* August 26, 1983, pp. 1, 28.

44. Bruce W. Jentleson, *Pipeline Politics: The Complex Political Economy of East-West Energy Trade* (Ithaca, NY: Cornell University Press, 1986).

45. General Accounting Office, *Iraq's Participation in U.S. Agricultural Export Programs,* p. 15.

46. Douglas Frantz and Murray Waas, "U.S. Loans Indirectly Financed Iraq Military," *Los Angeles Times,* February 25, 1992, p. A7.

47. Fessler, "Congress' Record on Saddam," p. 1073.

48. State Department memorandum, "U.S.-Iraqi Relations: Implications of Passage of Economic Sanctions Bill," October 18, 1988.

49. Letter from William T. Archey, Vice-President, International Affairs, U.S. Chamber of Commerce, to House Foreign Affairs Committee Chairman Dante B. Fascell, September 15, 1988.

50. This account is drawn from three interdependent sources: Joe Conason, "The Iraq Lobby," *The New Republic,* October 1, 1990, pp. 14–17; Murray Waas, "What We Gave Saddam for Christmas," *Village Voice,* December 18, 1990, included in U.S. Congress, House of Representatives, Committee on Government Operations, *U.S. Government Controls on Sales to Iraq,* hearing before the Commerce, Consumer and Monetary Affairs Subcommittee, 101st Congress, 2nd Session, September 27, 1990, pp. 300–310; Timmerman, *The Death Lobby,* pp. 219–23, 305–308.

51. Waas, "What We Gave Saddam for Christmas," p. 309.

52. "Sanctions Against Iraq: Let's Not be Stupid," Letter to the Editor by Marshall Wiley, *Washington Post,* October 22, 1988, p. A22.

53. Douglas Waller, "Glass House," *The New Republic,* November 5, 1990, pp. 13–14; Sciolino, *The Outlaw State,* p. 171.

54. State Department memorandum, "Iraq's Foreign Policy: Deeper Into the Mainstream," March 3, 1988 (emphasis added).

55. State Department memorandum, "U.S. Policy Towards Iraq and CW Use," September 19, 1988.

56. Letter from Assistant Secretary of State for Legislative Affairs J. Edward Fox to House Foreign Affairs Committee Chairman Dante B. Farcell, September 13, 1988.

57. Axelgard, *A New Iraq?,* pp. 14, 100.

58. Laurie Mylroie, "The Baghdad Alternative," *Orbis* (Summer 1988), pp. 339–40, 346, 348, 350.

59. Christine Moss Helms, *Iraq: Eastern Flank of the Arab World* (Washington, D.C.: Brookings Institution, 1984), p. 194.

60. State Department memorandum, "U.S.-Iraqi Relations: Implications of Passage of Economic Sanctions Bill," October 18, 1988.

61. Affidavit in U.S. Congress, House of Representatives, Committee on Foreign Affairs, *U.S. Exports of Sensitive Technology to Iraq,* hearing before the International Economic Policy Subcommittee, 102nd Congress, 1st Session, April 8 and May 22, 1991, p. 55.

62. "Approved Licenses to Iraq, 1985–1990," U.S. Department of Commerce.

63. Commerce Department memorandum, "Re-Export Application," August 8, 1988.

64. U.S. Congress, House of Representatives, Committee on Ways and Means, *Administration and Enforcement of U.S. Export Control Programs,* hearing before the Subcommittee on Oversight, 102nd Congress, 1st Session, April 18 and May 1, 1991, p. 466.

65. U.S. Congress, House of Representatives, Committee on Energy and Commerce, *Nuclear Nonproliferation,* hearings before the Subcommittee on Oversight and Investigations, 102nd Congress, 1st Session, April 24, 1991, p. 559.

66. In early October 1988, Special Agent Daniel Supnick, the Customs agent in charge of the operation, passed on the specifications of the order placed by Iraq to the Sandia National Laboratory, one of the government's main nuclear weapons labs. In a letter dated November 10, the Sandia scientists confirmed that the electronic capacitators in question had no civilian uses and that they did meet the specifications for nuclear bomb detonators. *Congressional Record,* February 18, 1993, p. H706.

67. *Jane's Defense Weekly,* January 9, 1988, p. 3; Eric Nadler and Robert Windrem, "Deadly Contagion," *The New Republic,* February 4, 1991, pp. 18–20.

68. Cordesman, "Creating Weapons of Mass Destruction," p. 56; David B. Ottaway, "U.S. Gave Iraq Bacteria, Sen. McCain Charges," *Washington Post*, January 26, 1989, p. A16.

69. Paul A. Gigot, "A Great American Screw-Up: The U.S. and Iraq, 1980–1990," *The National Interest* (Winter 1990–91), pp. 3–10; Don Oberdorfer, "Missed Signals in the Middle East," *Washington Post Magazine*, March 17, 1991, pp. 19–41; author interview, former Reagan administration official, March 9 and April 22, 1993.

70. Eisenstadt, *"The Sword of the Arabs,"* pp. 42–43.

71. Zalmay Khalilzad, "A Geo-Strategic Overview: Stability or New Aggressive Coalitions," in *Proceedings of the Washington Institute*, Third Annual Policy Conference, "U.S. Policy in the Middle East: Toward the Next Administration," September 16–18, 1988 (Washington, D.C.: Washington Institute for Near East Policy: 1988), pp. 12–13.

72. James M. Dorsey, "White House Urged to Drop Iran Sanctions," *Washington Times*, September 21, 1988, p. A1.

73. Shultz presents quite a different view in his memoirs (*Turmoil and Triumph*, p. 243). "I came to regard Iraq, once again, as one of the enemy states of the responsible world community. By the end of the Reagan years, after our reflagging policy had turned the Gulf War toward its conclusion, it was clear to me that no further reason existed for the United States to give Iraq the benefit of the doubt for balance-of-power purposes against Iran." However, both press reports and interviews support the account presented in this book. Shultz goes on to associate himself with another paper on Iraq written by Khalilzad, this one for the Bush transition team, "in which we sought . . . to point out that a new and tougher policy toward Saddam Hussein's Iraq was now appropriate." Here, too, there is no other supporting evidence that he took this position. In fact, as is discussed in Chapter 3, another Bush transition paper with a much more accommodationist thesis proved much more influential.

74. Gigot, "A Great American Screw-Up," p. 6.

75. State Department memorandum, "Administration Position on Proposed Iraq Sanctions," November 18, 1988.

76. Keith Bradsher, "Memo Cites Exception on Iraqi Trade to Protect Hussein," *New York Times*, May 23, 1991, p. D5.

77. Anthony Lewis, "Paying for Reagan," *New York Times*, October 5, 1990, p. A15.

78. State Department paper, "Curbing Proliferation of Chemical Weapons," June 19, 1985, p. 9.

79. House Ways and Means Committee, *Administration and Enforcement of U.S. Export Control Programs*, p. 39.

3: Bush's Strategy: The Making of NSD-26

1. National Security Directive 26, declassified version, dated October 2, 1989.
2. Judith Miller and Laurie Mylroie, *Saddam Hussein and the Crisis in the Gulf* (New York: Random House, 1990), p. 151.
3. "Guidelines for U.S.-Iraq Policy," Department of State, p. 1. The document has no date but its text clearly indicates that it was written during the transition period. Zalmay Khalilzad, the State Department Policy Planning Staff member who, as discussed in Chapter 2, wrote the "contain Iraq" paper right at the end of the Iran-Iraq war, also wrote a paper for the Bush transition team. But, as earlier, Khalilzad's analysis apparently was rejected. See Elaine Sciolino with Michael Wines, "Bush's Greatest Glory Fades as Questions About Iraq Persist," *New York Times,* June 27, 1992, pp. 1, 8.
4. Shaul Bakhash, "What Khomeini Did," *New York Review of Books,* July 20, 1989, p. 17.
5. Oles M. Smolansky, with Bettie M. Smolansky, *The USSR and Iraq: The Soviet Quest for Influence* (Durham, NC: Duke University Press, 1990), pp. 271–72.
6. Ibid., p. 274.
7. "Guidelines for U.S.-Iraq Policy," p. 4.
8. Ibid., p. 1.
9. Alexander L. George, *Bridging the Gap: Theory and Practice in Foreign Policy* (Washington, D.C.: U.S. Institute of Peace Press, 1993), pp. 45–60.
10. Testimony to House Banking Committee, May 8, 1992 (text from Legi-Slate data base).
11. Saddam, though, had tried to give the ACC also a military and collective security agenda, but was rebuffed by Mubarak. Dilip Hiro, *Desert Shield to Desert Storm: The Second Gulf War* (London: HarperCollins, 1992), p. 55.
12. Ibid., p. 56.
13. "Guidelines for U.S.-Iraq Policy," p. 4.
14. Lawrence Freedman and Efraim Karsh, *The Gulf Conflict: Diplomacy and War in the New World Order* (London: Faber and Faber, 1993), p. 16.
15. Secretary of State Baker, "Principles and Pragmatism: American Policy Toward the Arab-Israeli Conflict," May 21, 1989, Department of State, Bureau of Public Affairs, Current Policy No. 1176. Reaction to the Baker speech was intense. See John M. Goshko, "U.S. Faults Israel on Territories," *Washington Post,* May 23, 1989, pp. A1, A22; David S. Broder, "Shamir Rejects Baker's Suggestions on Mideast Approach as 'Useless,'" *Washington Post,* May 24, 1989; Jeanne Kirkpatrick, "Baker's Curious Neutrality," *Washington Post,* May 29, 1989.

16. "Guidelines for U.S.-Iraq Policy," p. 5 (emphasis in original).

17. Ibid., pp. 5–6.

18. Sandra L. Charles, NSC director for Near East and South Asian Affairs, quoted in R. Jeffrey Smith, "Selling to Scoundrels: Why We Won't Stop," *Washington Post,* November 15, 1992, pp. C1, C4.

19. U.S. General Accounting Office, *Iraq's Participation in U.S. Agricultural Export Programs,* November 1990, GAO/NSIAD-91-76, p. 4.

20. Kenneth R. Timmerman, *The Death Lobby: How the West Armed Iraq* (Boston: Houghton Mifflin, 1991), p. 348; testimony of Marshall Wiley, U.S. Congress, House, Committee on Banking, Finance, and Urban Affairs, *Banca Nazionale del Lavoro (BNL),* Hearings, 102nd Congress, 1st Session, April 9, 1991, p. 129.

21. "Imports from Iraq," U.S. Department of Energy, August 26, 1992; "Discount Prices on Imports of Iraqi Oil, 1988–1990," document provided by U.S. Congress, House of Representatives, Committee on Energy and Commerce, Subcommittee on Energy and Power.

22. "Guidelines for U.S.-Iraq Policy," p. 3 (emphasis in original).

23. Ibid., p. 6.

24. Stephen Engelberg, "Iraq Said to Study Biological Arms," *New York Times,* January 18, 1989, p. A7; David B. Ottaway, "Official Denies Iraq Has Germ Warfare Plant," *Washington Post,* January 19, 1989, p. A36.

25. *New York Times,* January 18, 1989; Seth Carus, *The Genie Unleashed: Iraq's Chemical and Biological Weapons Production* (Washington, D.C.: Washington Institute for Near East Policy, 1989), p. 29.

26. U.S. Department of Defense, *Conduct of the Persian Gulf War,* Final Report to Congress Pursuant to Title V of the Persian Gulf Conflict Supplemental Authorization and Personnel Benefits Act of 1991 (Public Law 101-25), Chapters I–VII, pp. 18–19.

27. *New York Times,* January 18, 1989.

28. U.S. Congress, Senate, Committee on Foreign Relations, *Chemical and Biological Weapons Threat: The Urgent Need for Remedies,* Hearings, 101st Congress, 1st Session, March 1, 1989, pp. 27–45.

29. U.S. Congress, House of Representatives, Committee on Armed Services, *HR 2461: Department of Defense Authorization for Appropriations for Fiscal Year 1990—Title I,* Hearings before the Subcommittee on Seapower and Strategic and Critical Materials, 101st Congress, 1st Session, February 22, 1989, pp. 39–41. See also Glenn Frankel, "Iraq Said Developing A-Weapons," *Washington Post,* March 31, 1989, pp. A1, A32, citing Israeli sources.

30. State Department memorandum, "Meeting with Iraqi Under Secretary Nizan Hamdun," March 24, 1989.

31. The account that follows is drawn from U.S. Congress, House of Representatives, Committee on Energy and Commerce, *Nuclear Nonproliferation,*

hearing before the subcommittee on Oversight and Investigations, 102nd Congress, 1st Session, April 24, 1991, pp. 32, 52, 54, 60, 476–90, 686.

32. Ibid., p. 353, and Department of Energy memorandum, "Comments on Iraq Export Control Initiative."

33. House Energy and Commerce Oversight Subcommittee, *Nuclear Nonproliferation*, pp. 8–11, 367–409, 420.

34. Gary Milhollin, Director of the Wisconsin Project on Nuclear Arms Control, testimony in U.S. Congress, Senate Committee on Banking, Housing and Urban Affairs, *United States Export Policy toward Iraq Prior to Iraq's Invasion of Kuwait*, Hearing, 102nd Congress, 2nd Session, October 27, 1992, p. 87.

35. House Energy and Commerce Oversight Subcommittee, *Nuclear Nonproliferation*, p. 9.

36. On the Consarc case, see U.S. Congress, House of Representatives, Committee on Government Operations, *U.S. Government Controls on Sales to Iraq*, hearing before the Commerce, Consumer and Monetary Affairs Subcommittee, 101st Congress, 2nd Session, September 27, 1990, and testimony of Henry M. Rowan, Consarc executive, to the Senate Banking Committee, *United States Export Policy toward Iraq*, p. 49.

37. Ibid., p. 110. The full deal included the high-performance "skull" furnace and an electron-beam furnace from Consarc, with heat treatment and vacuum induction furnaces from its British subsidiaries.

38. Ibid., p. 50.

39. Efraim Karsh and Inauri Rautsi, *Saddam Hussein: A Political Biography* (New York: Free Press, 1991), pp. 197–98.

40. Interview, former Bush administration official, April 4, 1992.

41. U.S. Congress, Senate, Committee on Foreign Relations, *United States Policy Toward Iraq: Human Rights, Weapons Proliferation, and International Law*, Hearing, 101st Congress, 2nd Session, June 15, 1990, pp. 56–70.

42. Karsh and Rautsi, *Saddam Hussein: A Political Biography*, pp. 197–98.

43. Amy Kaslow, "U.S. Eyes Sanctions Against Iraq," *Christian Science Monitor*, August 31, 1989, p. 6.

44. Timmerman, *The Death Lobby*, pp. 331–41.

45. Ibid., pp. 333–34.

46. William Lowther, *Arms and the Man: Dr. Gerald Bull, Iraq and the Supergun* (Novato, CA: Presidio Press, 1991); William Scott Malone, David Halevy, and Sam Hemingway, "The Guns of Saddam," *Washington Post*, February 10, 1991, pp. C1, C4; Congressman Henry Gonzalez, testimony and documents submitted to the Senate Banking Committee, *United States Export Policy toward Iraq*; Timmerman, *The Death Lobby*, pp. 70, 160–62.

47. Malone, Halevy, and Hemingway, "The Guns of Saddam," p. C4.

48. Ibid.

49. Voest Alpine also sold artillery to Iran. The whole ruse eventually was exposed, leading in 1990–91 to the most extensive criminal investigation in Austrian history. Two former Austrian chancellors and numerous cabinet ministers were among those implicated; see Malone, Halevy, and Hemingway, "The Guns of Saddam," p. C4.

50. Timmerman, *The Death Lobby*, pp. 283–84.

51. "President Says Iraq Working on Secret New Super Weapon," *Washington Post*, September 29, 1988, p. A35.

52. Gonzalez testimony, Senate Banking Committee, *United States Export Policy toward Iraq*, p. 70.

53. The actual sale later fell apart because the financing was to be provided by BNL.

54. Cable, American Embassy Baghdad to Secretary of State, May 21, 1989.

55. Included in *Congressional Record*, February 24, 1991, p. H521.

56. U.S. Export-Import Bank, "Country Review: Iraq," April 24, 1989, p. 1.

57. U.S. Export-Import Bank, "Country Review, Part Two: Iraq," June 13, 1989, p. 13.

58. Ibid., p. 2, Tables 1 and 2.

59. Ibid., p. 13.

60. Mike Eisenstadt, *"The Sword of the Arabs": Iraq's Strategic Weapons* (Washington, D.C.: Washington Institute for Near East Policy, 1990), pp. 41–44.

61. The full reports remain classified. Portions were released in the *Congressional Record* by Congressman Henry Gonzalez. See especially the *Record* for July 27, 1992, pp. H6696–H6704; August 10, 1992, pp. H7871–82; and September 21, 1992, pp. H8820–29.

62. *Congressional Record*, August 10, 1992, p. H7873.

63. *Congressional Record*, July 27, 1992, p. H6699.

64. W. Seth Carus, testimony to a joint hearing of the House Foreign Affairs Subcommittees on Arms Control, International Security, and Science and International Economic Policy and Trade, July 12, 1989, p. 5 (Xerox).

65. "Iraq Goes It Alone on Condor II," *MidEast Markets*, May 15, 1989, pp. 7, 11.

66. Commerce Department licensing records; *Congressional Record*, July 21, 1992, p. H6342; *Washington Post*, July 22, 1992; Clyde Farnsworth, "U.S. Company Linked to Iraqi Atom Program," *New York Times*, June 26, 1991, p. A5.

67. *Congressional Record*, September 14, 1992, p. H8823.

68. The British government went so far as to bring criminal charges of illegal sale of arms-making equipment to Iraq against the Matrix-Churchill Ltd. executives despite the fact that they had been working with British intelligence. The charges finally were dropped when the case came to trial in November 1992 amidst revelations of cabinet knowledge of and complicity in the scheme. The case quickly was dubbed the "British Iraq-gate." Wide

coverage was given in the American press. See, for example, Eugene Robinson, "Britain to Probe Cabinet Role in Iraqi Arms Sales," *Washington Post*, November 11, 1992, pp. A27, A31; Eugene Robinson and R. Jeffrey Smith, "Profits Lured Britain to Accept Iraqi Deals," *Washington Post*, November 24, 1992, pp. A1, A18; "British Leaders Implicated in Secret Arms Sales to Iraq," National Public Radio, *Morning Edition*, March 29, 1994.

69. Robinson, "Britain to Probe Cabinet Role in Iraqi Arms Sales."

70. Douglas Frantz and William Tuohy, "British Allowed Iraq to Acquire Tooling for High-Tech Weapons, Documents Say," *Los Angeles Times*, November 11, 1992, p. A5.

71. Robinson, "Britain to Probe Cabinet Role in Iraqi Arms Sales"; Dean Baquet, "Britain Drops a Case Against 3 Charged with Arms Sales to Iraq," *New York Times*, November 10, 1992, pp. A1, A13; R. Jeffrey Smith, "CIA Knew of British Iraq Deal," *Washington Post*, February 15, 1993, p. A22.

72. Statement by Congressman Gonzalez, *Congressional Record*, February 2, 1993, pp. H320–27.

73. Letter from Gordon Cooper, Vice-President, Matrix-Churchill Corporation, to the Al-Arabi Trading Company, Baghdad, May 18, 1988, included in *Congressional Record*, August 10, 1992, p. H7877.

74. Most of the equipment for the carbide tool factory was obtained from American companies, licensed by the Reagan and Bush administrations. One company employee gave sworn testimony that his firm's sales were financed by diverted CCC credit guarantees. Part of the deal also involved training Iraqi workers in the United States. The one piece of equipment the Bush administration refused to license, the Iraqis obtained from another source. Douglas Frantz and Murray Waas, "Iraq Used American-Built Plant to Develop A-Arms," *Los Angeles Times*, August 7, 1992, pp. A1, A22; John Murray Brown, "Turkey Says It Made Raids Inside Iraq; Kurdish Separatist Bases Were Targets," *Washington Post*, August 7, 1991, p. A17; *Congressional Record*, August 10, 1992, pp. H7874–75; Timmerman, *The Death Lobby*, pp. 311–13.

75. Cited in Douglas Frantz and Murray Waas, "U.S. Knew Firm Was Iraq's a Year Before It Was Closed," *Los Angeles Times*, July 24, 1992, p. A1.

76. Dean Baquet with Elaine Sciolino, "European Suppliers of Iraq Were Known to Pentagon," *New York Times*, November 2, 1992, p. A3; Douglas Frantz and Murray Waas, "CIA Told White House of Iraqi Arms Efforts," *Los Angeles Times*, August 6, 1992, pp. A1, A3.

77. Statement by Congressman Henry Gonzalez and accompanying documents, *Congressional Record*, February 18, 1993, pp. H703–13; testimony by Jerry Kowalsky, House Banking Committee, *BNL Hearings*, pp. 28–30.

78. *Congressional Record*, February 3, 1992, p. H213.

79. Kenneth Cline, "Lavoro Bank Scandal: The Inside Story," *Southern Banker*, June 1990, p. 7.

80. Timmerman, *The Death Lobby*, p. 228.
81. U.S. Congress, Senate, Select Committee on Intelligence, *The Intelligence Community's Involvement in the Banca Nazionale del Lavoro (BNL) Affair*, Staff Report, 103rd Congress, 1st Session, February 1993, p. 55.
82. Central Intelligence Agency, Directorate of Intelligence, "Iraq-Italy: Repercussions of the BNL-Atlanta Scandal," November 6, 1989, included in *Congressional Record*, July 31, 1992, pp. H7142–44; Gonzalez testimony, Senate Banking Committee, *United States Export Policy toward Iraq*, p. 159.
83. *Congressional Record*, September 25, 1992, pp. H9502–H9507, and July 21, 1992, pp. H6338–46; Frantz and Waas, "U.S. Knew Firm Was Iraq's a Year Before It Was Closed," pp. A1, A18–A19; Peter Mantius, "Firms Tied to BNL Shielded," *Atlanta Journal and Constitution*, September 13, 1992, pp. A1, A8.
84. Alan Friedman, *Spider's Web: The Secret History of How the White House Illegally Armed Iraq* (New York: Bantam Books, 1993), pp. 110, 132. For a contrasting view see Kenneth I. Juster, "The Myth of Iraqgate," *Foreign Policy*, 94 (Spring 1994), pp. 105–19.
85. Letter dated September 21, 1989, in *Congressional Record*, February 3, 1992, p. H213; *Congressional Record*, July 27, 1992, p. H6700.
86. State Department information memorandum, "Subject: The Banca del Lavoro Scandal and Trade with Iraq," September 22, 1989.
87. Federal Reserve Board, office correspondence, "Subject: Banca Nazionale de Lavoro's Atlanta Agency," September 28, 1989; Friedman, *Spider's Web*, p. 131.
88. Communiqué issued by Iraqi embassy in Rome, cited in Laura Colby, "Iraq Voices 'Surprise' in BNL Scandal, Says Export-Credit Pacts Date to 1982," *Wall Street Journal*, September 12, 1989, p. A8.
89. U.S. Congress, House of Representatives, Committee on Foreign Affairs, *United States–Iraqi Relations*, hearing before the Subcommittee on Europe and the Middle East, 101st Congress, 2nd Session, April 26, 1990, p. 1; interviews, congressional staff, December 4 and 12, 1992; R. Jeffrey Smith and John Goshko, "Ill-Fated Iraq Policy Originated Shortly After Bush Took Office," *Washington Post*, June 27, 1992, p. A7; Judith Miller and Laurie Mylroie, *Saddam Hussein and the Crisis in the Gulf* (New York: Times Books, 1990), pp. 148–49.
90. Bernard Roshco, *When Policy Fails: How the Buck Was Passed When Kuwait Was Invaded*, Harvard University, John F. Kennedy School of Government, Discussion Paper D-15, December 1992, p. 10.
91. The NAC was established in 1945 by the Bretton Woods Agreement Act. It is chaired by the Treasury Department and also includes representatives of State, Commerce, the Federal Reserve, the Export-Import Bank, the Agency for International Development (AID), and the U.S. Trade Representative (USTR). When CCC credits and other matters within its admin-

istrative jurisdiction are considered, the Agriculture Department (USDA) also participates in NAC meetings.

92. Minutes, NAC Staff Committee, October 3, 1989; Smith, "Selling to Scoundrels," pp. C1, C4.

93. Treasury Department memorandum, "CCC Credit Guarantees for Iraq" (no date); NAC October 3 minutes.

94. State Department, "Secretary's October 6 Meeting with Iraqi Foreign Minister Tariq Aziz," October 13, 1989, reprinted in *Congressional Record*, March 2, 1992, pp. H864–66.

95. State Department, cable from American Embassy Baghdad to Secretary of State, "CCC Negotiations," October 9, 1989.

96. State Department, "CCC Credits for Iraq," October 11, 1989.

97. Memorandum to file, Assistant U.S. Attorney Gale McKenzie, "Briefing of USDA-OIG by NDGA re: Criminal Investigation of BNL-Atlanta," June 16, 1992.

98. Agriculture Department, Foreign Agricultural Service, "Iraqi Credit Consultations" (no date).

99. Notes of Secretary Baker's senior staff meeting, October, 13, 1989, and other documents, Senate Agriculture Committee.

100. Interview, congressional staff, December 7, 1992; State Department memorandum of conversation, "USDA Comments on Investigations of Iraq and the Banca Nazionale del Lavoro, Atlanta Branch, Scandal," October 13, 1989; testimony of Frank M. Lemay, House Judiciary Committee, June 23, 1992 (Xerox).

101. Senate Agriculture Committee, document dated October 17, 1989 (emphasis in original).

102. State Department, "The Iraqi CCC Program," October 26, 1989.

103. Ibid.

104. Senate Agriculture Committee documents.

105. Included in *Congressional Record*, April 28, 1992, pp. H2699–H2700.

106. Ibid.

107. Agriculture Department, Foreign Agricultural Service, letter to Allen E. Clapp, National Advisory Council on International Monetary and Financial Policies, November 1, 1989.

108. R. Jeffrey Smith, "U.S. Overlooked Iraq's Loan Record," *Washington Post*, October 24, 1992, p. A15.

109. Michael Wines, "President Angrily Contests Charges Over Loans to Iraq," *New York Times*, July 2, 1992, p. A6.

110. Minutes, NAC Staff Committee, November 3, 1989 (emphasis added).

111. Letter dated November 8, 1989, included in *Congressional Record*, April 28, 1992, p. H2701 (emphasis added).

112. *Congressional Record*, April 28, 1992, pp. H2696, H2699.

113. Sharon LaFraniere and R. Jeffrey Smith, "Push for BNL Independent Counsel Likely After Disclosure of White House Call," *Washington Post,* July 9, 1992, p. A20; Elaine Sciolino, "Bush Staff Lawyer's Call on Iraq Is Reported," *New York Times,* July 9, 1992, p. A2, and "House Panel Urges Special Counsel for Iraq Inquiry," *New York Times,* July 10, 1992, p. A3; William Safire, "Obstructing Justice," *New York Times,* July 9, 1992, p. A21; R. Jeffrey Smith, "Memos on Iraq Loan Probe Criticized Administration," *Washington Post,* September 29, 1992, p. A3; U.S. Attorney's Office for Northern Georgia memorandum, Gale McKenzie to Gerrilyn Brill, "CCC Payments to Iraqi Owned Banks Resulting from Iraq's Repudiation of Its Debt to the U.S. Under the GSM Agricultural Credit Guarantee Program," April 9, 1992.

114. CIA, "Iraq-Italy," in *Congressional Record,* July 31, 1992, p. H7143.

115. Ibid.

116. Minutes, NAC Deputies Meeting, November 8, 1989.

117. Ibid.

118. Letter from Jack Parnell, Acting Secretary of Agriculture, to Treasury Secretary Nicholas Brady, November 8, 1989.

119. State Department, "Message to Iraqi Foreign Minister on CCC Credits," November 9, 1989.

120. State Department, "Message from Secretary to Iraqi Foreign Minister on CCC," November 9, 1989.

121. Ibid.

4: Saddam's Strategy: Into Kuwait, Not the Family of Nations

1. Anthony H. Cordesman, "Iraq and Weapons of Mass Destruction," included in *Congressional Record,* April 8, 1992, pp. S5062–74.

2. *Foreign Broadcast Information Service—Near East Section* (hereafter *FBIS-NES*), December 11, 1989, p. 22.

3. *FBIS-NES,* January 19, 1990, p. 22.

4. R. Jeffrey Smith, "Iraq's Nuclear Prowess Underestimated by U.S.," *Washington Post,* October 13, 1991, p. A45.

5. "Iraq and the Bomb," *MidEast Markets,* December 11, 1989.

6. *FBIS-NES,* December 7, 1989, pp. 28–29, and December 11, 1989, pp. 22–23.

7. *Keesing's Record of World Events,* "Middle East–Arab World," January 1990, p. 37199; *FBIS-NES,* January 5, 1990, p. 18.

8. Murray Waas and Douglas Frantz, "New Documents Show Bush Aides Favored Helping Iraq," *Los Angeles Times,* September 4, 1992, p. A1.

9. Memorandum dated November 21, 1989, included in *Congressional Record,* July 21, 1992, p. H6344.

10. Alan Friedman, *Spider's Web: The Secret History of How the White House Illegally Armed Iraq* (New York: Bantam Books, 1993), pp. 149–150.

11. Ruth Sinai, "Administration's Support for Iraq Ignored Multiple Early Warnings," Associated Press wire story, June 4, 1992.

12. State Department cables, American Embassy Baghdad to Secretary of State: "DAS Gnehm Call on Minister of Trade—CCC and BNL," December 10, 1989, and "U.S. Legislation Suspending Ex-Im Credits to Iraq," December 11, 1989.

13. State Department, "Memorandum of Justification for a Waiver of Export-Import Bank Restrictions with Respect to Iraq," January 2, 1990.

14. State Department memorandum, "Second Tranche of CCC Credits for Iraq," January 4, 1990.

15. State Department cable, December 10.

16. Ibid.

17. Don Oberdorfer, "Missed Signals in the Middle East," *Washington Post Magazine,* March 13, 1991, p. 22; interview, former Bush administration official, April 4, 1992.

18. Oberdorfer, "Missed Signals in the Middle East," p. 22.

19. "No More Secret Police," text included in Stanley Kober, *Appeasement and the Gulf War,* Progressive Policy Institute, July 1992 (emphasis added).

20. William Safire, "Broadcast to Baghdad," *New York Times,* September 10, 1990, p. A23.

21. Efraim Karsh and Inauri Rautsi, *Saddam Hussein: A Political Biography* (New York: Free Press, 1991), p. 208.

22. U.S. Congress, House of Representatives, Committee on Foreign Affairs, *Country Reports on Human Rights Practices for 1989,* 101st Congress, 2nd Session, February 1990, pp. 1411–15.

23. William M. Carley, "How Iraq Attempted to Kill a Dissident in the United States," *Wall Street Journal,* February 27, 1991, pp. A1, A4.

24. State Department cable, "Iraqi Protest: VOA Editorial," February 27, 1990, included in Kober, *Appeasement and the Gulf War.*

25. Letter dated February 28, 1990, in ibid.

26. Senator Simpson's statement is from the transcript of the meeting released by Iraq and included in *FBIS-NES,* April 17, 1990, pp. 5–13. While the veracity of Iraqi versions of transcripts is subject to question, Senator Simpson was reported to have confirmed that this one "accurately reflected his statements." R. Jeffrey Smith, "Saddam's Beef with the Press: The Despot Got Plenty of Sympathy from His American Visitors," *Washington Post,* September 30, 1990, p. D5.

27. NAC Alternates Meeting, Minutes, February 22, 1990; State Department memorandum, "CCC Program for Iraq," February 22, 1990; Douglas Frantz

and Murray Waas, "Secret Effort in '89 Helped Hussein Build Iraq's War Machine," *Los Angeles Times,* February 24, 1992, pp. A1, A6.

28. Letter from Senator Leahy to Agriculture Secretary Yeutter, February 12, 1990; letter from Secretary Yeutter to Senator Leahy, February 20, 1990.

29. State Department memorandums, "Status of Iraq CCC Program," February 28, 1990, and "NAC Meeting on Iraq CCC Program," March 5, 1990.

30. State Department, *Current Policy,* No. 1259, Bureau of Public Affairs, 1990.

31. *FBIS-NES,* February 20, 1990, pp. 1–6, and February 27, 1990, pp. 1–5; "Kuwait: How the West Blundered," *The Economist,* September 29, 1990.

32. Interview of Egyptian Ambassador-at-Large Tahseen Bashir by Professor Janice Gross Stein of the University of Toronto. See her article, "Deterrence and Compellence in the Gulf, 1990–91: A Failed or Impossible Task?," *International Security,* 17 (Fall 1992), p. 163, footnote 57.

33. *FBIS-NES,* February 6, 1990, p. 24, and February 27, 1990, pp. 1–5.

34. *FBIS-NES,* March 15, 1990, p. 27.

35. Lawrence Freedman and Efraim Karsh, *The Gulf Conflict: Diplomacy and War in the New World Order* (London: Faber and Faber, 1993), p. 45.

36. Elaine Sciolino, *The Outlaw State: Saddam Hussein's Quest for Power and the Gulf Crisis* (New York: John Wiley and Sons, 1991), p. 199.

37. Christine Moss Helms, "Arab Perspectives of the Gulf Crisis," in Robert F. Helms II and Robert H. Dorff, eds., *The Persian Gulf Crisis: Power in the Post–Cold War World* (Westport, CT: Praeger, 1993), p. 75.

38. These sites eventually would contain 28 operational launchers, and would be used extensively in the 1991 war against Israel and Saudi Arabia. U.S. Department of Defense, *Conduct of the Persian Gulf War,* Final Report to Congress, April 1992, p. 16.

39. State Department cable, "Possible Iraqi Missile and Nuclear-Related Procurement," February 12, 1990.

40. "Approved Licenses to Iraq," records submitted to the House Government Operations Subcommittee on Commerce, Consumer and Monetary Affairs, March 7, 1991; *Congressional Record,* July 21, 1992, p. H6342.

41. U.S. Congress, House of Representatives, Committee on Government Operations, *U.S. Government Controls on Sales to Iraq,* hearing before the Commerce, Consumer and Monetary Affairs Subcommittee, 101st Congress, 2nd Session, September 27, 1990, p. 306.

42. State Department memorandum, "Licensing for Iraq," late February or early March 1990.

43. "I followed up on your suggestion about a possible connection between Banca Nazionale del Lavoro ('BNL') and the nuclear triggers that were seized in London. As you suspected, there is a connection." Federal Reserve Bank of New York memorandum, "Subject: Lavoro," April 5, 1990.

44. Kenneth Timmerman, *The Death Lobby: How the West Armed Iraq* (Boston: Houghton Mifflin, 1991), pp. 319–20, 361–62, 371–79.

45. U.S. Congress, House of Representatives, Committee on Energy and Commerce, *Nuclear Nonproliferation,* hearing before the Subcommittee on Oversight and Investigations, 102nd Congress, 1st Session, April 24, 1991, pp. 339–41.

46. *Keesing's Record of World Events,* News Digest for March 1990, "Iraq," p. 37332.

47. Timmerman, *The Death Lobby,* pp. 378–79.

48. Ibid., pp. 357–58, 375–76; William Safire, "Object: Survival," *New York Times,* November 5, 1990, p. A21.

49. *Keesing's Record of World Events,* March 1990, p. 37332; Nigel Hawkes, "Major in Plea for Observer Reporter," *Observer,* October 1, 1989, p. 1; Timmerman, *The Death Lobby,* p. 376.

50. Bernard Roshco, *When Policy Fails: How the Buck Was Passed When Kuwait Was Invaded,* Harvard University, John F. Kennedy School of Government, Discussion Paper D-15, December 1992, pp. 14–15.

51. Oberdorfer, "Missed Signals in the Middle East," p. 36.

52. *FBIS-NES,* April 3, 1990, pp. 32–37 (emphasis added).

53. Bob Woodward, *The Commanders* (New York: Simon and Schuster, 1991), p. 201.

54. Ibid., p. 202.

55. *Keesing's Record of World Events,* News Digest for April 1990, p. 37390.

56. Woodward, *The Commanders,* pp. 203–204.

57. State Department cable, Secretary of State to American Embassy Baghdad, "Tensions in U.S.-Iraqi Relations," April 12, 1990.

58. *Congressional Record,* April 20, 1990, p. S4678.

59. State Department memorandums, "Note to the Secretary: DC Meeting on Iraq," April 17, 1990, and "NSC Deputies Committee Meeting on Iraq, April 16, 1990."

60. Testimony in U.S. Congress, House, Committee on Foreign Relations, *U.S. Exports of Sensitive Technology to Iraq,* hearing before the Subcommittee on International Economic Policy and Trade, 102nd Congress, 1st Session, April 8 and May 22, 1991; also letter and attachments from Under Secretary of Commerce Kloske to Congressman Gejdenson, May 2, 1990.

61. State Department memorandum, "Possible New Trade Controls on Iraq and other Chemical-Biological Warfare Proliferators," April 16, 1990, and "Discussion Paper for Iraq PCC" (n.d.), emphases in original.

62. Staff of U.S. News and World Report, *Triumph Without Victory: The History of the Persian Gulf War* (New York: Times Books, 1993), pp. 17–18.

63. Oberdorfer, "Missed Signals in the Middle East," p. 36; Robert S. Greenberger, "How the Baker Plan for Early Sanctions Against Iraq Failed," *Wall*

Street Journal, October 1, 1990, pp. A1, A12; *Los Angeles Times,* February 24, 1992, pp. A1, A6; Friedman, *Spider's Web,* pp. 161–62.

64. Kimmitt testimony, House Foreign Relations Committee, *U.S. Exports of Sensitive Technology to Iraq,* p. 90.

65. U.S. Congress, House of Representatives, Committee on Foreign Affairs, *Consideration of Miscellaneous Bills and Resolutions (Volume II),* Markup, 101st Congress, 2nd Session, 1989–90; Kitty Dumas, "Iraq: Hill Members Renew Attempts to Impose Sanctions," *Congressional Quarterly Weekly Report,* April 28, 1990, pp. 1281–82; *Congressional Record,* July 9, 1992, p. H6242.

66. "Senator Dole: I assume [President] Bush will object to the sanctions. He may veto them, unless something provocative occurs. Ambassador Glaspie: As an American ambassador, I can confirm this is the U.S. Government policy. Senator Dole: We in Congress also try to exert our utmost efforts in this direction." *FBIS-NES,* April 17, 1990, p. 9.

67. *Congressional Record,* July 9, 1992, pp. H6237–41; William Safire, "Into the Shredder," *New York Times,* September 24, 1992, p. A29; Agriculture Department press releases and other documents, Senate Agriculture Committee.

68. Douglas Frantz and Murray Waas, "U.S. Loans Indirectly Financed Iraq Military," *Los Angeles Times,* February 25, 1992, pp. A1, A7.

69. U.S. Congress, House of Representatives, Committee on Foreign Affairs, *United States-Iraqi Relations,* hearing before the Subcommittee on Europe and the Middle East, 101st Congress, 2nd Session, April 26, 1990, pp. 1, 22–23.

70. State Department cable, "American Embassy Baghdad to Secretary of State, Hamilton Subcommittee," April 25, 1990 (emphasis added); letter from Human Rights Watch, *Consideration of Miscellaneous Bills and Resolutions,* pp. 475–76.

71. Alexander L. George, *Bridging the Gap: Theory and Practice in Foreign Policy* (Washington, D.C.: U.S. Institute of Peace Press, 1993), p. 37.

72. State Department memorandum, "Options Paper on Iraq," included in *Congressional Record,* March 9, 1992, pp. H1111–12.

73. Treasury Department memorandum, May 25, 1990, included in House Banking Committee, "BNL Chronology," document obtained from staff.

74. Agriculture Department, "USDA Administrative Review of Iraq GSM-102 Program," May 21, 1990; *Congressional Record,* July 9, 1992, pp. H6237–41; *Congressional Record,* April 28, 1992, pp. H2694–702.

75. *Congressional Record,* July 9, 1992, p. H6241.

76. Commerce Department memorandums, "Interagency Meeting on Iraq," June 11, 1990, and "The NSC and Iraq," May 29, 1991.

77. *Congressional Record,* July 27, 1992; R. Jeffrey Smith, "U.S. Cleared Factory Sale to Iraq Despite Own Ban," *Washington Post,* July 27, 1992, pp. A1, A14.

78. *U.S. News and World Report,* June 4, 1990.

79. *FBIS-NES*, May 29, 1990, pp. 2–7.

80. *Keesing's Record of World Events*, News Digest for May 1990, pp. 37472–73.

81. Quoted in Alex Roberto Hybel, *Power Over Rationality: The Bush Administration and the Gulf Crisis* (Albany, NY: State University of New York Press, 1993), pp. 29–30.

82. State Department cable, Secretary of State to American Embassy Baghdad (and other Middle East embassies), "Iraq and Terrorism," June 27, 1990.

83. Bruce Hoffman, *The Ultimate Fifth Column: Saddam Hussein, International Terrorism and the Crisis in the Gulf,* Rand Corporation, P-7668, August 1990, p. 3.

84. June 27 cable (Secretary of State to American Embassy Baghdad), "Iraq and Terrorism."

85. Ishan A. Hijazi, "PLO and Iraq Cooperate on Hard-Line Strategy," *New York Times*, May 13, 1990.

86. Hoffman, *The Ultimate Fifth Column*, p. 2.

87. State Department cable, Secretary of State to American Embassy Baghdad, "Demarche on Abu Abbas," June 20, 1990.

88. June 27 cable (Secretary of State to American Embassy Baghdad), "Iraq and Terrorism."

89. State Department cable, American Embassy Baghdad to Secretary of State, "Iraq and Terrorism," June 27, 1990.

90. *U.S. Exports of Sensitive Technology to Iraq*, p. 49.

91. State Department memorandum, "Returning Iraq to the Terrorism List," September 1, 1990.

92. Paul K. Davis and John Arquilla, *Deterring or Coercing Opponents in Crisis: Lessons from the War with Saddam Hussein* (Rand Corporation, 1991), pp. 5–7.

93. Ibid., p. 5; Woodward, *The Commanders*, p. 217.

94. Freedman and Karsh, *The Gulf Conflict*, pp. 47–49; Oberdorfer, "Missed Signals in the Middle East," pp. 37–38.

95. John K. Cooley, "Pre-War Gulf Diplomacy," *Survival*, 33 (March/April 1991), p. 127.

96. Freedman and Karsh, *The Gulf Conflict*, p. 49; Cooley, "Pre-War Gulf Diplomacy," p. 127.

97. While wanting Iraq to notice, the UAE also had its sensitivities about open military cooperation with the United States. When the Pentagon publicly confirmed the operation, the UAE protested to Washington that it had wanted it kept secret. Woodward, *The Commanders*, p. 210; Stein, "Deterrence and Compellence in the Gulf," p. 151; U.S. Congress, House of Representatives, Committee on Foreign Affairs, *Developments in the Middle East, July 1990*, hearing before the Subcommittee on Europe and the Middle East, 101st Congress, 2nd Session, July 31, 1990, p. 56.

98. Aside from the innumerable articles and commentaries on the Glaspie-

Saddam meeting, the key sources for the primary documents are as follows: Excerpts from the Iraqi version of the transcript were published in the *New York Times*, September 23, 1990, p. 19. Excerpts from the July 24 cable from Secretary of State Baker and the July 25 cable from Ambassador Glaspie reporting on her meeting with Saddam were published in the *Washington Post*, October 21, 1992, p. A17. See also Ambassador Glaspie's congressional testimony: U.S. Congress, House of Representatives, Committee on Foreign Affairs, *United States–Iraqi Relations*, hearing before the Subcommittee on Europe and the Middle East, 102nd Congress, 1st Session, March 12, 1991, and the "informal public discussion" with the Senate Foreign Relations Committee on March 20, 1991, never officially published but available through the Federal Information Systems Corporation data base.

99. House Foreign Affairs Committee (1991), *United States–Iraqi Relations*, p. 9.

100. Roshco, *When Policy Fails*, p. 20.

101. Woodward, *The Commanders*, pp. 214–15.

102. Excerpts from text of the cable, *Washington Post*, October 21, 1992. See also Michael R. Gordon, "Pentagon Objected to a Message Bush Sent to Iraq Before Its Invasion," *New York Times*, October 25, 1992, pp. 1, 14; Woodward, *The Commanders*, pp. 215–16; Jim Hoagland, "Hiding Behind April Glaspie," *Washington Post*, October 21, 1992, p. A19.

103. *Congressional Record*, July 26, 1990, p. S10832, and July 27, 1990, p. S10907. The differences between the House and Senate bills had yet to be worked out by conference committee when they were superseded by the post-invasion sanctions imposed through executive order by President Bush.

104. Reports cited and quoted in *Congressional Record*, July 21, 1992, p. H6342, and July 27, 1992, p. H6700.

105. State Department memorandum, "Foreign Policy Controls for Proliferation-Related Exports to Iraq," July 19, 1990 (emphasis added); letter to Secretary of Commerce Mosbacher from Secretary of State Baker, July 25, 1990.

106. In a meeting ostensibly to reassure Ambassador Glaspie that his father-in-law would not invade Kuwait, Hussein Kamil also asked if the ambassador could "spring our furnaces for us." House Foreign Affairs Committee (1991), *United States–Iraqi Relations*, p. 4.

107. Patrick J. Sloyan, "Bush Ignored Satellite Tip-Off of Invasion," *Cleveland Plain-Dealer*, September 21, 1990, pp. 1A, 4A.

108. Woodward, *The Commanders*, pp. 216–17.

109. Testimony during confirmation hearings for Robert Gates, U.S. Senate, Select Committee on Intelligence, *Nomination of Robert Gates*, Hearings, 102nd Congress, 1st Session, September 24, 1991, pp. 29–30.

110. Michael Wines, "A Cassandra of the Gulf Is Sidelined by the CIA," *New York Times*, January 24, 1991, p. A15; Woodward, *The Commanders*, pp. 216–20;

Oberdorfer, "Missed Signals in the Middle East," p. 40. In his memoirs General Schwarzkopf claims that based on his own military intelligence, "shortly after noon on the last day of July, we notified Washington that war between Iraq and Kuwait appeared imminent." He acknowledges, however, that "I didn't believe Saddam would grab the entire country." H. Norman Schwarzkopf, *Autobiography: It Doesn't Take a Hero* (New York: Bantam Books, 1992), pp. 294–95.

111. House Foreign Affairs Committee, *Developments in the Middle East*, pp. 6, 14.

112. Staff of U.S. News and World Report, *Triumph Without Victory*, p. 25.

113. Michael A. Palmer, *Guardians of the Gulf: A History of America's Expanding Role in the Persian Gulf, 1833–1992* (New York: Free Press, 1992), p. 160.

114. Woodward, *The Commanders*, pp. 218–19; Freedman and Karsh, *The Gulf Conflict*, pp. 60–61.

115. Defense Department, *Conduct of the Persian Gulf War*, pp. 7–9.

116. Palmer, *Guardians of the Gulf*, p. 159; Davis and Arquilla, *Deterring or Coercing Opponents in Crisis*, pp. 47–48.

117. Oberdorfer, "Missed Signals in the Middle East," p. 40.

118. Speech to a joint session of Congress, September 11, 1990.

119. This is not in any way to lend credence to the attempts by such critics as Ramsey Clark to blame the United States for the costs of the war. The "blame America always and especially" ideology of such leftism is no more genuinely analytic than the "blame America never" ideology of many ardent conservatives. See, for example, the commentary by Jim Hoagland, "Ramsey Clark: Wrong Again," *Washington Post*, March 23, 1993, p. A21.

120. Joseph Albright, "Iraqi Threat Still Serious, CIA Believes," *Atlanta Journal-Constitution*, January 16, 1992, pp. A1, A10.

5: The Enemy of My Enemy May Still Be My Enemy, Too: Lessons for Foreign Policy Strategy

1. Testimony of Lawrence Eagleburger, U.S. Congress, House of Representatives, hearing before the Committee on Banking, Finance, and Urban Affairs, *Banca Nazionale Del Lavoro (BNL) Scandal and the Department of Agriculture's Commodity Credit Corporation (CCC) Program for Iraq, Part I*, 102nd Congress, 2nd Session, May 21, 1992, pp. 29–39.

2. Walid Khalidi, "Iraq vs. Kuwait: Claims and Counterclaims," in Micah L. Sifry and Christopher Cerf, eds., *The Gulf War Reader* (New York: Random House, 1991), p. 57.

3. Robert O. Keohane, "Reciprocity in International Relations," *International Organization*, 40 (Winter 1986), p. 8.

4. The classic statement of the "free-rider" dilemma remains Mancur Olson, *The Logic of Collective Action* (Cambridge, Mass.: Harvard University Press, 1965).

5. John E. Rielly, "America's State of Mind," *Foreign Policy*, 66 (Spring 1987), p. 42.

6. Khalidi, "Iraq vs. Kuwait," p. 58.

7. State Department, "Secretary's October 6 Meeting with Iraqi Foreign Minister Tariq Aziz," October 13, 1989, reprinted in *Congressional Record*, March 2, 1992, pp. H864–66.

8. Alexander L. George, *Bridging the Gap: Theory and Practice in Foreign Policy* (Washington, D.C.: U.S. Institute of Peace, 1993), p. 47.

9. Letter dated June 20, 1985, from Secretary of State George Shultz to Congressman Howard L. Berman (D-California); State Department memorandum, "Administration Policy on Proposed Iraq Sanctions," October 18, 1988.

10. Gary Hufbauer and Jeffrey Schott, *Economic Sanctions Reconsidered: History and Current Policy* (Washington, D.C.: Institute for International Economics, 1985); Bruce W. Jentleson, *Pipeline Politics: The Complex Political Economy of East-West Energy Trade* (Ithaca, NY: Cornell University Press, 1986).

11. Johan Galtung, "On the Effects of International Sanctions, with Examples from the Case of Rhodesia," *World Politics*, 19 (April 1967), pp. 378–416.

12. There also was the instance mentioned in Chapter 1 when, as part of the arms-for-hostages gambit, the Iraqis were given additional intelligence data to encourage them to step up their bombing raids so that, unknowingly, they might make Iran want U.S. arms enough to release all the American hostages.

13. Staff of U.S. News and World Report, *Triumph Without Victory: The History of the Persian Gulf War* (New York: Random House, 1993), p. 14; "Options Paper on Iraq," *Congressional Record*, March 9, 1992, pp. H1111–12.

14. *Congressional Record*, July 21, 1992, p. H6341; Murray Waas and Douglas Frantz, "Iraq Got U.S. Technology After CIA Warned Baker," *Los Angeles Times*, July 22, 1992, p. A10; Douglas Frantz and Murray Waas, "U.S. Documents Dispute Bush on Iraq A-Arms," *Los Angeles Times*, July 2, 1992, pp. A1, A22.

15. CBS, "This Morning," July 1, 1992.

16. Testimony of David Kay as well as Gary Milhollin and Kenneth Timmerman in U.S. Congress, Senate Committee on Banking, Housing, and Urban Affairs, *United States Export Policy toward Iraq Prior to Iraq's Invasion of Kuwait*, Hearing, 102nd Congress, 2nd Session, October 27, 1992, p. 81, emphasis in original; see also pp. 54, 85. R. Jeffrey Smith, "Dozens of U.S. Items Used in Iraq Arms," *Washington Post*, July 22, 1992, pp. A1, A28. Among the equipment found at the Al Atheer complex, one of the facilities blown up by the IAEA because of its centrality to the whole Iraqi nuclear weapons program, was the carbide-tipped machine tool factory which American firms and BNL financing had helped build (Chapter 3). In addition, UNSCOM found equipment from 11 American companies in Iraqi missile and chemi-

cal weapons plants. Some of those 17 bacterial and viral cultures licensed for export by the Reagan and Bush administrations also turned up at the Salman Pak site as part of what UNSCOM found to be a "major military research program . . . concentrating on anthrax and botulism."

17. *Congressional Record*, July 21, 1992, p. H6346. At an April 1991 congressional hearing, two Bush administration officials, Commerce Under Secretary for Export Administration Dennis Kloske and Defense Deputy Under Secretary for Trade Security Policy William N. Rudman, were questioned by Republican congressman Toby Roth as to whether U.S. technology exports helped Saddam's military forces: "Mr. Kloske: I think in some instances it is quite clear that it probably contributed to his military capabilities. Mr. Roth: Mr. Rudman, how would you answer that? Mr. Rudman: I would answer yes." U.S. Congress, House of Representatives, Committee on Foreign Affairs, *U.S. Exports of Sensitive Technology to Iraq*, hearing before the International Economic Policy and Trade Subcommittee, 102nd Congress, 1st Session, April 8 and May 22, 1991, p. 42.

18. Elaine Sciolino, *The Outlaw State: Saddam Hussein's Quest for Power and the Gulf Crisis* (New York: John Wiley and Sons, 1991), p. 139.

19. Anthony H. Cordesman, "Iraq and Weapons of Mass Destruction," included in *Congressional Record*, April 8, 1992, pp. S5062–74.

20. Gary Milhollin, "The Iraqi Bomb," *The New Yorker*, February 1, 1992, pp. 47–56.

21. *Restoring the Balance: U.S. Strategy and the Gulf Crisis*, Initial Report of the Washington Institute's Strategic Study Group (Washington, D.C.: Washington Institute on Near East Policy, 1991), p. 13.

22. Alexander George and Richard Smoke, "Deterrence and Foreign Policy," *World Politics*, 41 (January 1989), p. 182. See also their earlier and classic book, *Deterrence in American Foreign Policy: Theory and Practice* (New York: Columbia University Press, 1974), especially Chapter 21.

23. Evan Luard, "Conciliation and Deterrence: A Comparison of Political Strategies in the Interwar and Postwar Periods," *World Politics*, 19 (January 1967), p. 185. Luard applies this to the 1938 Munich agreement, arguing that "the fault was that the British and others attempted conciliation without a sufficient reserve of deterrence as an inducement against alternative courses. Conceivably, it is true, no degree of armed strength on their part could have convinced Hitler that they really meant business or could have deterred him from war. . . . On the other hand . . . conciliation unbacked by strength was certain to fail" (p. 186).

24. Paul Huth and Bruce Russett, "Deterrence Failure and Crisis Escalation," *International Studies Quarterly*, 32 (March 1988), pp. 29–45; Paul Huth, *Extended Deterrence and the Prevention of War* (New Haven, CT: Yale University Press, 1988); Noel Kaplowitz, "Psychopolitical Dimensions of Interna-

tional Relations: The Reciprocal Effects of Conflict Strategies," *International Studies Quarterly,* 28 (December 1984), pp. 373–406.

25. Robert Jervis, *Perception and Misperception in International Relations* (Princeton: Princeton University Press, 1976); Richard Ned Lebow, *Between Peace and War: The Nature of International Crises* (Baltimore: Johns Hopkins University Press, 1981); Richard Ned Lebow and Janice Gross Stein, "Rational Deterrence Theory: I Think, Therefore I Deter," *World Politics,* 41 (January 1989), pp. 208–24.

26. U.S. Congress, Senate, Select Committee on Intelligence, *Nomination of Robert M. Gates,* Hearings, 102nd Congress, 1st Session, September 24, October 1, 2, 1991, Volume II, p. 30.

27. Bob Woodward, *The Commanders* (New York: Simon and Schuster, 1991), p. 217.

28. Douglas Frantz and Murray Waas, "U.S. Loans Indirectly Financed Iraq Military," *Los Angeles Times,* February 25, 1992, p. A7.

29. Lawrence Freedman and Efraim Karsh, *The Gulf Conflict, 1990–1991: Diplomacy and War in the New World Order* (London: Faber and Faber, 1993), p. 58.

30. Paul K. Davis and John Arquilla, *Deterring or Coercing Opponents in Crisis: Lessons from the War with Saddam Hussein* (Santa Monica, CA: Rand Corporation, 1991), R-4111-JS, p. 70.

31. Bruce W. Jentleson, "The Pretty Prudent Public: Post Post-Vietnam American Opinion on the Use of Military Force," *International Studies Quarterly,* 36 (March 1992), pp. 49–74.

32. Ibid., pp. 65–67.

33. Charles Allen testimony, Senate Select Committee on Intelligence, *Nomination of Robert Gates,* pp. 80–81.

34. Murray Waas and Douglas Frantz, "New Documents Show Bush Aides Favored Helping Iraq," *Los Angeles Times,* September 4, 1992, p. A1.

35. Janice Gross Stein, "Deterrence and Compellence in the Gulf, 1990–91: A Failed or Impossible Task?," *International Security,* 17 (Fall 1992), pp. 147–79; Freedman and Karsh, *The Gulf Conflict* pp. 42–63; Milton Viorst, "Report from Baghdad," *The New Yorker,* June 24, 1991, pp. 55–73.

36. Stein, "Deterrence and Compellence in the Gulf," p. 148.

37. State Department cable, American Embassy Baghdad to Secretary of State, "DAS Gnehm Call on Minister of Trade—CCC and BNL," December 10, 1989.

38. Viorst, "Report from Baghdad," p. 67.

39. Cited in Norman Cigar, "Iraq's Strategic Mindset and the Gulf War: Blueprint for Defeat," *Journal of Strategic Studies,* 15 (March 1992), p. 3.

40. Cited in Martin Indyk, "The Postwar Balance of Power in the Middle East," in Joseph S. Nye, Jr., and Roger K. Smith, eds., *After the Storm: Lessons from the Gulf War* (New York: Madison Books, 1992), p. 110, footnote 16.

41. Stein, "Deterrence and Compellence in the Gulf," p. 147.

42. Davis and Arquilla, *Deterring or Coercing Opponents in Crisis,* p. 6.

43. Woodward, *The Commanders,* p. 239.

44. George, *Bridging the Gap,* p. 16.

45. Ibid., pp. xxiv–xxv, 16.

46. Ibid., pp. 117–18.

47. See, for example, Bernard Brodie, ed., *The Absolute Weapon: Atomic Power and World Order* (New York: Harcourt Brace, 1946) and *War and Politics* (New York: Macmillan, 1973); Herman Kahn, *On Thermonuclear War* (Princeton: Princeton University Press, 1960); Albert Wohlstetter, "The Delicate Balance of Terror," *Foreign Affairs,* 37 (January 1959), pp. 211–34; Henry Kissinger, *Nuclear Weapons and Foreign Policy* (New York: Harper and Row, 1957); Thomas Schelling, *The Strategy of Conflict* (Cambridge, MA: Harvard University Press, 1960); and the accounts in Fred Kaplan, *The Wizards of Armageddon* (New York: Simon and Schuster, 1983).

48. Robert Axelrod, *The Evolution of Cooperation* (New York: Basic Books, 1984); Charles E. Osgood, "Suggestions for Winning the Real War with Communism," *Journal of Conflict Resolution,* 3 (December 1959), pp. 295–325; Alexander L. George, "Strategies for Facilitating Cooperation," in A. L. George, Philip J. Farley, and Alexander Dallin, eds., *U.S.-Soviet Security Cooperation* (New York: Oxford University Press, 1988), pp. 692–711.

49. Axelrod, *Evolution of Cooperation,* p. 119.

50. Cited in Hans Morgenthau, *Politics Among Nations,* 5th edition (New York: Alfred A. Knopf, 1985), p. 10.

51. George Liska, *Nations in Alliance: The Limits of Interdependence* (Baltimore: Johns Hopkins University Press, 1962), p. 12.

6: Premises, Processes, and Politics: Lessons for Foreign Policy Making

1. Baker's statement on October 29, 1990, cited in Thomas L. Friedman, "Baker Seen as Balancing Bush's Urge to Fight Iraq," *New York Times,* November 3, 1990, p. 6; Bush statement during the third presidential debate, see transcript, *New York Times,* October 20, 1992, p. A24.

2. Irving L. Janis, *Victims of Groupthink* (Boston: Houghton Mifflin, 1972); Peter Wyden, *The Bay of Pigs: The Untold Story* (New York: Simon and Schuster, 1979); Richard E. Neustadt and Ernest R. May, *Thinking in Time: The Use of History for Decision Makers,* (New York: Free Press, 1986), pp. 134–56.

3. Larry Berman, *Planning a Tragedy: The Americanization of the War in Vietnam* (New York: W.W. Norton, 1982); Stanley Karnow, *Vietnam: A History* (New York: Viking, 1983); Neil Sheehan, *The Pentagon Papers* (New York: Quadrangle Books, 1975).

4. Gary Sick, *All Fall Down: America's Tragic Encounter with Iran* (New York: Viking Penguin, 1985); Zbigniew Brzezinski, *Power and Principle: Memoirs of the National Security Advisor, 1977–1981* (New York: Farrar, Strauss and Giroux, 1983); Cyrus Vance, *Hard Choices: Critical Years in America's Foreign Policy* (New York: Simon and Schuster, 1983); Jimmy Carter, *Keeping Faith: Memoirs of a President* (New York: Bantam Books, 1982); Bruce W. Jentleson, "Discrepant Responses to Falling Dictators: Presidential Belief Systems and the Mediating Effects of the Senior Advisory Process," *Political Psychology*, 11 (June 1990), pp. 353–82.

5. Bruce W. Jentleson, "The Lebanon War and Soviet-American Competition: Scope and Limits of Superpower Influence," in Steven L. Spiegel, Mark Heller, and Jacob Goldberg, eds., *The Soviet-American Competition in the Middle East* (Lexington, MA: Lexington Books, 1986); Thomas Friedman, *From Beirut to Jerusalem* (New York: Farrar Straus Giroux, 1989).

6. This section draws on Jentleson, "Discrepant Responses to Falling Dictators," pp. 355–57.

7. Kenneth Waltz, *Theory of International Politics* (Reading, MA: Addison-Wesley, 1979).

8. Hans Morgenthau, *Politics Among Nations: The Struggle for Power and Peace* (New York: Alfred A. Knopf, 1961), p. 5 and passim.

9. Bruce Bueno de Mesquita, *The War Trap* (New Haven, CT: Yale University Press, 1981); Bruce Bueno de Mesquita and David Lalman, "Reason and War," *American Political Science Review*, 80 (December 1986), pp. 1113–29; Duncan Snidal, "The Game Theory of International Politics," *World Politics*, 37 (October 1985), pp. 35–57.

10. Robert Jervis, *Perception and Misperception in International Politics* (Princeton: Princeton University Press, 1976), p. 28.

11. Richard Betts, "Analysis, War and Decision," *World Politics*, 31 (October 1978), p. 961.

12. Alexander L. George, "Criteria for Evaluation of Foreign Policy Decisionmaking," *Global Perspectives*, 2 (Spring 1984), pp. 59–60, and *Presidential Decisionmaking in Foreign Policy: The Effective Use of Information and Advice* (Boulder, CO: Westview Press, 1980).

13. Jervis, *Perception and Misperception*, pp. 112–15; Irving Janis and Leon Mann, *Decision-Making: A Psychological Analysis of Conflict, Choice and Commitment* (New York: Free Press, 1977), pp. 128–30; Richard Ned Lebow, *Between Peace and War: The Nature of International Crises* (Baltimore: Johns Hopkins University Press, 1981), pp. 101–19.

14. Glenn Frankel, "Deepening Confrontation with Iraq Rooted in U.S. Obsession with Iran," *Washington Post*, August 19, 1990, p. A33.

15. *New York Times*, November 13, 1984, p. 14, and November 27, 1984, p. 1.

16. Laurie Mylroie, "The Baghdad Alternative," *Orbis* (Summer 1988), pp. 339–

40, 346, 348, 350; Christine Moss Helms, *Iraq: Eastern Flank of the Arab World* (Washington, D.C.: Brookings Institution, 1984), p. 194.

17. John Bulloch and Harvey Morris, *Saddam's War: The Origins of the Kuwaiti Conflict and the International Response* (London: Faber and Faber, 1991), p. 27; Kenneth R. Timmerman, *The Death Lobby: How the West Armed Iraq* (Boston: Houghton Mifflin, 1991), pp. 67–68, 344–45.

18. Efraim Karsh and Inauri Rautsi, *Saddam Hussein: A Political Biography* (New York: Free Press, 1991), p. 4.

19. There were the 131-feet-tall bronze "Victory Arches" built along the road to Baghdad from Saddam International Airport, and consisting of crossed swords being held by disembodied forearms and fists made from plaster casts of Saddam's own forearms and hands, "even down to his fingerprints and hair follicles." Christopher Walker, "Ubiquitous Saddam Turns to Iraq's Past in Pursuit of His Ambitions," *London Times*, November 21, 1989; Elaine Sciolino, *The Outlaw State: Saddam Hussein's Quest for Power and the Gulf Crisis* (New York: John Wiley and sons, 1991), pp. 183–84.

20. Karsh and Rautsi, *Saddam Hussein: A Political Biography*, p. 195.

21. U.S. Congress, Senate, Committee on Foreign Relations, *United States Policy Towards Iraq: Human Rights, Weapons Proliferation, and International Law*, Hearing, 101st Congress, 2nd Session, June 15, 1990, pp. 56–70.

22. Sciolino, *The Outlaw State*, p. 139.

23. State Department memorandum, "Countering Iraqi Weapons of Mass Destruction: The Gulf Crisis and Beyond," July 10, 1990.

24. Sciolino, *The Outlaw State*, p. 140.

25. Lawrence Freedman and Efraim Karsh, *The Gulf Conflict: Diplomacy and War in the New World Order* (London: Faber and Faber, 1993), p. 45.

26. Testimony during confirmation hearings for Robert Gates, U.S. Senate, Select Committee on Intelligence, *Nomination of Robert Gates*, Hearings, 102nd Congress, 1st Session, September 24, 1991, pp. 29–30.

27. Dean Baquet with Elaine Sciolino, "European Suppliers of Iraq Were Known to Pentagon," *New York Times*, November 2, 1992, p. A3; Douglas Frantz and Murray Waas, "CIA Told White House of Iraqi Arms Efforts," *Los Angeles Times*, August 6, 1992, pp. A1, A3.

28. Ariel Levite, *Intelligence and Strategic Surprise* (New York: Columbia University Press, 1987).

29. "X," "The Sources of Soviet Conduct," *Foreign Affairs*, 25 (July 1947), pp. 566–82.

30. Mohammed Ayoob, "The Third World Security Problematic," *World Politics*, 43 (January 1991), pp. 257–83; Michael N. Barnett and Jack Levy, "Domestic Sources of Alliance and Alignment: The Case of Egypt," *International Organization*, 45 (Summer 1991), pp. 369–95.

31. Adeed Dawisha, *The Arab Radicals* (New York: Council on Foreign Rela-

tions), pp. 60–61; Charles Tripp, "The Consequences of the Iran-Iraq War for Iraqi Politics," in Efraim Karsh, ed., *The Iran-Iraq War: Impact and Implications* (New York: St. martin's 1989), pp. 72, 76.

32. Bob Woodward, *The Commanders* (New York: Simon and Schuster, 1991), p. 202.

33. Dawisha, *The Arab Radicals,* pp. 3, 41.

34. Ole Holsti, "Foreign Policy Formation Viewed Cognitively," in Robert Axelrod, ed., *The Structure of Decision: Cognitive Maps of Political Elites* (Princeton: Princeton University Press, 1976), pp. 52–53.

35. Charles O. Jones, "Meeting Low Expectations: Strategy and Prospects of the Bush Presidency," in Colin Campbell and Bert A. Rockman, eds., *The Bush Presidency: First Appraisals* (Chatham, NJ: Chatham House, 1991), p. 59.

36. This paragraph draws from Larry Berman and Bruce W. Jentleson, "Bush and the Post–Cold War World: New Challenges for American Leadership," in Campbell and Rockman, *The Bush Presidency,* pp. 99–103.

37. Jentleson, "Discrepant Responses to Falling Dictators," pp. 353–84.

38. See, for example, Freedman and Karsh, *The Gulf Conflict,* pp. 55–56; Woodward, *The Commanders,* p. 214; and Alan Friedman, *Spider's Web: The Secret History of How the White House Illegally Armed Iraq* (New York: Bantam Books, 1993), pp. 32–33.

39. State Department cable, American Embassy Baghdad to Secretary of State, "DAS Gnehm Call on Minister of Trade—CCC and BNL," December 10, 1989.

40. Jentleson, "Discrepant Responses to Falling Dictators"; Sick, *All Fall Down.*

41. Martin Indyk, "The Postwar Balance of Power in the Middle East," in Joseph S. Nye, Jr., and Roger K. Smith, eds., *After the Storm: Lessons from the Gulf War* (New York: Madison Books, 1992), p. 98.

42. Judith Miller and Laurie Mylroie, *Saddam Hussein and the Crisis in the Gulf* (New York: Times Books, 1990), p. 149.

43. Ibid.

44. Douglas Jehl, "Assertion India and Pakistan Faced Nuclear War Is Doubted," *New York Times,* March 23, 1993, p. A4; Alexander L. George, *Bridging the Gap: Theory and Practice in Foreign Policy* (Washington, D.C.: U.S. Institute of Peace, 1993), p. 46.

45. National Academy of Sciences, *Finding Common Ground: U.S. Export Controls in a Changed Global Environment* (Washington, D.C.: National Academy Press, 1991); U.S. Congress, House of Representatives, Committee on Government Operations, *Strengthening the Export Licensing System,* House Report 102–137, 102nd Congress, 1st Session, July 2, 1991.

46. Commerce Department memorandum, "Re-Export Application," August 8, 1988.

47. U.S. Congress, House of Representatives, Committee on Foreign Affairs, *U.S. Exports of Sensitive Technology to Iraq,* hearing before the International Economic Policy and Trade Subcommittee, 102nd Congress, 1st Session, April 8 and May 22, 1991, p. 40.

48. Memorandum dated November 21, 1989, included in *Congressional Record,* July 21, 1992, p. H6344.

49. Graham T. Allison, *The Essence of Decision: Explaining the Cuban Missile Crisis* (Boston: Little, Brown, 1971); Morton Halperin, *Bureaucratic Politics and Foreign Policy* (Washington, D.C.: Brookings Institution, 1974); Roger Hilsman, *The Politics of Policy Making in Defense and Foreign Affairs: Conceptual Models and Bureaucratic Politics* (New York: Prentice-Hall, 1986); Christopher M. Jones, "American Prewar Technology Sales to Iraq: A Bureaucratic Politics Explanation," in Eugene R. Wittkopf, ed., *The Domestic Sources of American Foreign Policy: Insights and Evidence,* 2nd. ed. (New York: St. Martin's Press, 1994), pp. 279–96.

50. State Department memorandum, "Computers for Iraq: DOD's Concerns," April 3, 1986.

51. Elaine Sciolino, "Justice Dept. Role Cited in Deception on Iraq Loan Data," *New York Times,* October 10, 1992, pp. 1, 4, and "CIA and Justice Feud over Inquiry in Iraq Loan Case," October 11, 1992, pp. 1, 12; William Safire, "Panic on Ninth Street," *New York Times,* October 12, 1992, p. A19; *The Intelligence Community's Involvement in the Banca Nazionale del Lavoro (BNL) Affair,* report prepared by the Staff of the Select Committee on Intelligence, United States Senate, 103rd Congress, 1st Session, February 1993.

52. Quoted in Senate Select Committee on Intelligence, *The Intelligence Community's Involvement in the BNL Affair,* p. 5.

53. Bruce Russett and Harvey Starr, *World Politics: The Menu for Choice* (San Francisco: Freeman, 1981), pp. 237–38.

54. See my article, "American Diplomacy: Around the World and Along Pennsylvania Avenue," in Thomas E. Mann, ed., *A Question of Balance: The President, Congress and Foreign Policy* (Washington, D.C.: Brookings Institution, 1990), pp. 146–200.

55. Berman and Jentleson, "Bush and the Post–Cold War World," p. 104.

56. Ibid., pp. 105–106.

57. Letter dated June 20, 1985.

58. Letter from J. Edward Fox, Assistant Secretary of State for Legislative Affairs, to Congressman Dante B. Fascell, Chairman of the House Foreign Affairs Committee, September 13, 1988; letter from the Acting Secretary of State to Congressman David Obey, Chairman of the House Appropriations Subcommittee on Foreign Operations, September 30, 1988.

59. Berman and Jentleson, "Bush and the Post–Cold War World," pp. 105–106.

60. The authors of the congressional Iran-Contra report refer to a passage from *A Man for All Seasons*, in which William Roper says he would cut down every law in England to attack the Devil. Sir Thomas More replies: "And when the last law was down, and the Devil turned round on you—where would you hide, Roper, the laws all being flat? This country's planted thick with laws from coast to coast—Man's laws, not God's—and if you cut them down—and you're just the man to do it—d'you really think you could stand upright in the winds that would blow then?" *Report of the Congressional Committees Investigating the Iran-Contra Affair with Supplemental, Minority, and Additional Views,* H. Rept. 100–433, S. Rept. 100–216, 100th Congress, 1st Session (Washington, D.C.: Government Printing Office, 1987), p. 411.

61. Letter dated June 20, 1985; State Department memorandum, "Iraq's Retreat from Terrorism," July 1, 1986.

62. For an excellent theoretical development of this thesis and its application to trade policy, see Robert A. Pastor, *Congress and the Politics of U.S. Foreign Economic Policy, 1929–1976* (Berkeley, CA: University of California Press, 1976).

63. Compare J. William Fulbright's "American Foreign Policy in the 20th Century under an 18th-Century Constitution," *Cornell Law Quarterly,* 47 (Fall 1961), pp. 1–13, with his "Congress and Foreign Policy," included in *Commission on the Organization of the Government for the Conduct of Foreign Policy,* Volume 5 (Washington, D.C.: Government Printing Office, 1975).

64. Edward S. Corwin, *The President: Office and Power, 1787–1957,* 4th revised edition (New York: New York University Press, 1957), p. 171; Louis Henkin, "Foreign Affairs and the Constitution," *Foreign Affairs,* 66 (Winter 1987–88), p. 287.

65. I.M. Destler, Leslie H. Gelb, and Anthony Lake, *Our Own Worst Enemy: The Unmaking of American Foreign Policy* (New York: Simon and Schuster, 1984).

66. Jentleson, "American Diplomacy," pp. 177–84.

67. Michael Doyle, "Liberalism and World Politics," *American Political Science Review,* 80 (December 1986), pp. 1151–1169.

68. Miroslav Nincic, *Democracy and Foreign Policy: The Fallacy of Political Realism* (New York: Columbia University Press, 1992); Bruce W. Jentleson, "The Pretty Prudent Public: Post Post-Vietnam American Opinion on the Use of Military Force," *International Studies Quarterly,* 36 (March 1992), pp. 49–74.

Index